Gordon Noble is Professor and Head of Archaeology at the University of Aberdeen. He has undertaken landscape research and directed field projects across Scotland. He is author of *Neolithic Scotland: Timber, Stone, Earth and Fire* (Edinburgh University Press, 2006) and *Woodland in the Neolithic of Northern Europe: The Forest as Ancestor* (Cambridge University Press, 2017). He was recently awarded a Leverhulme Research Leadership Award for a project entitled *Comparative Kingship: The Early Medieval Kingdoms of Northern Britain and Ireland*.

Nicholas Evans is a Research Fellow on the Leverhulme Trust-funded *Comparative Kingship: The Early Medieval Kingdoms of Northern Britain and Ireland* project at the University of Aberdeen. He is a historian whose research and teaching have focused on the medieval Celtic-speaking societies of Britain and Ireland and the texts they produced. He is the author of *The Present and the Past in Medieval Irish Chronicles* (Boydell Press, 2010), and *A Historical Introduction to the Northern Picts* (Aberdeen University/Tarbat Discovery Centre, 2014).

Author proceeds from this volume will go to the Tarbat Discovery Centre, Easter Ross. The Tarbat Discovery Centre is a museum, learning and activity centre dedicated to displaying and preserving the heritage of the Tarbat peninsula in northern Scotland. Housed in the refurbished Old Parish Church, it is the site of the only Pictish monastic settlement found in Scotland to date. The centre displays many of the spectacular artefacts and Pictish sculpture uncovered during the extensive archaeological investigations by the University of York.

Find out more about the centre at: www.tarbat-discovery.co.uk

The King in the North

THE PICTISH REALMS OF FORTRIU AND CE

Collected essays written as part of the University of Aberdeen's Northern Picts project

GORDON NOBLE and NICHOLAS EVANS

with Ewan Campbell, Martin Goldberg, Meggen Gondek, Derek Hamilton, Alistair McPherson, Juliette Mitchell, Oskar Sveinbjarnarson and Simon Taylor

BIRLINN

First published in Great Britain in 2019 by
Birlinn Ltd
West Newington House
10 Newington Road
Edinburgh
EH9 1QS

www.birlinn.co.uk

Reprinted in 2020

ISBN: 978 1 78027 551 2

British Library Cataloguing-in-Publication Data
A catalogue record for this book is available
on request from the British Library.

Typeset by Hewer Text UK Ltd, Edinburgh
Printed and bound by PNB, Latvia

The volume is dedicated to Don and Elizabeth Cruickshank and to all the students, volunteers and supporters who have made the fieldwork of the Northern Picts project possible.

Contents

List of plates and figures

Frontispiece
The Tarbat Discovery Centre, Portmahomack

Plates

Figures

Abbreviations

AU   Mac Airt, S. and Mac Niocaill, G. (eds and trans.) 1983 *The Annals of Ulster (To A.D. 1131) Part I Text and Translation* (Dublin: Dublin Institute for Advanced Studies).

CKA   Anderson, M.O. (ed.) 2011 'The Chronicle of the Kings of Alba', in M.O. Anderson (ed.), *Kings and Kingship in Early Scotland* (Edinburgh: John Donald), pp. 249–53.

HE   Colgrave, B. and Mynors, R.A.B. (eds and trans.) 1969 *Bede's Ecclesiastical History of the English People* (Oxford: The Clarendon Press).

VSC   Sharpe, R. (trans.) 1995 *Adomnán of Iona: Life of St Columba* (Harmondsworth: Penguin Books).

Acknowledgements

The studies that are included in this volume are edited versions of published work in a range of journals and edited volumes, but they are brought here together for the first time to provide a concentrated body of work for the specialist and general reader. An extended version of Chapter 2, 'A historical introduction to the northern Picts', was first published as a booklet in a University of Aberdeen series produced for the Tarbat Discovery Centre. The present version is a substantially cut-down version that focuses on the main sources and debates involved in understanding the nature of early medieval society in northern Pictland. Chapter 3 was first published as a chapter in a volume edited by Neil Christie and Hajnalka Herold, entitled *Fortified Settlement in Early Medieval Europe* and published by Oxbow books. The chapter has been edited and updated to reflect on more recent work and to more closely integrate with the contents of the other chapters in this volume. The study weekend organised by Neil Christie and Hajnalka Herold that led to this volume was an extremely stimulating event for pursuing the wider context of northern Pictish sites like Rhynie and Burghead. Chapter 4 is a shorter version of a paper in the journal *Medieval Archaeology*. The journal article outlines in much greater detail the dating and historical context which the version published here is based upon. Readers who would like more detail on these dimensions of the site are referred to the *Medieval Archaeology* article. Chapter 5 is again based on an article published in *Medieval Archaeology*. The article once more includes greater detail, with tables of identified sites. Chapter 6 is based on an article in *Antiquity*. The *Antiquity* article dwelt more on the implications for how we approach antiquarian finds and findspots, but the majority of the text is the same as in Chapter 6. Likewise, Chapter 7 follows a published version in *Antiquity* but does not include the detailed Bayesian modelling upon which the chronology is based, nor the data tables published in online supplements for the *Antiquity* article. Chapter 8 was specifically written for this volume. Thus, while much of the text is available elsewhere, the volume brings this material together for a first time to produce a cohesive extended narrative for considering the nature and development of society in northern Pictland in the period *c.* AD 300–1000.

The authors of the book would like to extend many thanks. To all the landowners who gave permission for work on their land, we send the warmest thanks. Bruce Mann of Aberdeenshire Council Archaeology Service has provided continual support and advice. Gail Drinkall, Curator of Orkney Museum, helped arrange dating of samples from Orkney for Chapter 6. Members of the Historic Environment Scotland Survey Team provided help in the transcription and identification of sites for Chapter 5. John Borland produced and helped source images for Chapters 7 and 8.

The Northern Picts project has been funded through the University of Aberdeen's Development Trust, Historic Environment Scotland Archaeology Programme, the Leverhulme-funded Comparative Kingship project, The Strathmartine Trust, British Academy, the Society of Antiquaries of Scotland and Aberdeenshire Council Archaeology Service. The work on the Gaulcross hoard has also been supported by the ongoing Glenmorangie Research project at National Museums Scotland.

The writing of this volume was supported by a Leverhulme Trust Research Leadership Award (RL-2016-069).

The volume was funded by Elizabeth and Don Cruickshank, both born and educated in the north-east of Scotland, graduates of the University of Aberdeen and supporters of the Tarbat Discovery Centre in Portmahomack.

CHAPTER ONE

Introduction: The king in the north – The Pictish realms of Fortriu and Ce

Gordon Noble

This book brings together a number of studies that demonstrate the ways in which new historical perspectives and recently discovered archaeological evidence can underpin fresh understandings of the development of Pictish society in northern Scotland. More specifically, the volume tracks the rise of Pictish society from the first references in the late Roman period to the development of the powerful Pictish kingdoms in the early medieval era. The focus in the book is on the modern local government regions of Aberdeenshire, Moray, Inverness-shire and Easter Ross, areas that were probably included in the Pictish territories of Fortriu and Ce (See Chapter 2) (Fig. 1). The volume builds on the work of the University of Aberdeen's Northern Picts project, which was established to explore the archaeology and early history of 1st-millennium AD northern Scotland. The volume collects together scholarship compiled over the first five years of the project, representing the first consolidated book-length publication of the project. It is hoped that bringing together a series of publications based on the early results of the project will provide fresh perspectives on the Pictish period and the important roles that northern Pictland played in shaping the early kingdoms of Scotland, even though the work of Northern Picts is ongoing and the picture will undoubtedly change.

Historical interest in northern Pictland has been hugely invigorated in the last decade. Just over ten years ago, the historian Alex Woolf wrote an article that fundamentally challenged our understandings of the sociopolitical geography of Pictland (Woolf 2006). The most commonly cited Pictish kingdom is that of Fortriu, and for over a century Fortriu was assumed to be located in southern Pictland in central Scotland. Woolf persuasively argued that Fortriu was actually in northern Pictland, centred on the southern shores of the Moray Firth, showing that this region was actually the core of the Pictish

1. Pictland with some of the major sites of northern Pictland referenced in the text.
© Crown Copyright/database right 2018. An Ordnance Survey/EDINA-supplied service.

kingdom rather than a periphery (see Chapter 2). In terms of the archaeology of northern Pictland, until recently, work had been relatively piecemeal, with few projects that specifically focused on elucidating information regarding the structure of northern Pictish society and there were few relevant historical sources or named sites to help target archaeological work. Nonetheless, previous archaeological work had established the presence of fortified settlements of the Pictish period in northern Pictland. For example, seven seasons of excavation at Cullykhan by Colvin Greig and his team identified Pictish phases at a major Iron Age enclosure complex near Pennan, Aberdeenshire (Greig 1970, 1971, 1972). Excavations at Green Castle, Portknockie, by Ian Ralston also identified a defended settlement of the Pictish period, with the remains of a timber-laced rampart and post-built structures identified within the interior of another coastal promontory (Ralston 1980, 1987). At Burghead, Alan Small, lecturer in the Geography Department at Aberdeen and latterly Dundee, excavated areas of the interior and ramparts of the fort in the late 1960s, and retrieved the first radiocarbon dating samples for a site which had long been identified as a major centre of the northern Picts (Oram 2007; Small 1969). As well as work on the coastal sites, there were also projects on inland forts. Alan Small, for example, also excavated at Craig Phadrig, Inverness-shire, discovering sherds of E-ware and metalworking moulds, and demonstrated that an Iron Age vitrified fort had been reoccupied in the 7th century AD (Small and Cottam 1972). There was also archaeological work at a small number of Pictish cemeteries – with cairns excavated at Garbeg (Wedderburn and Grime 1984) and Pityoulish (Rae and Rae 1953). These post-war excavations built on limited antiquarian work (e.g. MacDonald 1862; Young 1891, 1893).

Apart from the excavations of forts or cemeteries highlighted above, much of the work on the Picts north of the Mounth focused on an iconic element of Pictish archaeology – the symbol stone monuments that are found from Fife to the Shetland Isles. The symbol stones are carved with a distinctive group of symbols, some abstract, others naturalistic, such as striking animal designs or recognisable objects such as mirrors and combs (Henderson and Henderson 2004, 167). In their magisterial corpus, Allen and Anderson highlighted the importance of northern Pictland, with the majority of Class I monuments, symbols carved on unshaped boulders, being found here,

particularly in Aberdeenshire (Allen and Anderson 1903, civ). Isabel
Henderson, in her early work, followed Allen and Anderson in
favouring a northern origin for the tradition, although she sought the
origins in the inner Moray Firth, around Golspie in the southernmost
part of Sutherland rather than in Aberdeenshire (Henderson 1958).
Few commentators followed this line of reasoning, and in subsequent
decades the northern Pictish corpus was generally not pursued as a
body of evidence in its own right, but subsumed within wider studies
on the patterns and distributions of particular artistic motifs and
particular styles of symbol more generally.

In more recent decades, major new progress on northern Pictland
in the area stretching from Easter Ross to Aberdeenshire began to
occur particularly from the 1990s onwards, with a number of important archaeological projects. The most prominent has been the 14
seasons of excavation at Portmahomack on the Tarbat Peninsula,
Easter Ross (Carver 2016a; Carver *et al.* 2016). Building on the
discovery of a large cropmark enclosure surrounding the church at
Portmahomack and evaluative work by Jill Harden in 1991, the
University of York project at Portmahomack revealed a Pictish
monastery and secular settlement, and tracked its demise in the
Viking Age (Chapter 8). Further developments on the archaeology of
the Picts occurred in the 2000s, with a series of excavations on
enclosed settlements undertaken as part of Murray Cook's *The
Hillforts of Strathdon* project revealing important new evidence for
early medieval enclosed settlement. Cook's work built on the important Royal Commission for Ancient and Historical Monuments of
Scotland (RCAHMS) survey of central Aberdeenshire *In the Shadow
of Bennachie* (RCAHMS 2007). In the RCAHMS survey, a typology
of forts and enclosures was developed, with a sixfold scheme based
on size and rampart type postulated (RCAHMS 2007, 100–1). Cook's
work involved testing by spade the RCAHMS typology, using keyhole
excavation to retrieve dating samples. Six seasons of excavation were
conducted on nine enclosures. These excavations revealed Pictish
occupation or construction phases at a range of new sites. The results
of this project were used to extrapolate wider Pictish settlement
patterns across Aberdeenshire and led to renewed interest in the
nature of early medieval settlement and power structures in north-
east Scotland (e.g. Cook 2011a, b). Other smaller-scale investigations
through development-led work have also contributed, such as the

dating of the interior deposits of the Mither Tap, Bennachie, which revealed early medieval occupation (Atkinson 2007) and the excavation of the Pictish cemetery at Greshop in advance of development (Dunbar 2012).

These recent projects and the historical work of Woolf (2006, 2007a) set the scene for the University of Aberdeen's Northern Picts project, the results of which this volume showcases. The Northern Picts project was established in 2012 to investigate the early medieval archaeology and early history of an area stretching from Aberdeenshire to Easter Ross, covering the probable extent of the Pictish provinces and kingdoms of Fortriu and Ce (Fig. 1). The Northern Picts project was designed to investigate sites of potential early medieval date through survey and excavation and in addition was developed to help support local museums such as the Tarbat Discovery Centre by curating exhibitions and providing new information for visitor films and a booklet series. The earliest phases of the project mainly involved work on sites on the Tarbat peninsula in the environs of the Pictish monastery at Portmahomack. A series of enclosed and unenclosed sites were targeted for excavation and revealed a largely Iron Age settlement sequence with some indications of later reuse of these sites in the 3rd and 4th centuries AD – in the period when the Picts are first mentioned in late Roman sources. The focus of the Northern Picts project shifted in 2013 to Moray and Aberdeenshire, with work undertaken at sites such as Rhynie (in collaboration with the universities of Chester and Glasgow), Burghead and Dunnicaer and a series of other enclosed settlement sites, symbol stone locations and cemetery sites. The project also helped identify a major portion of a silver hoard at Gaulcross, Banffshire, dating to the 5th–7th century AD, working in this case with the National Museum of Scotland (Noble et al. 2016) (Chapter 6).

This volume represents a synthesis of the work that Northern Picts has conducted in the first five years of the project in the period 2012–17 and brings together work that has been published elsewhere along with work from scholars who have worked alongside the Northern Picts team. Few syntheses on northern Pictland exist. Isabel Henderson considered the topic of 'North Pictland' in the 1971 volume *The Dark Ages in the Highlands*, but the text largely dwelt on the historical texts with little contribution from archaeology (Henderson 1971). In the 1980s Ralston and Inglis reviewed the evidence for north-east Scotland

for an exhibition at Marischal Museum, Aberdeen, and while the text
was more archaeologically focused there were few definitively dated
archaeological assemblages and sites to draw upon (Ralston and Inglis
1984). In the 1990s Ian Shepherd reviewed the evidence for the Picts
in Moray and was able to consider the emerging aerial evidence for
Pictish cemeteries, but the number of sites he was able to cite was
again very limited. In Wainwright's earlier seminal publication *The
Problem of the Picts* (1955a), a small number of northern Pictish sites
were mentioned, such as the fort at Burghead and a number of carved
stone monuments, but the archaeological evidence for all of Pictland
was generally thought to be thin on the ground and the focus was on
historically documented sites in the south. Recent historical syntheses
of Pictland have foregrounded northern Pictland in more detail, drawing on Woolf's important 2006 article (e.g. J.E. Fraser 2009a). The
2007 RCAHMS volume *In the Shadow of Bennachie* also partly drew
together some of the information from north-east Scotland relating to
the Pictish period and made important contributions on the setting
and context of Pictish symbol stones, settlement and early Christian
sites. The excellent *Studies on the Book of Deer* provided interdisciplinary views on this important manuscript, with wide-ranging and
multidisciplinary reviews of archaeological, place-name, sculpture
and historical perspectives centred on understanding the Book of Deer
in its wider context (Forsyth 2008a). However, this volume represents
the first attempt to summarise major aspects of the archaeological and
historical record of a significant part of northern Pictland.

The volume is not comprehensive in the way that the last academic
volume on Pictland, *Pictish Progress* (Driscoll *et al.* 2011), attempted
to be. *Pictish Progress* provided summaries of recent historical, art-
historical, archaeological and place-name studies, discussing past
scholarship and avenues for future research. This volume is more
restrictive in that it focuses on one part of Pictland and largely focuses
on the archaeological and historical evidence, but it includes new
syntheses of the social and political framework, religion and sculpture, alongside the results of major recent archaeological discoveries
helping illuminate northern Pictland to a new level of detail.

The book is structured as follows. In Chapter 2, Nick Evans sets
the scene by reviewing the historical records we can draw upon for
understanding northern Pictland in its wider context. He interprets
the evidence we have for the sociopolitical geography of northern

Pictland, drawing on chronicles, histories, literary texts, saints' lives, king-lists and place-names.

Chapter 3 moves on to provide an overview of one major category of archaeological evidence we have for Pictland: fortified or enclosed settlements. In northern Britain, fort and enclosure building proliferated in the early medieval period after a hiatus of construction during the late Iron Age in many areas of Scotland. The chapter draws on evidence from across Pictland, with a focus on the north, to show that this phenomenon gained particular traction in the 5th–6th centuries AD with the construction of a range of enclosed architectural forms. It is archaeological evidence such as from these forts that can help us trace the material dimensions of the exercise of power that made the social conditions of the early medieval period possible.

Chapter 4 zooms in to examine a specific case study on a newly identified power centre of northern Pictland – the enclosure complex and wider landscape at Rhynie, Aberdeenshire. Rhynie has long been known for its particular concentration of Class I Pictish stones (see, for example, Henderson 1958, 55). Fieldwork from 2011 onwards has revealed that the symbol stones were associated with a high-status settlement and ceremonial complex of the 4th–6th centuries AD. The Rhynie evidence includes traces of large-scale metalwork production, the construction of various enclosures and internal buildings, and the evidence for long-distance connections that ultimately connected Rhynie to the Byzantine and Frankish empires. In this chapter, the sources that we have available, including place-name and later historical evidence, are also explored to try to reconstruct the significance of an elite centre that clearly had roles in the production and redistribution of wealth and the exercise of power in this part of Pictland at a relatively early date.

Chapter 5 leads us on to consider the burial traditions of northern Pictland. The rich aerial evidence for the areas of Fortriu and Ce is reviewed to reveal the elaborate barrow and cairn cemeteries that existed in the study area. These included enormous monuments that extended to over 20m in size – square mounds, cairns and enclosures. The emergence of formal cemeteries is a notable feature of the early medieval period in northern Britain, replacing the diffuse and difficult to identify mortuary traditions of the Iron Age. Chapter 5 suggests that these cemeteries marked significant transitions in the marking of more formal ties to land and its inheritance in the 5th–7th centuries

AD. The phenomena of creating linked monuments and more elaborate monuments through time were particular features of these Pictish
cemeteries. It may have been one way in which particular individuals
and lineages were marked as being important and their history and
legitimacy grounded in the particular landscapes in which these cemeteries were constructed.

Chapter 6 changes tack to look at material culture in more detail
and, in particular, the (re)discovery of the metalwork hoard from
Gaulcross, to consider how a detailed analysis of material culture can
help illuminate the late Roman and early post-Roman period of
northern Scotland. Many finds of early medieval objects were uncovered in the 19th century, but often these are uncontextualised and
poorly understood. New archaeological work can help us better
understand these important assemblages of metalwork, and Chapter
6 outlines how recent archaeological survey and excavation led to the
discovery of a larger part of a silver hoard first identified during agricultural improvements in the first half of the 19th century. Chapter 7
moves the focus to the most iconic feature of Pictish archaeology –
the symbol tradition. The Pictish symbol tradition and Pictish symbol
stones hold an enduring fascination for scholars and members of the
public alike, but their study has been hampered by an absolute chronology and the tendency to study symbol stones in isolation or from
an art-historical perspective alone.

Chapter 7 relates the symbol system of Pictland to wider northern
European traditions such as runes and ogham, which originated
through cultural contact with the Roman Empire. The chapter
explores the significance the symbol system had for the development
of 1st-millennium AD society in Pictland, drawing on a new chronology derived from the work of the Northern Picts project. The volume's
core ends with a consideration of the evidence for the early Church
in northern Pictland in Chapter 8. The excavations at Portmahomack
were a game-changer for the study of the early Church in northern
Britain.

The evidence for the early Church in the early medieval period
from Easter Ross to Aberdeenshire is reviewed in Chapter 8 to reveal
the range of evidence we can now draw upon. The chapter outlines
the results of recent work on early church sites in northern Pictland
and evidence for how Christianity began to impact on major elite
centres and on the orchestration of power.

The volume concludes in Chapter 9 with a short summary of the evidence and reflections on what all the new evidence might reveal about the rise and demise of the northern Picts and its rulers.

A great deal more could have been included in this volume, but the large body of evidence outlined here, much of which will be new to the non-specialist, provides ample material for creating new narratives concerning the northern Picts. The lack of archaeological evidence has repeatedly been highlighted in reviews of Pictish archaeology, from Wainwright to more recent periods (Carver 2011; Crawford 2011, 7; Wainwright 1955a). Now archaeology, alongside new historical perspectives and the contributions of a wide range of disciplines, can increasingly contribute to our understanding of the Picts. While we have still much to do, the Pictish evidence can also increasingly contribute to northern European narratives due in no small part to the rich sculptural and iconographic evidence from Pictland that is increasingly well understood thanks to the new contextual approaches of the kind outlined in this volume. The Picts, often marginalised in wider European narratives, can now begin to take a more central role in our understandings of early medieval society in Britain, Ireland and beyond.

CHAPTER TWO

A historical introduction to the northern Picts

Nicholas Evans

The 1st millennium was a period of major change in northern Scotland. When this era began, northern Scotland was organised into a large number of local polities, but by the year 1000 a consolidated Gaelic kingship of Alba had formed, although large areas of the north and west were also controlled by Scandinavians. By looking at the termini of the millennium, however, we neglect another people, the Picts, who emerged during the time of Roman rule in Britain, and whose culture lasted for at least 500 years, until their identity and language disappeared. They are the last major ethnic identity in the British Isles to become extinct. Nevertheless, in their own time they played a major role in the history of northern Europe and had a profound impact on the successor society of Alba, which formed the basis for Scotland.

The nature of the written evidence

As with most early medieval peoples of Britain, the written evidence for the Picts is fragmentary, so there will always be large gaps in what it can tell us, although archaeological investigation offers a chance to obtain a greater understanding of many areas. The texts we have provide a few shards of light in a generally dark chamber, but it is important to understand how to interpret these sources. In general, very little written material from the Picts survives. As well as the important and expanding corpus of inscriptions, there are the Pictish king-lists, which derive from a source written in Pictland before AD 900, but they survive in later versions, and there are also fragments of Pictish information in texts from outside Pictland. In spite of this evidence, the claim that the Picts did not write texts and relied more on an oral tradition than other contemporary societies is popular, but mistaken; as with other peoples of the time, like the Britons of

Strathclyde around Glasgow, whose languages died out before the medieval literacy explosion of the 12th century, the later lack of interest in Pictish vernacular texts ensured that they were not copied. Therefore, those that once existed are now virtually all lost to us (Evans 2011, 59–61; Forsyth 1998; Hughes 1980, 1–21).

As a result, we are largely reliant on two main source groups: first, contemporary works from neighbouring societies, by Romans, Irish and English people who included the Picts in their texts; and secondly, later texts that contain discussion of the Picts or include relevant evidence, for instance Pictish place-names. With each of these groups of evidence, much of the work of historians is concentrated on identifying what from these sources actually derives from the Picts and what was created later. It is now recognised that texts are to a large extent artefacts of the period of composition; often sources were changed over time to fit different contemporary purposes, such as supporting political aims. This was sometimes achieved by creating or adapting historical traditions where necessary, but usually it was also based on received views of the past. So it is only when, through close textual study, we can identify earlier elements contemporary with the Picts that reliable evidence for Pictish society can be obtained: to claim that a later source represents a 'good tradition' is a recipe for disaster with the Picts. Interpreting these fragments is likewise fraught with potential pitfalls, such as relying on preconceived ideas, but through a careful comparison with analogous societies, especially of the same era, we can gain a greater understanding of the ways in which the Picts were similar to and also different from their contemporaries. The following is largely intended as a guide through these potential minefields, using much of the innovative work undertaken in the last few decades.

The Roman period

The Picts, *Picti* in Latin, are first mentioned as a people by classical authors in AD 297 or 298 referring anachronistically to the Picts as pre-existing enemies of the Britons before Julius Caesar (Nixon and Rodgers 1994, 4–5; Ritchie 1994, 3–4). Overall, inferring from the Roman-period references, the Picts clearly were inhabiting Britain to the north of the Roman province, although their territory was not defined exactly (Ireland 1986, 152–60; Ritchie 1994, 4–5; Rivet and

Smith 1979, 76). Before the Picts appear in sources, the people of northern Britain were described either as 'Britons' or as 'Caledonians'. After the Roman retreat from what is now Scotland in AD 86/7, the extent of Roman rule in northern Britain varied; often Hadrian's Wall or the Antonine Wall between the firths of the Clyde and Forth marked the main boundary, but there were forts further north, and among the locals the Romans maintained a network of agents to prevent trouble from developing. As a result, the people between the Hadrianic and Antonine walls retained a British identity, like the inhabitants of the Roman province to the south, and spoke a Celtic language of the Brittonic branch (which evolved into modern Welsh, Cornish and Breton) (J.E. Fraser 2009a, 35–7). In the medieval period, the term 'British' was used for these Brittonic languages and 'Britons' and 'British' related to the people who spoke them; unlike in the modern era, these words did not refer to the island or all inhabitants of Britain or the UK. To avoid confusion, the terms 'British' and 'Britons' will be used here according to the medieval usage.

As in other frontier zones, like Germany (Heather 2009, 36–93), the written evidence indicates that one result of the Roman presence may have been that the population groups bordering Roman Britain became amalgamated, so that fewer but larger political units developed. In northern Britain, according to the mid 3rd-century account of Cassius Dio, from AD 208–11 the Romans under Septimius Severus launched major campaigns against two large groups, the *Maiatai* and beyond them the *Caledonii*, into which the names of other British groups had been merged (Cary 1927, 262; J.E. Fraser 2009a, 15–17, 23–9). In the 4th century, according to the *Res Gestae* of Ammianus Marcellinus written shortly after 391, 'the Barbarian Conspiracy' of 367 involved Picts, 'divided into two nations (*gentes*), called Dicalydones and Verturiones', as well as *Scotti*, *Attacotti*, Franks and Saxons, taking part in a coordinated attack on the Roman province of Britain (Elliott 1983, 1; J.E. Fraser 2009a, 54–61; Rolfe 1972, xxvii.8). It is likely that various groups north of the Roman frontier rose to prominence in the Roman period at different times, and that by 367 the term *Picti* could be used by the Romans as a collective term for these. While the situation may have been more complex than indicated by classical writers, with the continuation of local identities (indicated by the survival to the 6th century of the *Maiatai*), a growth in power of a few elite groups, dominating the others, is indicated by the written texts (for a different view, see Hunter 2007a).

Who were the Picts mentioned in these sources? There is no reliable written evidence that they arrived in Britain in this period from elsewhere. It is unlikely that *Picti* had been the main name for these peoples much before *c*.300 because classical writers probably would have mentioned it, and there was another term they used, *Caledonii*, for the northern Britons. So the rise of the name *Picti* seems to reflect a change in terminology in the 3rd century AD. In Latin the word means 'painted people', and it is traditionally considered to refer to the practice of tattooing or body painting, although it has been suggested that the Romans encountered a similar-sounding Pictish word and interpreted it as *Picti* (Watson 1926, 67–8).

Based on the former explanation, James Fraser has recently proposed that *Picti* was a term created and used by the Romans, coined for the more 'barbaric' people outside of the Roman cultural sphere, but only employed by the Picts themselves in the late 7th century, when a single Pictish overkingship was being established (J.E. Fraser 2009a, 44–54; J.E. Fraser 2011). A new term was needed because the Britons under Roman influence no longer seemed to the classical world to fit in the same category as those to the north. This increasingly popular view has largely replaced the previous opinion that, even before the Roman intervention, the Picts (and their Caledonian predecessors) were in essence a separate people and had a different culture from the Britons.

Part of this scholarly shift is based on changing linguistic views relating to the Picts. In the 1950s, the pre-eminent Celtic linguist Kenneth Jackson argued that two languages were spoken by the Picts: one was most closely related to Gaulish, a form of Celtic spoken on the Continent, while the other was unrelated to any known language (Jackson 1955). Jackson did not claim to understand any of this second language, but he suggested it was non-Celtic, and not any other known language either, on the basis of unintelligible sections of inscriptions and names from sources, such as Ptolemy's 'Geography'. In the last few decades, Katherine Forsyth has argued that Jackson was too willing to discount a Celtic interpretation of the evidence in many instances, and that our inability to understand text does not necessarily mean that it is in a different language (Forsyth 1997a). In addition, place-name evidence, which was not really studied by

Jackson, shows that Pictish place-name elements, like *aber-*, 'confluence, river mouth' (as found in Aberdeen), and *pert-*, 'wood, grove' (as in Perth), are nearly all also found in British-speaking areas (for instance Aberystwyth in Wales, and Partick in Glasgow) (Taylor 2011), providing evidence for close ties with Brittonic rather than Gaulish. Non-Celtic Pictish elements have not yet been identified, although the lower number of recognisable Celtic Pictish elements north of the Mounth has been noted. The debate on language in Pictland has not been decisively resolved, but it is significant for how we interpret the culture and society of the Picts, even if we no longer firmly correlate language and ethnicity as we once did before the late 20th century.

Fortriu, the Pictish overkingship and socio-economic structures

The rise of Fortriu to become the pre-eminent Pictish province is one of the most notable developments of early medieval Scotland. By the end of the 7th century, after their victory at the battle in 685 called *Nechtanesmere* in Old English, *Dún Nechtain* in Gaelic, when King Bridei son of Beli defeated and killed King Ecgfrith of Northumbria, the kings of Fortriu had established a hegemony over most, if not all, of the Picts. Indeed, James Fraser has even suggested that these kings adopted the word *Picti*, 'Picts', for their realm's inhabitants in order to justify this expansion, turning an external term into one used by people in northern Britain themselves (J.E. Fraser 2009a, 224–7). Under Onuist son of Uurguist (732–61), this kingdom invaded and conquered the Gaels of Dál Riata in Argyll after a number of campaigns. This conquest was not permanent; kings of Dál Riata appear again in the 770s until 792, in a period in which Pictland was itself divided, but by the 9th century Dál Riata again seems to have come under Pictish rule. It is clear that the emergence of a powerful Pictish kingship dominating much of northern Britain and seemingly focused on Fortriu among the northern Picts was a major development. What caused this change and what impact did it have on the nature of society? When did the power of Fortriu start to expand, and what was its basis? Were there different ideological and physical underpinnings to this kingship compared to others among the Picts? We have a few fragments of evidence for regional rulers in places like the Orkneys. Can we identify whether there were changes to local power structures? The written evidence on its own cannot answer most of these questions, but from it an interpretative framework can be produced, so long as we recognise that the processes involved are likely to be far more complex than can be inferred from the texts.

Models of interpretation

Given the fragmentary nature of the Pictish written evidence, modern scholars have often interpreted the evidence in terms of how they compare with their neighbours. Utilising such a perspective, there are a number of models from other countries for how Pictland might have developed under Fortriu's suzerainty. One potential scenario is that it displayed similar political and economic changes to those found in Anglo-Saxon England. By the end of the 7th century, a number of Anglo-Saxon kingdoms of varying power had developed. The Anglo-Saxon elite had converted to Christianity, enabling them to take full advantage of literacy and the cultural contacts which developed with the rest of Europe. Political consolidation continued in the 8th and early 9th centuries so that kingdoms such as Kent were assimilated into the kingdoms of the Northumbrians, Mercians, West Saxons and East Angles, but it is questionable whether England would have been created without Scandinavian intervention (Bassett 1989, 26–7).

Former royal dynasties which survived often provided the local nobility and clergymen under the patronage of their overlords. In some kingdoms, the administration of localities changed, with the creation of local official positions, such as *ealdormen* among the West Saxons. These were appointed by the king, and combined with kings promulgating laws and utilising charters to grant or consent to the donation of land and rights, they represented increased royal control of the localities, rather than allowing a local king to rule on his behalf according to their own laws and customs. The evidence for some Anglo-Saxon kingdoms clearly indicates that elite structures had changed by the 9th century, with ultimate authority and patronage in local areas often derived directly from the king.

Such political changes may have been accompanied by socio-economic changes at a local level: Chris Wickham has argued that the Anglo-Saxons participated in a more general European transforma-tion around this time away from a 'peasant' mode of production, whereby the local community controlled the means of production and gave nothing or virtually nothing to an overlord, to a 'feudal' mode of production, in which communities provided substantial renders of produce to their lords (Wickham 2005). This meant that lords gradually increased their power and estates, reducing the independence of their subordinates, leading to greater social stratification, a process probably closely related to the political developments of the same era.

Another potential model for the Picts is provided by Ireland (for which, see Byrne 1973; Charles-Edwards 2000). Here, there were at least 100 kingships at any one time throughout the early medieval period, although possibly there were fewer in 1100 than at the beginning. At the local level there was the *túath*, a kingdom and people sometimes covering a territory of less than ten miles square. However, more powerful kings of a *túath* were able to dominate and gain the submission of others: a king receiving the submission of three or four other kings was called a *ruirí*; and above the *ruirí* were greater kings including rulers of the Irish provinces of *Mumu* (Munster), *Laigin* (Leinster), *Connachta* (Connaught), *Ulaid* (part of Ulster), and the powerful Uí Néill confederation in the north and midlands. Theoretically, and maybe occasionally in reality, there was also a 'High-king of Ireland' (also sometimes called 'King of Tara' after the ritual centre in modern County Meath). Often kings were related, because minor kingdoms were frequently formed from branches of powerful royal dynasties, although sometimes such genealogical connections were fabricated according to political circumstances. Kindreds were important, but contests for power among rival related claimants were a constant feature. A somewhat simplified but nevertheless generally valid view is that, unlike in Anglo-Saxon England, kings did not deal directly with the people subject to their client kings, so they were dependent on the loyalty of the client kings. Overkingship was personal and not necessarily inherited, so the power of a kingdom was very reliant on the abilities of a particular monarch. As a result, the Irish political system was very unstable with complex and constantly changing overkingship structures and alliances, even if certain kingdoms tended to be dominant. Only in the mid 9th century with the growth of Uí Néill power and the late 10th-century rise of Munster under Brian Boru (d. 1014) was a more substantial consolidation of power turned into reality, albeit not permanently.

It is easy to view the Irish kings as weaker than those in England, but it is important to note that powerful Irish kings could sometimes control large armies, and that one of the most significant Anglo-Saxon kingships, Mercia, had large areas where charters were not (or were little) used, seemingly because the king of Mercia allowed local rulers to govern these areas for them as more or less autonomous units (Keynes 2001, 314–20). Charters and royal officials did not necessarily make the governance of a region more effective or secure, especially if their introduction transformed established loyal power structures.

The rise of Fortriu

When we consider the development of the Pictish overkingship, we should not expect the evidence to follow one or other comparative case exactly, but the two models should be borne in mind. The first reference we have to Fortriu is when Ammianus Marcellinus named the Verturiones (hence the adjective 'Verturian') as one of the two Pictish peoples, along with the Dicalydones, involved in the 'Barbarian Conspiracy' of 367. In the late Roman period (Ritchie 1994, 3–5), in the writings of the 5th-century St Patrick (Hood 1978, 35–8, 55–9), and the 6th-century Gildas (Winterbottom 1978, 21–5), there are general, usually negative comments on the Picts. From 550 to 650, we do know the names of some Pictish kings, and from the 650s or 660s until 685 presumably at least a considerable proportion of Pictland south of the Mounth was under the domination of the Anglo-Saxon rulers of Northumbria.

Near the end of this period, we start to get references in the Irish chronicles to Fortriu (the first is in 664), the Gaelic territorial name related to the earlier Verturiones. On his death in 692, Bridei son of Beli, the victor at Nechtanesmere in 685, was called *rex Fortrenn*, 'king of Fortriu' (AU [693].1). Fortriu itself used to be located by scholars in southern Pictland, but in 2006 Alex Woolf persuasively argued that Fortriu was actually a region including the Findhorn and Strathdearn rivers, in northern Pictland (Woolf 2006). This relocation means that Bridei's career makes much more sense; from 671 he was a ruler among the Picts, possibly a sub-king of the Northumbrians while they dominated Pictland (AU [672].6). In 680 Dunnottar was besieged (AU [681].5), and in 681 the Irish chronicles record that Bridei attacked the Orkneys (AU [682].4). Both these events are likely to represent the extension of Bridei's power, although it is unclear when exactly he challenged the Northumbrians, provoking the invasion that culminated in the destruction of the Northumbrian army and king at Nechtanesmere. Given Bede's description of the Northumbrian advance into a mountainous area, Woolf's suggestion that this battle was probably located at Dunachton in Speyside is preferable to the traditional identification with Dunnichen Moss in Angus (Woolf 2006, 183–7).

The overlordship of northern Pictland that Bridei may have established by 685 was probably not an unheralded development; the 'Life of St Columba' (*VSC*) includes an episode (*VSC* II.42) in which St Columba in the late 6th century goes to the other side of *Druim Alban* to see the Pictish king Bridei son of Mailcon and obtain protection for a monk who wanted to settle in the Orkneys. When he made this request of Bridei, the *sub-regulus*, literally 'little under king', of the Orkneys was present. Other episodes in the 'Life' (*VSC* II.33–5) indicate that Bridei son of Mailcon was based in a stronghold somewhere by or close to Loch Ness – the location favoured by scholars is the hillfort of Craig Phadrig, just west of Inverness. While the account may represent the situation when the 'Life' was written in *c*.700, it could well indicate that by then rulers around the northern part of the Great Glen had long claimed overlordship of the Orkneys, and that local areas were sometimes ruled by kings, albeit of diminished status.

The territories of northern Pictland

The extent and location of Fortriu (and the people who inhabited it) have not been firmly established, partly because Fortriu could have multiple meanings: it is used as a synonym for the overkingship of the Picts in the Irish chronicles, and as a term in the 'Northern Recension' of the 'Anglo-Saxon Chronicle' denoting the northern Picts (Woolf 2006, 197–9), as well as a smaller territory. In the prehistoric section of the *Series longior* Pictish king-list added in the reign of Constantín son of Cináed (862–76), the text states that Cruithne (Gaelic for 'Pict') son of Cinge had seven sons: *Fib, Fidach, Floclaid/Foltlaid, Fortrenn, Got/Cat, Ce* and *Circinn* (Anderson 2011, 245–89; Evans 2011, 46–51). These sons, given names of Pictish provinces, are then listed and included as kings ruling one after the other. Fortriu (as *Fortrenn*) is listed alongside them, its pre-eminence indicated by the fact that *Fortrenn* is given the longest reign of all of Cruithne's sons.

Alex Woolf has argued convincingly that Fortriu included Strathdearn where the River Findhorn flows, suggesting that Fortriu may have included Nairnshire and the Black Isle, but also possibly other areas of Ross, Inverness and Moray, but there are a few other pieces of evidence for its extent (Woolf 2006). *Mag Fortrenn*, the 'plain of Fortriu', appears in a Gaelic text, in *Senchas Síl hÍr*'s account of the settlement of the Cruithni (Dobbs 1923, 64–6), the Gaelic name for Picts, which although subject to a later alteration has a core dating from the mid 10th century or earlier. This text states that the Cruithni settled *Mag Fortrenn* first and also *Mag Circin* (probably the plain south of the Highland line including at least the Mearns, Strathmore and Strathearn). The text seems to be pairing the most significant plain south of the Mounth with the most prominent one to the north, indicating that the plain of Fortriu was extensive, perhaps including much of the coastline south of the Moray Firth (Evans 2013). In support of the view that Fortriu extended north beyond Moray, it has been suggested by Simon Taylor that the place-name Fortrose on the Black Isle may contain a form of Fortriu plus *ros*, 'headland', meaning 'the headland of Fortriu', presumably an older name for Chanonry Ness (Taylor (forthcoming); see also Ross 2011, 73).

The other main reference to Fortriu appears in *Historia Regum Anglorum*, attributed to Symeon of Durham, regarding the Anglo-Saxon king Æthelstan's campaign in Alba in 934, in which he wasted *Scotia* 'as far as Dunnottar and *Wertermorum*' (*usque Dunfoeder et Wertermorum*) (Woolf 2006, 197). *Werter* is the same element as *Uerturiones*, displaying a Brittonic rather than Gaelic form, and *morum* is Old English *mōr* meaning either 'a moor, waste and damp land', or 'high waste ground, a mountain'. *Wertermorum* has been interpreted as the Braes of Angus or the Mounth in Kincardineshire, because of their proximity to Dunnottar and to southern Pictland, but a more northern location is potentially possible (Woolf 2006, 197).

Some evidence for regions which were not part of Fortriu may be obtained from other northern territories present along with Fortriu in the Pictish king-lists: Cat, Ce and perhaps Fidach. Cat included not only Caithness, 'the promontory of Cat', with Norse *ness*, but also Sutherland, which is *Cataibh* in Scottish Gaelic, from *i Cataibh*, 'among the Cats'. The same word, perhaps denoting the Cat-people, is found in the medieval Gaelic name for the Shetlands, *Innse Catt*, 'Isles of the Cats' (Watson 1926, 29–30, 117).

Ce is found in the title of two stories in the 10th- and 11th-century medieval Irish tale-lists (Dobbs 1949, 137–8; Mac Cana 1980, 46, 47, 61, 63). In addition, in a tale about a person called Frigriu, this character is described as 'the artificer of *Cruthmag Cé*', 'the Cruithnean plain of Ce', confirming that it was in Pictland (it is unlikely that it refers to Cruithnean territory in Ireland) (Watson 1926, 115). Bennachie in Aberdeenshire is likely to include Ce, from *Beinn Ce* (or *Beinn a Che*), 'mountain/hill of Ce'. Ce, therefore, presumably included Bennachie and at least some of the lowland area around it in Garioch, Donside and the coastal plain of Aberdeenshire to the east.

Fidach has been tentatively explained by Watson as a word containing the Gaelic element *fid*, 'wood', probably meaning '(people) of the wood', so it could have been created for the *Series longior* Pictish king-list, as has been proposed by Dauvit Broun (Broun 2007, 79; Watson 1926, 115). If it was not coined for this text, it could, as Watson also suggested, possibly survive as Glen Fiddich in Banffshire, which may or may not have been part of Fortriu. Given the alliterative quality of the provincial names included in the Pictish king-list, we do not know whether the writer in desperation would have included area names inside the more local territory of Fortriu.

A number of other regional names in northern Pictland, most notably Ross, Moray and Buchan, may have origins in the Pictish period, but only appear in later sources. The main point relevant here is that while Fortriu was a significant region (and potentially an expanding one, as landowners in Fortriu extended their holdings into neighbouring areas), it was not the only territory in northern Pictland. It is difficult to determine the bounds of Fortriu at the end of its usage; the medieval bishoprics or earldoms of both Moray and Ross (at least Easter Ross) might have been based on Fortriu, but that is highly speculative, involving back-projecting post-1100 units to the early 10th century and before (Grant 2005, 89–90; Ross 2011, 64–80).

Pictish kingship and power structures

The evidence indicates that by the 680s, and possibly for periods from the late 6th century onwards, Fortriu had come to dominate northern Pictland. How this was achieved is not indicated in the sources, although similar methods to the military campaigns of the 680s are hinted at in the portrayal of Bridei son of Mailcon as resident in a *munitio*, 'fortress', in Adomnán's *VSC* II.35, and perhaps in the obscure event, 'The flight before the son of Mailcon', recorded in AU under 558 (duplicated at 560). However, the appearance of a *sub-regulus* of the Orkneys in *VSC* indicates that some regions could retain local rulers. This is supported by the existence of a king of Atholl, but the circumstances of the title's usage in AU 739.7 – the drowning of Talorgan son of Drostan, king of Atholl, by Onuist son of Uurguist, king of the Picts – do not perhaps provide the best example of local power in action!

The nature of Pictish kingship and succession can offer us some clues about how Verturian power was consolidated. Before the late 8th century no sons succeeded their fathers, although brothers did, and it is very difficult to reconstruct a family tree of the royal dynasty of Fortriu or for the Pictish overkingship (Evans 2008). Explanations have been that succession was matrilineal, passing through the female line (Anderson 2011; Miller 1982; Sellar 1985), or that it rotated between different royal kindreds (Ross 1999; Smyth 1984), or simply that kings were repeatedly deposed, preventing dynastic continuity (Woolf 1998). There is potentially some truth in all these ideas, but most of the analyses do not account for all the evidence. In particular, there is the very unusual fact that none of the fathers of kings had the same name as any of the kings; there were royal names and non-royal names, used to distinguish between people in the same lineage who could and could not become king (Evans 2008). The most likely explanation for this is that the naming system was designed to prevent sons from succeeding their fathers to the kingship, since any attempt by a person of the royal dynasty with a royal name himself to give his son a similar name (such as Talorgan, Bridei or Drust) would immediately demonstrate an intention to break the succession system.

There are a number of implications stemming from this, although much is speculative. One is that the royal dynasty was large, so that enough suitable candidates existed. The system meant that no narrow lineage could dominate, enabling the kingship to gain wider support, as there were more opportunities for local areas to intermarry with the royal kindred and have the chance to provide kings of Fortriu. Another likely consequence of the succession system was that, to prevent the king from distributing royal lands to their kinsmen, there was presumably a relatively strict distinction between the property of the kingship and the private possessions of the people who became kings. Such a distinction is also found in the 7th century AD in Visigothic Spain, where the king was chosen from a small group of noble families and father-to-son succession was also prevented (often by deposition). This differs from narrower single-kindred dominated kingships where presumably the basis of royal power was the private land and support that the king was able to muster, with less of a boundary between royal and private property.

The succession system outlined above survived until the 720s or 730s, when infighting allowed one kindred to become dominant. In the 720s, a sequence of succession and deposition culminated in a civil war in 728 and 729 fought between rival claimants: Nechtan son of Derilei, Drust and Elpin. Another important figure who supported Nechtan in this war was Onuist son of Uurguist. His origins are obscure (although he was probably from southern Pictland), but he defeated Drust and Elpin and re-established Nechtan on the throne. After Nechtan's death, Onuist became king (732–61), following this up by killing other local rulers, such as the king of Atholl in 739, and conquering Dál Riata in the west by 741. Since both his brothers and children had royal names, and Onuist's own name was not used by any earlier Pictish king, he may well have been from outside the royal dynasty. When he obtained power, it is likely that Onuist attempted to change the succession system so that sons could succeed their fathers. He was not immediately successful, since there were some later kings of the Picts seemingly unrelated to him, but many of the following kings were probably part of his kindred, including a certain Talorgan son of Onuist in the 780s (Broun 1998, 81–2). The royal and non-royal name pattern was broken; we get sons clearly succeeding their fathers in the early 9th century, albeit not immediately following the death of their fathers.

The gradual restriction of the kingship to a smaller kin-group in the late 8th century probably also marked a major change in local power structures, as the activities of Onuist and others in the 720s and 730s probably eliminated many potentates and rivals who presumably had claims according to the earlier succession system. As well as the Irish chronicle reference to his killing of the king of Atholl in 739, the obituary notice for Onuist in *Continuatio Bedae* in 761 is: 'Óengus, king of the Picts, died. From the beginning of his reign right to the end he perpetuated bloody crimes, like a tyrannical slaughterer' (Colgrave and Mynors 1969, 577; Forsyth 2000, 22). The lands of those attacked by Onuist were presumably either kept by the kings or distributed to close kinsmen or supporters. We may want to connect this change to Stephen Driscoll's hypothesis that in the late 8th and early 9th centuries there was a move away from hillforts to elite residences on lower ground and monastic patronage tied into pre-existing foci of activity, as seen at sites such as Forteviot and Scone (Driscoll 1998b). It may be that the new elite abandoned the hillforts maintained by more independent political groups and replaced them with undefended centres less threatening to the royal dynasty. This more restricted royal dynasty, which monopolised the kingship from *c.*788 to 834, also may over time have merged public royal possessions with their own landholdings, although the alternation of the kingship between two main branches may have provided a check on such appropriations.

How exactly localities were administered under the new system is uncertain; such areas could have been run by kindreds and supporters providing food renders for the king (who presumably also had his own estates). Alternatively, royal officials worked at a local level on behalf of the king, collecting dues and maintaining royal supervision of local elites. The debate about this has centred on the roles of people called *mormaer* (plural *mormaír*; a Gaelic word probably very similar to a Pictish one), *thane* and *toísech* (plural *toísig*) in later sources but which have sometimes been regarded as Pictish in origin. The *mormaer* first appears in an AU entry for the year 918, *toísech* first appears in Scotland in 11th-century transactions in the Book of Deer, while thanes and thanages, the territory of the thanes, are found in documents after 1100 (see Fig. 2). Until the last decade, the consensus was that *mormaír* (translated as 'great stewards' or 'sea-stewards') of areas like Moray and Buchan originated as royal officials, as did thanes, and that *toísig* were either leaders of a kindred or another, Gaelic, name for thane (Broun 2008, 315–26; Ross 2011, 47–55). Most notably, it has been suggested that *mormaír* were created in Argyll during the reign of Onuist son of Uurguist (732–61), and from there spread to Pictland (J.E. Fraser 2009a, 357–8). Similarly, Alexander Grant argued that the thane, although linguistically from Old English *thegn* and so possibly created after Lothian was conquered by Alba in the late 10th century, was a translation of an earlier official title for the administrators of *villae regiae*, royal multiple estates, in the Pictish period (Grant 2000, 63–4).

2. Thanages and provinces of Scotland (after Grant 1993, Map (A)).

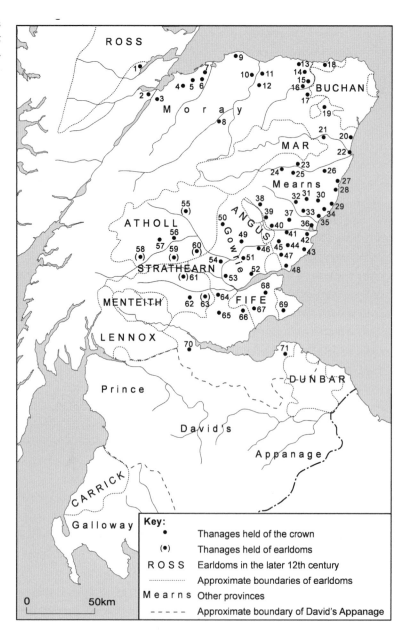

In the last decade, while the position of *mormaer* has been accepted as having Pictish origins, the view that the *mormaer*, thane and *toísech* were significant royal officials has been challenged. Alex Woolf has argued that the *mormaer* did not have much more status than a thane and should probably be regarded as first-among-equals in an area (Woolf 2007b, 344–9), and Broun has suggested that in the 11th and 12th centuries *mormaír*, thanes and *toísig* in the Book of Deer in Buchan were all local lords of varying status and not royal officials (Broun 2008, 353–6). Therefore, considerable doubt has been cast over the claim that the kingdom of Alba, and perhaps its Pictish predecessor, had developed state-like structures before 1100. However, even if the *mormaer* was simply a powerful local figure by the 11th century, the derivation of the name, including the term for 'steward', indicates that *the mormaer* was initially intended to be a royal official (Taylor with Márkus 2012, 438–9). As with many such positions, it can be suggested that over time it became embedded in local society, with dues going to the *mormaer*, later the earl, rather than the monarchy, but the king often limited the power of the *mormaer* by holding considerable landholdings in the *mormaer*'s territory. Understanding the origins of the thane is more difficult, although Ross has pointed out that every thanage in Moray consists of an exact multiple of davochs (usually six), showing that the thanage, like the parish, was later than the creation of the davochs (Ross 2006; 2011, 52). Unfortunately, though, without dating the davochs, this does not assist much with dating the thanages (and hence the thane).

Overall, in the Pictish era there were considerable changes in power structures relating to the royal dynasty, potentially reflected in transformations in material culture, but this still remains to be tested. Before the late 11th century, we have no evidence for the systematic creation of royal documentary records or for the existence of a substantial royal bureaucracy similar to that in England. The role of *mormaer* had probably been created by AD 900, and thanes could also have earlier Pictish antecedents, although there is still considerable debate about the origins and roles of these positions. The general impression is that the Pictish kingship derived from Fortriu shared features common to both Irish and Anglo-Saxon kingships. As in Anglo-Saxon regions, Pictish kings probably had royal officials, but like the Irish, they did not generally use formal administrative documents to define power relations. The result, however, was not a middle position: in terms of the creation of a powerful single kingship, the Picts followed the English, not the Irish, pattern.

The Gaelicisation and Scandinavianisation of northern Pictland

The end of the Picts and the creation of the Gaelic kingdom of Alba, the forerunner of the kingdom of Scotland, are processes which have sparked debate for generations. A number of sub-issues are involved, such as the ethnicity of rulers of the Picts and Dál Riata, the degree of migration and ethnic antagonism involved, and the impact of the Vikings. All these relate to the northern Picts, although in some ways the change was ostensibly even more striking than further south, because the north contained Fortriu, the territory which was identified with the Pictish overkingship, and Scandinavian settlement in some areas wiped out any linguistic trace of the Picts, producing another significant transformation.

When, how and why these changes happened, and their significance, are not agreed upon. Nevertheless, our understanding of the subject is increasing, and there are areas of common ground shared by scholars. One is that the Pictish language (or languages) was replaced by Gaelic and Norse, with variations depending on the area. For the elites this linguistic transition had taken place by AD 1000 at the latest, but at a local level pockets of Pictish speakers could potentially have survived much later. In the period from the late 8th to the 10th century, significant Scandinavian settlement took place in the Northern and Western Isles of Scotland, in some areas of the mainland, in particular Caithness, but also in Sutherland, Ross and on the western seaboard. In addition, by the end of the 10th century the elite of the kingdom of Alba (*Scotia*) no longer regarded themselves primarily as Picts but as Gaels, men and women of Alba, and *Scotti* (apart from in Lothian, which had never been Pictish and remained predominantly English-speaking). The kings and the leading noble families mainly traced their ancestry back to the Gaelic kindreds of Dál Riata and thence back to Ireland. As a result, Pictishness was replaced by other local, Gaelic and Scandinavian identities throughout the former Pictish realm.

However, this took place in a context in which it was Pictland, not Dál Riata, which survived to provide the core territory of the later kingdom. There is good evidence indicating that, after a period of separation beginning perhaps in the 770s, by the early 9th century Dál Riata and Pictland were reunited. The same people ruled both areas, the first of these being King Constantine son of Uurguist (d. 820), described on his death as 'king of Fortriu' in the Irish chronicles, although there may also have been subordinates ruling in Dál Riata. In 839 the Vikings fought against 'the men of Fortriu' and killed the current joint king (called Eóganán in Gaelic, Unen in Pictish) and other leaders. In 842 or 843 a person named Cináed mac Alpín in his contemporary Gaelic form, Cinioid in Pictish, now often known as Kenneth mac Alpine, became king of the Picts. His origins, ethnic identity and whether he was already king of Dál Riata have all been called into question. Cináed was an ancestor of the royal dynasty which dominated the kingship of the Scots until the late 13th century, when Alexander III died.

By the end of the 10th century the Gaelic kingdom of Alba, which was definitely in existence by 900, was firmly established, but it controlled less than half of what is now Scotland; the core territory was north of the Forth, east of *Druim Alban*, 'the ridge of Britain', the mountain watershed which divided it from Argyll, and south and east of the River Spey. Its control further north was less certain; the kings of Alba certainly did not control the Scandinavian-held lands of Caithness and Sutherland (and perhaps also Ross), but it is likely that they attempted to be overlords of the rulers of Moray, although there control was only effective sporadically (Ross 2011, 82–95; Woolf 2007b, 220–71). In the west, the Hebrides and much, if not all, of Argyll was under Scandinavian rule, and in the south the British kings of Strathclyde maintained power from Clydesdale down into Cumbria.

These more certain aspects still leave a large number of areas of contention. The main arguments have been over the nature and timing of the cultural and political transitions outlined above, from Pictish to Gaelic or Norse. Is the older interpretation of conquests from outside followed by rapid colonisation and cultural transformation correct, or were these processes more peaceful? When did the elite change from being Pictish to Gaelic? It has always been thought that there must have been considerable Scandinavian settlement in

Scotland in this period, but to what extent were similar movements of Gaelic speakers taking place from Argyll into Pictland, and was this a longer process, beginning much earlier than the 9th century?

There is also the question of Fortriu's position over the Pictish period. It had been the centre of the Pictish kingship in the late 7th century, but our sources for the 9th century mainly mention royal centres in the south, close to the Tay estuary and river located from St Andrews to Dunkeld. Had the focus of royal power changed from Fortriu to the south, and how were power structures altered at a local level? Also, not only was Pictish identity replaced by a Gaelic one, but many Pictish territorial names, most notably Fortriu, fell out of use; why was this the case?

In terms of the Gaelicisation process, it is increasingly the view of scholars that there was considerable continuity from Pictish to Gaelic culture, and that the transition may have already been taking place in the centuries before the 9th century, rather than primarily in the reign of Cináed mac Alpín (842/3–58). The significance of Gaelic ecclesiastics in the conversion and establishment of the Church in Pictland by the 7th century at least has long been regarded as one factor that would have facilitated change later. Among the northern Picts, it has been suggested that the cluster of Gaelic *cill* place-names around the west and north of the Great Glen, in south-east Sutherland, Ross, the Black Isle and Strathglass represents early churches founded around 700 by Curetán/Boniface (see Fig. 3) (MacDonald 1994; Taylor 1996, 94, 102–3). Moreover, the Pictish ogham inscriptions, found in both northern and southern Pictland, indicate perhaps more secular influence, since ogham was a Gaelic cipher system, converting letters of the alphabet to lines and notches along a baseline. The conquest of Dál Riata by Onuist son of Uurguist (732–61) and the subsequent joint rule of both Pictland and Dál Riata by the same kings in the early 9th century provide a context whereby cultural contacts could have been increased and the elites of the two regions welded together. Therefore, while we do have increased evidence for Gaelic culture (in terms of Gaelic personal names and cultural ideas and contacts) in the period from 842 to 900, this need not have been a dramatic change. The rule of Cináed mac Alpín was not accompanied by the replacement of ethnic or territorial terminology which would reflect a new Gaelic identity; that happened a generation or so afterwards.

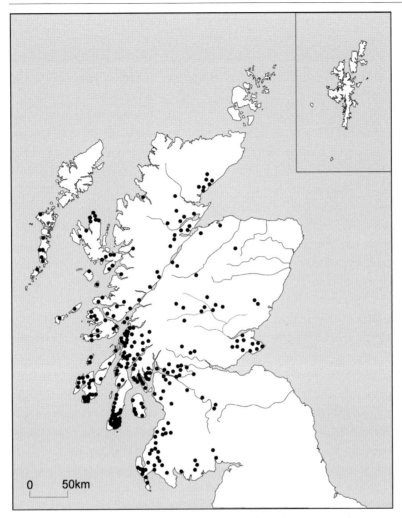

3. Location of place-names containing *cill* (after Taylor 1996, Fig. 5.2).

0   50km

Our last certain contemporary chronicle reference to the Picts occurs when AU 878.2 described Áed son of Cináed mac Alpín as 'king of the Picts'. When the same text next records the death of a king in AU 900.6, Domnall son of Constantín is called 'king of Alba', *rí Alban*. A similar change occurs in the *Chronicle of the Kings of Alba* (CKA) where the territory is called *Pictavia* in Domnall son of Constantín's reign (889–900), but has become *Albania* when events in 903 are recounted (CKA, 251). In the 10th century, Gaelic *Goídil* ('Gaels') and *Albanaig* or *fir Alban* ('men of Alba'), as well as the Latin term *Scotti*, come to be used for the inhabitants of Alba, replacing *Picti* and 'men of Fortriu', while for the territory Latin *Albania* and *Scotia* (which had originally denoted Ireland), Gaelic *Alba* and

English *Scottaland* appear instead of *Pictavia* and Gaelic *Cruithentúath* (Broun 2007, 71–97; Charles-Edwards 2008). This seems like a radical transformation, dateable to the late 9th and early 10th centuries, involving the rejection of Pictish identity in favour of a new Gaelic Albanian one.

Indeed, by the end of the 10th century the kings and leading noble families of Alba traced their ancestry from the kindreds of Dál Riata, rather than from the Picts, and by the 12th century the idea that the Picts were destroyed by Cináed mac Alpín had arisen. The idea of ethnic destruction is exemplified by the tale of the 'Treachery of Scone' in which Pictish nobles were invited to a feast by Cináed and then treacherously massacred by his followers (Anderson 1922, 1:271–4). In modern times it has been difficult to understand how the complete loss of the Pictish language took place without discrimination and ethnic replacement. Ethnic conflicts and cleansing are possible, as has been seen in Rwanda, the former Yugoslavia and elsewhere in recent decades. In the case of the Picts, based on comments in CKA, it has been suggested that their defeats at the hands of the Vikings in the 9th century may have been regarded by the growing Gaelic *Céli Dé* reform movement as heavenly punishment for their sins. This interpretation of events was thus used to legitimise the replacement of a Pictish elite with a Gaelic aristocracy and clergy, a Christian reading of history similar to that used to justify the British to Anglo-Saxon transition (Wormald 1996, 131–60).

However, it is possible that the transition from Pictland to Alba was less dramatic than this. There was a word related to Gaelic *Alba* in Pictish, *Albidosi* ('people of Albidia'), found in CKA in the account of Máel Coluim mac Domnaill's reign (943–54); both *Alba* and *Albidosi* derive from an ancient word for Britain, found as *Albion* in classical sources (Broun 2007, 71–97; Dumville 1996; Woolf 2007b, 177–80). Therefore, the name Alba could have united both Picts and Gaels by including all of Gaelic and Pictish Britain, and maybe a broader hegemony even if political reality meant that the term later became restricted mainly to former Pictish territory. There is, then, little reason to regard the appearance of *rí Alban* for the kings as an abrupt change.

There is some evidence that Fortriu also continued to be a term used after AD 900. AU 904.4 records that the men of Fortriu killed Ímar grandson of Ímar. It is not certain whether the men of Fortriu referred to were only inhabitants of the province in northern Pictland or the wider Pictish realm, but the appearance of Fortriu in an Irish text, which had four years earlier started to use the title *rí Alban*, demonstrates at least that the term Fortriu was still relevant to the Irish chroniclers. Later, in 934, according to the northern English *Historia Regum Anglorum*, the English King Æthelstan wasted *Scotia* 'as far as Dunnottar and *Wertermorum*' (see above p. 19), with the use of *Werter-* indicating that the Pictish form of Fortriu was still known and was the basis for more local (albeit substantial) features of the landscape then (Woolf 2007b, 161). After this, Fortriu no longer appears in contemporary chronicles, but we do have Gaelic sources employing the term for events in the past. There is little indication that the transition to Albanian and Gaelic terminology was accompanied by a conscious rejection of names based on Fortriu.

Otherwise, the degree of continuity in the northern Pictish territories is difficult to quantify, since although Cat survived in Caithness and the Gaelic name for Sutherland, it is uncertain whether Ross and Moray have Pictish or Gaelic origins. Ross either means the moor or plain (if Pictish) or the promontory (if Gaelic) of Easter Ross, but it first appears as a *regio* ('kingdom' or 'region') and as a river name in the 'Life of St Cadróe' of Metz, which focuses on Cadróe, a nobleman of the kingdom of Alba who in the mid 10th century went to the Continent and became a monk and significant Church reformer, before dying between 971 and 976 (Ó Riain 2009). The text contains an account of the settlement of northern Britain which includes the following:

> Many years passed until, crossing the sea nearest to them, they occupied the island of Euea, now called Iona. Not yet content, after surveying the nearby sea of Britain, they settled along the river *Rosim* in the kingdom [or 'region'] of Rossia. Heading for the towns of Rigmonath [St Andrews] and Bellethor, which are not far from one another, they took possession of them. (Ó Riain 2009, 41; with a few emendations)

This text, while written on the Continent and displaying a very faulty understanding of geography, contains some genuinely contemporary information and indicates that Ross existed as a territorial name by the early 11th century.

Moray could derive from Pictish or Gaelic, although a Pictish origin is preferable given that the spelling is closer to Welsh and Cornish cognates *moreb* and *morab*, meaning 'low-lying land near to the sea' (Woolf 2007b, 177–8), a better translation than W.J. Watson's 'sea-settlement', based on a supposed derivation from **mori-treb-* (Watson 1926, 115–16). Moray first appears in CKA in Máel Coluim mac Domnaill's reign (943–54), when the king of Alba with his army 'crossed into *Moreb* and slew Cellach' (Woolf 2007b, 177). There is also little to support the view that Cenél Loairn in Dál Riata migrated up the Great Glen, replacing Pictish Fortriu with Gaelic territories, while the Cenél nGabráin kindred further south conquered southern Pictland. It is plausible, however, that a similar process of territorial fragmentation happened in northern Pictland as in the south, where we start in the period from 900 to 1100 to find references to areas like Angus, the Mearns, Gowrie and Strathearn (see Fig. 2), where previously in Pictish times we simply know of Circin (Evans 2013).

In the north, lesser territories, which may already have existed before 900, like Ross, Moray, Buchan and Marr, may have risen to prominence at the expense of larger units like Fortriu and Ce, possibly reflecting changes in the political structure of Alba compared to Pictland. The derivation of Buchan and Marr is uncertain, but they could potentially be early in date (Watson 1926, 115, 119). Another late medieval territory, Badenoch, means 'the drowned land' in Gaelic, referring to the flooding in the area once caused by the River Spey (Watson 1926, 118), while other names in northern Scotland, such as Elgin, Banff and the River Deveron, may contain Gaelic words for Ireland (Clancy 2010; Nicolaisen 1993; Watson 1926, 225–33). Whether Pictish or Gaelic in origin, these units only start to appear in our sources after 900, possibly reflecting a reorganised landscape of lordship. This could simply reflect the existence of more evidence for local units after 900, but the disappearance of Fortriu and Ce indicates that some transformation had taken place.

In general, the place-name evidence for northern Scotland potentially related to the end of the Picts can be divided into two zones: the first where Gaelic clearly succeeded Pictish, south and east of the Beauly and Strathglass; the second contains Scandinavian and Gaelic place-names on top of the Pictish stratum. In the first zone, Pictish place-names are quite common, as are *pett* names (often now *pit*), used for a piece of land (Taylor 2011, 77–80, 103, 105). *Pett* appears in Scotland north of the Forth (with a few examples to the south of it) and generally on the east side of the Highlands, although there are two on the west coastal region opposite Skye (See Fig. 4, from Nicolaisen 2001, 198, noting that more instances exist in south-east Sutherland and that the two cases included in Glenelg are actually only one name (Taylor 2011, 79–80)). *Pett* names are mainly now thought to date from after the Pictish period, after the element had been adopted by Gaelic speakers. However, since *pett* was adopted by the Gaels from the Picts, the presence of this element indicates that an area was once Pictish or was influenced considerably in the following centuries by people from Pictland.

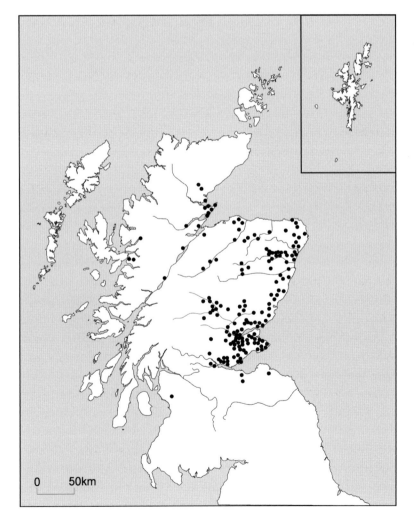

4. Location of place-names containing *pit* (after Nicolaisen, 2001, Fig. 17).

In the second zone, with Scandinavian and Gaelic names, Pictish survivals are less frequent, with none north of southern Sutherland or on the far north-west coast, a result of extensive Scandinavian settlement in the northern mainland of Scotland. The Scandinavian place-names occur along the coast, for instance around the north-west, reflecting the sea-routes travelled by Scandinavians, but there are also some inland, indicating that more substantial settlement took place (Fraser 1995). The lack of Pictish place-names and the high density of Scandinavian names in coastal areas of Caithness might indicate that there was greater disruption during settlement compared to Sutherland and further south to the Beauly valley where Scandinavian and some Pictish names survive (Fig. 5). Scandinavian place-names have not so far been identified on the southern side of the Moray Firth, so it is fairly safe to argue that there was little or no long-term Scandinavian settlement in Moray and further east.

In some areas of Scandinavian settlement on the mainland, such as Ross and Sutherland, Scandinavian place-names are intermixed with Gaelic and Pictish names (Crawford and Taylor 2003; Gammeltoft 2001). The cluster of *pett* names on the Tarbat peninsula is intriguing. What does the existence of Pictish Peffer close to Norse Dingwall, or the appearance of Scandinavian Arboll, Cadboll and Shandwick close to Gaelic place-names such as Pitcalnie, Portmahomack and the name Tarbat indicate? The later existence of Pictish and possibly also Gaelic names (depending on when Gaelic arrived) implies a degree of continuity of non-Scandinavian languages greater than in other regions, such as the Orkneys, which lack these Celtic place-name survivals. Given the existence of similar concentrations south of the Mounth around the monasteries of Abernethy and Dunfermline, it is possible, as scholars have suggested, that at least some of the *pett* names in Ross can be explained similarly. While the monastery of Portmahomack may have ceased to exist as a community in the 9th century, and the general view is that the *pett* names are not that early, perhaps the landholdings of the monastery continued under the supervision of a different ecclesiastical establishment (Carver 2016a, 67–70), so the *pett* names might reflect some continuity. Further research combining place-name research and investigations of the landholding, archaeology and environment might produce a clearer picture of the area's linguistic, social and political development.

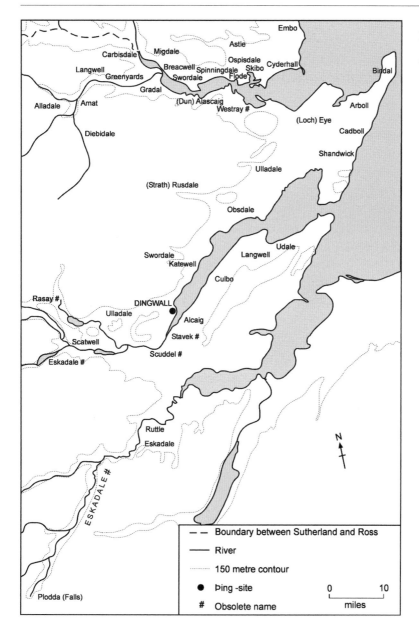

5. Norse names in Easter Ross and South Sutherland (after Crawford and Taylor 2003, Fig. 2).

There are still many questions remaining about the change from Pictland to Alba. Given our uncertainty in dating Scandinavian settlement, and associated conquests, it is not currently possible to declare whether or not this was a major factor in the cultural and linguistic shift which ended Pictish identity and language. There is good evidence to suggest that the process was long and not abrupt in terms of the core names of the kingdom and people. However, the period from about 850 to 950 does seem to have been when a mainly Pictish culture shifted to become a majority Gaelic one, at least in terms of the elite. If Cináed mac Alpín's rise to power in Pictland is no longer regarded as the catalyst for this change, the Scandinavian impact is left as the main suspect. The period of transition coincided with the height of Viking depredations in northern Britain. If Woolf's suggestion that the southern Hebrides were conquered in the late 840s is correct, then this would have had a knock-on effect on Pictland, since Pictish kings had dominated Dál Riata for most of the preceding half-century. The result of these attacks could have been an influx of Gaelic-speaking refugees, including members of the clerical and secular elite, to the lands of their Pictish overlords, altering the balance of Picts and Gaels in Pictland. In the following decades, especially in the 860s, 870s and around 900, substantial Viking attacks were made on Pictland itself. The Viking campaigns in the 860s and 870s were conducted by the same leaders who broke the power of the Anglo-Saxon kings of East Anglia, Northumbria and Mercia, allowing Scandinavian conquest. The attacks on the Picts threatened the very basis of the Pictish overkingship, since they questioned the ability of Pictish kings to provide defence, while royal revenues were also diverted to the Viking horde.

According to CKA and the Irish chronicles, on maybe three occasions, in 839, perhaps 876 and 900, the Vikings killed kings of the Picts or Alba; they raided and plundered extensively, and took tribute and hostages (AU 839.9; CKA, 250, 251). They also stayed in Pictland for considerable periods in 866 and 875. These occupations would have involved living off the Picts and forcing them to pay tribute, causing substantial strains on Pictish resources and undermining royal power, but this need not have led to any settlement. The geographical extent of some of these episodes is not clear; where details are given the places tend to be in southern Pictland, but, where the entries only vaguely state that they faced Picts or the men of Fortriu, a more northern location for Scandinavian activity cannot be dismissed.

The way to respond successfully to these attacks was through transformation (Woolf 2007b, 116–34, 312–42). Apart from the Pictish kingdom, the other realm in Britain that succeeded in defeating the Vikings, after first paying tribute and experiencing occupation, was that of the West Saxons. Under King Alfred and their successors, they reorganised their defence, through the creation of *burhs* which provided places of refuge and safety. It is also likely that they, as well as other rulers in western Europe, appropriated Church lands to provide themselves with more patronage and revenues; when the whole of society, including Christianity, was at risk, confiscation of Church property became legitimate for the greater cause. While there is little direct evidence for this in northern Britain, the reduction in sculptural patronage in the 10th century compared to previous centuries could reflect a Church with a lower level of available resources. Such lands, and others which became available, could have been used by the kings to reward loyal followers, perhaps favouring Gaels who had previously come from Dál Riata. Alex Woolf has suggested that the key period for this process was the reigns of Giric son of Dúngal (king with Eochaid son of Rhun, 878–89), Domnall son of Constantín (889–900) and the first years of the reign of Constantín son of Áed (900–43). Giric (along with Eochaid) may have been a leader of a Gaelic faction which gained the kingdom after the dynasty of Alpín had failed to defeat the Vikings, but when Domnall and Constantín, descendants of Alpín dynasty, reigned after Giric their experience as exiles in Ireland may have ensured that they continued the process of Gaelicisation. Woolf (2007b, 321–6, 340–2) views this as the context in which kindreds from Dál Riata became the established elite in the kingdom of Alba, with Cenél Loairn moving to Moray, and considers that the *pett* and *baile* place-names were coined during tenurial changes which formed part of this process.

While there is much to recommend in this interpretation, it is unlikely that the Gaelic kindreds of Dál Riata reconstituted themselves unaltered as the elite of Alba; they would have been weakened by the loss of much of the Hebrides by the mid 9th century, and the repeated wars against the Vikings in Pictland would have involved adaptation, and have favoured some groups and destroyed others, perhaps propelling some people from relative obscurity. We should, therefore, be very wary of 11th-century sources, such as a genealogical tract from the reign of Máel Coluim II son of Cináed (1005–34) which claimed Gaelic royal ancestry for many of those ruling the main territories in Alba; it is preferable to view them as statements explaining the 11th-century political situation (Woolf 2007b, 226).

This text may, however, be significant in displaying the shift in power which had taken place in Pictland as a whole. It focuses on the royal kindred of Alba, with the main territorial families related to the main royal line through lineages descended from figures supposed to have lived in 6th-century Dál Riata. As with all royal dynasties, the closer the relationship to the current king, the greater the prestige, so the fact that the nearest kindreds to the kings of Alba were the noble families of Gowrie, Fife and Strathearn, whereas Moray and Angus were more distantly related, and Ross and Buchan were not mentioned, is indicative of the status of the regions of Alba. The text demonstrates that by this time Alba north of the Mounth was not as significant to these kings as the southern half of the realm, a marked shift from the period when Fortriu was the dominant polity among the Picts. When exactly this movement took place is not known; by the second half of the 9th century there is already good evidence for the significance of southern centres like Forteviot, Dunkeld and maybe *Cennbelathoir* (whose location is possibly just north of Perth), and by the early 10th century also Scone. Were northern centres still important at the same time, just not recorded, or had they gone into decline by the mid 9th century, as indicated by excavations at the Pictish monastery at Portmahomack? To what extent were the Scandinavians part of this process?

In recent decades, advances in the study of the written sources have enabled us to understand better the origins, development and eclipse of Pictish identity and society. While one result has been to encourage scepticism about the evidence and how it used to be interpreted, the effect is that it is clearer what we can and cannot expect the texts to indicate. Hopefully, archaeological investigation will allow us to pursue many of the lines of enquiry thrown up by the historical evidence, as well as filling in some of the large holes in our knowledge, bringing out new facets of the society of the northern Picts. However, although it is difficult to do well, research that enables the integration of evidence from different disciplines, for instance of place-names, landholdings and archaeology in their landscape context is also needed to identify the nature of the complex interactions and developments of the early medieval period. Only then can some of the important remaining questions about the northern Picts be answered.

CHAPTER THREE

Fortified settlement in northern Pictland

Gordon Noble

The post-Roman centuries in northern Britain have long been identified as a new phase of hillfort building, and the emergence of such architecture can be identified as a key development in the social and political hierarchies that emerged in the early medieval period. This chapter outlines the evidence for the development of hillforts and defended enclosures in northern Britain and in particular the areas of eastern and northern Scotland that came to define the core of the kingdoms of the Picts. The evidence for Pictland, particularly from northern Pictland, increasingly suggests a diverse range of enclosed architecture was implicated in the developing frameworks of power and governance in an early medieval context. The character of the defended sites also increasingly suggests that the defensive dimension to such locations was only one element of the significance of these sites in creating and defining new forms of social and political groupings in northern Britain.

The emergence of fortified enclosures in northern Britain

The 5th and 6th centuries in northern Britain are a key period when historical sources increase in frequency for the societies that had lived north of the Roman frontier (Chapter 2 of this volume; Evans 2008, 2014; Fraser 2009a; Woolf 2007b). The literary sources suggest that this was a transformative period with the emergence of more developed systems of rulership and social structure. Important changes can also be identified in the archaeological record in this same chronological horizon: for example, after more than 1,000 years of very limited burial evidence, the dead become a more prominent part of the archaeological record (Chapter 5 of this volume; Maldonado 2013; Mitchell and Noble 2017). As well as cemeteries, memorials to the dead and traditions of monumental carved stone monuments emerged and played notable roles in creating and maintaining new forms of personal and group affiliation (e.g. Forsyth 1997a, b; Goldberg 2012, 155–9; Henderson and Henderson 2004; Samson 1992).

However, one of the most significant changes visible in early medieval northern Britain was the re-emergence of fortified enclosures and settlements (Alcock 2003, 179–99). As in Ireland and western England and Wales, the hillfort formed the material manifestation of power, a northern alternative (or addition) to the hall as symbol of more developed social hierarchies in a post-Roman context. In this chapter, the types of fortified sites that emerged in the early medieval period in northern Britain are outlined and the important role they played in early medieval society is explored, notably their role in establishing and reinforcing new and emergent cultural identities. Reference will be made to sites across early medieval Scotland, but the role of fortified sites among the Picts, particularly northern Pictland, will be foregrounded. As noted in Chapter 2, the Picts are first mentioned in the later 3rd century AD by late Roman writers who recorded attacks on Britain's northern frontier by aggressors they called *Picti*, or 'painted people' (see also Fraser 2009a, 43–67). Throughout the 4th century, military campaigns were waged against the Picts as they caused repeated trouble north and south of Hadrian's Wall. After the Roman withdrawal, across the period *c.* AD 400–900, the kingdoms of the Picts became some of the most powerful political groups in northern Britain. At the height of Pictish cultural expansion, Pictish influence was felt across a large area (and perhaps territory) that stretched from the Firth of Forth in the south to Orkney and Shetland in the north and from the east coast to the northern Hebrides in western Scotland. The Picts were just one of the many early medieval peoples of what we now identify as Scotland or northern Britain – this was an intense period of competing social, political and cultural identities: to the west lay the Scots, Gaelic-speaking peoples with strong connections to Ireland (Campbell 2001); in the south-west of modern Scotland were the Strathclyde Britons; and in the south-east was the Anglo-Saxon kingdom of Bernicia (Woolf 2007b, 5). From the late 8th century onwards commenced Viking intrusion and subsequent settlement, and these had a huge impact on all of the existing king-doms, but particularly in the far north where the earldoms of Orkney and Caithness were established in areas that were either part of Pictland or strongly influenced by Pictish overlords (Woolf 2007b, 275–311). All of the early medieval societies of Scotland, with the possible exception of the Vikings, were united by – or rather shared in – the construction of defended settlements from at least the 5th or 6th century AD onwards.

Fortified settlements in Pictland

Research on the Picts, once seen as the darkest of the 'Dark Age' soci-eties in northern Britain, is now slowly beginning to drive important research agendas on the character of defended settlement in early medieval Scotland. At least three main types of fortified enclosure can be identified in Pictland, and many of the recent advances have been made in northern Pictland (Noble *et al.* 2013). Following this work, we can identify a range of enclosed sites from 'nuclear' hillforts, to smaller 'ringforts' or settlement enclosures to coastal promontory forts. These types of enclosure closely match similar forms found across northern and western Britain and Ireland in the early medieval period.

'Nuclear'/multiple enclosure forts

The best-known of the Pictish fortified enclosures are the hilltop enclosures often known as 'nuclear' hillforts. These sites are charac-terised by multiple ramparts, with a series of terraces and enclosures, but with a central (and higher) enclosure of seemingly greater signifi-cance and a series of lower enclosures radiating or extending from this central nucleus (a site type first labelled and explored by Stevenson 1949). Enclosures of this form exist beyond Pictland, of course, with a prominent example being Dunadd in western Scotland, a multival-late fort on a prominent rocky hill, identified as the principal seat of the Scots of Dál Riata (Lane and Campbell 2000) (Fig. 6). In terms of numbers, fewer than ten hilltop enclosed sites in Pictland have been radiocarbon dated, but more have been proposed through their morphology (Ralston 2004). The most extensively investigated are Dundurn in Perthshire and Clatchard Craig, Fife, both in southern Pictland.

6. Plans of fortified sites
in Pictland compared
with Dunadd in western
Scotland (after Alcock 2003,
Figs. 55, 56 and 60).

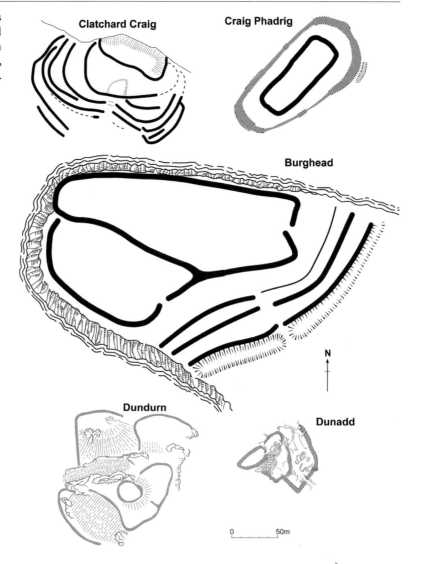

Clatchard Craig

Craig Phadrig

Burghead

N

Dundurn

Dunadd

0   50m

Excavations at the nuclear hillfort at Dundurn, Perthshire in 1976–77 (Figs. 6, 7) were conducted as part of Leslie Alcock's long-term programme of excavating historically documented early medieval fortifications in western and northern Britain. His programme of work in Scotland was conceived in 1973 and involved 'keyhole' excavation with the objective of documenting early medieval activity (Alcock and Alcock 1990, 216). Dundurn is one of the few Pictish sites referred to in early documents – the Annals of Ulster document a siege in AD 682 (AU 683.3). At Dundurn, Alcock's keyhole excavations revealed evidence for a prominent summit citadel enclosure with a series of lower enclosures on top of a craggy outcrop overlooking the upper Earn river valley (Alcock *et al.* 1989). Like most early medieval forts in Scotland the overall site was small – the outer terraces occupy an area covering three hectares in maximum extent, but the defences may not all date to the same period. The summit itself was only around 35m × 25m in diameter, with 4m-thick timber-laced walls.

7. Aerial view of Dundurn fort looking down Strathearn.

Alcock suggested that the site may have originated as a palisaded enclosure in the 5th or 6th centuries AD, subsequently replaced with the construction of the stone-built summit citadel. The fort was then later expanded through the construction of terrace walls and the rebuilding of the citadel defence over the coming centuries, with the entire sequence extending into the 8th or 9th century AD. Evidence of the primary palisade consisted of rock-cut grooves across the upper terrace as well as preserved timbers found in waterlogged deposits in a trench cut across the upper terrace defences. These timbers included a massive oak beam and thinner oak planks, some with evidence for wooden peg fasteners.

The wooden elements of the timber-laced rampart of the upper citadel at Dundurn had been secured using large iron nails or spikes up to 170 mm long – over 100 of these were found in

Alcock's small trench over the summit enclosure. The front face of the rampart consisted of horizontal timbers laid in rock-cut grooves. This nailed-timbered rampart was in turn destroyed and replaced by a more massive stone-built rampart. Inside, reused Roman masonry and other structural evidence suggested a number of buildings. The evidence for material culture from Dundurn was limited owing to the scale of excavation. However, one sherd of E-ware, another sherd of a vessel from the Rhineland and two sherds of imported glass indicate Continental connections. Other finds, which included quern stones and whetstones, a glass boss, a spindle whorl, bone pins and a leather shoe, hint at some of the activities carried out in the fort (Alcock *et al.* 1989, 214–21). Given the very limited nature of Alcock's excavations, it is hard to say much about the distribution of material culture – preservation on site was also very poor apart from in one waterlogged section of the site.

Very few other Pictish forts are named in historical sources, and few have been excavated on any scale. The most extensive modern excavations on a hillfort of the nuclear type in Pictland were conducted at Clatchard Craig in Fife, again in southern Pictland (Figs. 6, 8), in advance of its total destruction by quarrying (Close-Brooks 1986). Excavations carried out by Ritchie in the early 1950s and by R Hope-Simpson in 1959 and 1960, showed that the hill had been enclosed by no fewer than seven individual defences, but covered an area of less than two hectares. The inner ramparts defined a summit 'citadel' comprising a relatively small internal area. Below, two further ramparts enclosed an upper terrace, while a further series of ramparts seemingly reinforced the upper terrace enclosure. All of the ramparts excavated showed evidence of stone facing-walls and timber lacing. Excavations in the interior of the fort revealed little apart from a hearth and floor surface in the upper terrace enclosure. Clay mould fragments were found in association with, and under the floor and hearth of the possible building here. These moulds were for brooch manufacture of a type probably dating to the 8th century AD. Two sherds of E-ware, spindle whorls, bone pins and animal bones suggest occupation in this upper enclosure (Close-Brooks 1986, 146–7).

There are a number of other examples of nuclear forts in Pictland, including sites such as East Lomond in Fife, which recall the

8. Clatchard Craig fort © Historic Environment Scotland.

hierarchical organisation and extensive defences found at Dundurn and Clatchard Craig (Driscoll 2011, 256; Feachem 1955). In northern Pictland, there have been few excavations of hillforts of this character. However, one site of this type recently confirmed as featuring deposits of early medieval date is the Mither Tap, Bennachie, in Aberdeenshire (Fig. 9; Plate 1): here small-scale excavations conducted as part of path improvement by Forestry Commission Scotland have confirmed occupation in the 1st millennium AD at a hillfort long suspected to be a Pictish stronghold given its morphological form (Atkinson 2006, 2007; Feachem 1955, 76; RCAHMS 2007, 105–7; Shepherd 1993).

Undoubtedly the so-called 'nuclear' form of some of the forts outlined above emerged through time and through the reuse of earlier remains in some cases. Other major hillforts in Pictland also utilised the remains of Iron Age defences, such as Craig Phadrig, Inverness (Fig. 6), where finds of E-ware and a fragment of a mould for an escutcheon from a hanging bowl, plus a radiocarbon date from an occupation layer of the 5th–6th century AD, and more recent 5th–6th century dates from a palisade on top of the Iron Age ramparts, all reveal an early medieval phase to the use of this fort in northern

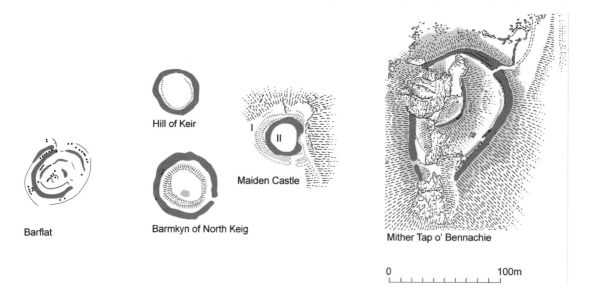

Hill of Keir

Maiden Castle

Barflat

Barmkyn of North Keig

Mither Tap o' Bennachie

0   100m

9. Plans of Pictish enclosed sites in Aberdeenshire: the palisade at Barflat (Rhynie), 'ringforts' at Maiden Castle, Hill of Keir and Barmkyn of North Keig and the hillfort at the Mither Tap (after RCAHMS 2007).

Pictland. There was also tentative evidence for the reconstruction of the lower rampart during the fort's secondary historic-period phase of use (Cook 2010; Small and Cottam 1972). The reuse of Iron Age hillforts may have been common; another fort from northern Pictland, the Doune of Relugas, Moray, has recently been confirmed to have early medieval phases of occupation as well as Iron Age.

Coastal promontory forts

Much more numerous in northern Pictland are coastal promontory forts, found throughout north-east Scotland. The most sustained archaeological work has been along the Moray Firth coast where a number of sites show evidence of use or construction of defended enclosures in the 1st millennium AD. To date, coastal promontory forts seem to be a particularly prominent phenomenon in northern Pictland.

The most spectacular example of these defended coastal communities is undoubtedly Burghead (Figs. 6, 10). The early medieval archaeology at Burghead is perhaps more impressive than any other site in Pictland despite the fact that a large portion of the fort was damaged in the early 19th century with the construction of a planned village and harbour over the remains of the fort (see Oram 2007 for a full account). The fort appears to have covered an area of around 5.5 hectares – the largest Pictish fortified site known (Alcock 2003,

193; Foster 2014, 43). Well-known finds from Burghead include nearly 30 bull carvings and an impressive well (Oram 2007; Ralston 2004; RCAHMS 2007, 104; Young 1890, 1891, 1893). Excavation at the site has had a long history, extending back to the work of James MacDonald, who excavated the ramparts of the upper and lower citadel enclosures in the 1860s (MacDonald 1862, 348). Thirty years later, the local antiquarian Hugh Young recounted, in a quite remarkable series of reports, the most detailed evidence for the ramparts, suggesting that they were of exceptional scale and workmanship (1891, 189). In the lower fort, the ramparts were composed of an inner and outer drystone wall utilising dressed and carefully quarried stone. Between the facing-walls was a core of earth, stone and midden material (Young 1891, 436). The two facing-walls were linked or at least bonded to the rampart core by oak planks and logs riveted together in places by iron nails or spikes up to 0.2m long. Young identified that the lower citadel rampart had been over 7m wide and perhaps as much as 6m high. Further work in the late 1960s by Alan Small (1969) focused on the upper citadel and showed that the character of the defences may have differed across the site. The most recent studies at Burghead by Edwards and Ralston (1978) and latterly by Ralston (2004) have provided valuable additional chronological and environmental information focusing on the rampart construction and dating.

The evidence from Burghead can be set alongside that from a limited number of further examples of promontory forts with secure evidence for construction or use in the 1st millennium AD; these include much more modest forts such as Portknockie on the Banffshire coastline (Ralston 1980, 1987) (Plate 2). Like the hillforts outlined earlier, promontory forts also reused Iron Age sites, as evident at Cullykhan, Aberdeenshire, where Pictish period reuse included both occupation and refortification (Greig 1970, 1971). Recent work at Dunnicaer, near Stonehaven, has also identified a 1st-millennium AD phase (see Chapter 6).

'Ringforts'/settlement enclosures

One further type of enclosure can be highlighted. In a classic volume, *The Problem of the Picts* (Wainwright 1955a), the archaeologist Richard Feachem suggested that a series of small circular enclosures or 'ringforts' found in Pictland were also likely to be early medieval

10. Aerial image of Burghead fort showing the upper citadel with later buildings on top and the lower citadel (left).

in date (Feachem 1955). Excavation has been slow to establish that this is the case, but the Pictish sites can now be considered alongside other northern British examples of ringforts or duns such as the evidence from western Scotland in Argyll. The latter evidence includes renewed phases of construction of smaller fortified settlements in the second half of the 1st millennium AD, again in some cases reusing earlier Iron Age sites (Harding 2004, 129–32). In Pictland, excavations at two sites in southern Pictland at Litigan and Queen's View first suggested early medieval occupation of small settlement enclosures with substantial outer stone walls (Taylor 1990). The Perthshire sites are usually around 15–30m in diameter with stone walls up to 3m thick. Excavations at Aldclune, also in Perthshire, show that Iron Age homesteads could also be revamped. At Aldclune, one of a pair of ringforts (Site 1), originally constructed in the last centuries BC and early centuries AD, was perhaps reoccupied in the second half of the

1st millennium AD; its latest phase included construction of a walled enclosure, which finds close parallel in sites dated to the 5th–6th centuries AD in Aberdeenshire (Hingley *et al.* 1997, Illus. 2 and 3).

The emerging evidence for settlement enclosures of the character outlined above has been significantly advanced by more recent work carried out in northern Pictland in Aberdeenshire. While most excavations have been keyhole in nature, these reveal that a series of sites identified by the Royal Commission on the Ancient and Historical Monuments of Scotland Donside survey (RCAHMS 2007) as a distinctive class of small stone-walled defined sites date to the early medieval period. Sites investigated include Maiden Castle on the slopes of Bennachie in Aberdeenshire (Cook 2011a) (Fig. 9), which featured remains of at least two successive enclosures – a thick stone-walled enclosure (around 20m in internal diameter) with perhaps successive phases of surrounding ramparts and ditches (max. 40m in overall diameter). It is uncertain whether the stone-walled enclosure was roofed, or perhaps more likely surrounded internal buildings (Cook 2011a, 27). Test-pits around the fortified site found evidence for unenclosed settlement around the enclosure. Other sites dated to this period include a multivallate stone-walled enclosure at Cairnmore in western Aberdeenshire and, potentially, a series of surveyed, but as yet unexcavated, sites in the Don Valley (Cook 2011b) (Fig. 9).

Perhaps closely related to these smaller series of fortified settlements is a very recently identified site at Rhynie (also Aberdeenshire) (see Chapter 4). In 2011 and 2012 a lowland enclosure with traces of internal buildings was firmly dated to the early medieval period at Rhynie (Noble *et al.* 2013; Noble and Gondek 2011) (Fig. 9; Plate 3) (Chapter 4). The excavations revealed two ditched enclosures and a third outer timber-defined enclosure measuring *c.*60m in maximum diameter. The outer enclosure consisted of a deep foundation trench (up to 1.5m deep) which held huge oak planks and was flanked by an inner setting of postholes. This arrangement probably defined an elaborate timber-laced rampart or box-rampart, perhaps with a wall-walk. The construction of this outer defence may have strengthened or replaced a slightly earlier earthwork enclosure consisting of two surviving ditches, which morphologically would have closely resembled the upstanding enclosures at Maiden Castle and Cairnmore (RCAHMS 2007, 101). Inside the enclosures a series of beam slots, postholes and destruction layers indicate the presence of a number of timber buildings. The complex has been dated to the 4th–6th centuries AD.

The (re)emergence of fortified enclosure in northern Britain

The short summary above highlights the different types of fortified enclosure that emerged in Pictland, each with plan forms recognised over a much wider geographical frame in the second half of the 1st millennium AD. What is particularly striking (and is seemingly a much broader trend elsewhere in northern and western Britain and Ireland) is that the range of fortified sites that characterised early medieval society in these areas was in existence by at least the 5th and 6th centuries AD and included the emergence (or re-emergence) of major hillforts, ringforts, promontory forts and more unusual lowland sites like Rhynie (Fig. 9). The site at Dunnicaer suggests that a smaller number of sites emerged in the late Roman period (Chapter 7).

Ireland shows a similar rise of sites dating to the 5th–6th centuries AD, with ringfort sites proliferating from the 7th century onwards (Stout 1997, 22–31). However, in Pictland or northern Pictland at least, a reverse trend is evident with apparently fewer sites established from the 7th century onwards. The data here are provisional, but the recently identified settlement enclosure sites in Aberdeenshire, for example – sites at the smaller end of the spectrum – show limited sign of continued occupation beyond their initial construction phases. However, larger sites such as the major hillforts and promontory forts do, in contrast, endure and show repeated expansion or refortification into the 8th and 9th centuries AD, possibly under the influence of/in response to the new Viking invaders of the north towards the end of the 1st millennium AD (Noble et al. 2013). What is also clear from the overall spread of dates is that the phenomenon of fort construction began after a hiatus of perhaps up to four centuries in many areas: for example, at sites that show clear reuse of earlier Iron Age hillforts such as Craig Phadrig and Cullykhan there was a distinct gap between Iron Age construction (ending by the 1st century BC at the latest) and the rebuilding/re-occupation sometime in the 5th–6th centuries AD (Noble et al. 2013, 1143).

The focus on the 5th and 6th centuries as a major period of defended settlement construction in Pictland tallies well with the first documented references to Pictish kings in sources such as the Irish Annals and the earliest kings recorded in the Pictish king-lists that can be independently verified from other sources (Evans 2008; Chapter 2). The apparent focus of construction and use on larger and more complex fortified sites such as Burghead from the 7th century onwards also coincides with the impact of Christianity and, in northern Pictland at least, the emergence of the documented 'overkingdom' of Fortriu. Certainly, the larger hillforts of Pictland and early medieval northern Britain more generally have traditionally been linked to changes in political structure in the mid 1st millennium AD. Thus the identification of Pictish sites such as Dundurn or Burghead as the major 'capitals' of kingdoms goes back to 19th-century scholarship at least (Alcock *et al.* 1989, 190; Oram 2007). In the mid 20th century, Stevenson, in his definition of the nuclear hillfort, saw these 'citadels' as royal strongholds akin to the castles of later medieval Scotland (Stevenson 1949). Feachem (1955), too, continued the idea that these sites functioned as capitals, though this was a view later cautioned against by Alcock *et al.* (1989, 209) who rightly pointed out that the much later concept of a 'capital' is inappropriate in an early medieval context; rather, kings would have probably had a number of royal strongholds or 'central places' among which they would have made periodic circuits or progresses.

Other hillforts in northern Britain such as Dunadd in western Scotland have long been connected to overkingship, in this case in relation to the Gaelic kingdom of Dál Riata. The hillfort at Dumbarton Rock on the Clyde has likewise been identified as a 'seat' of the Britons in south-western Scotland (Lane and Campbell 2000, 259) – a claim/identification aided by the Venerable Bede in the 8th century who referred to Dumbarton Rock (Alt Clut), as a strongly defended political centre of the Britons – *civitas munitissima Brettonum quae vocatur Alcluith* and *urbs Alcluith* (*HE*, I.11 and I.12). While *urbs* in classical Latin would refer to a walled town, the meaning of these terms as used by Bede is uncertain in an early medieval context (Alcock and Alcock 1990, 116).

The references to fortified sites in Pictland are frustratingly vague and altogether brief. Adomnán refers to Columba visiting the stronghold of Bridei, son of Mailcon, by the River Ness in northern Pictland.

His account records that there was a royal hall within the fortress where the king and his council resided, and Adomnán also refers to a royal treasury (*VSC* II.33, 35). The site Adomnán refers to is as yet unidentified, though Craig Phadrig, located on the outskirts of modern Inverness, has often been proposed. However, the extent to which Adomnán's description of a Pictish fort would have been an accurate one is unknown. Place-names can perhaps play some role in identifying the status and role of the defended sites of Pictland. The place-name Bennachie, site of the elaborate nuclear hillfort of the Mither Tap, for example, has been translated as 'Mountain of the people of Ce' (Dobbs 1949). As Dobbs and Evans have highlighted, the Ce is mentioned in the Pictish king-lists as one of the 'sons' of Cruithne, father of the Picts (Dobbs 1949; Chapter 1). The place-name evidence suggests Bennachie was perhaps the pre-eminent site in this region of Pictland. The place-name of Rhynie (Chapter 4) also suggests pre-eminent connections and status for the enclosures here.

The place-name evidence can be related to the historical and, increasingly, archaeological evidence, which suggests that the fortified sites of Pictland were connected to emerging social and political hierarchies. Nonetheless, the exact role that these forts played among the new forms of early medieval society remains debated. Despite the oft-mooted role as seats of kings, there have been difficulties in identifying actual settlement evidence at many of these sites. At Dundurn, the excavated evidence of settlement included midden and floor levels and a stone-slab water tank covered by a mass of bracken, moss and detritus preserved by waterlogging on the upper terrace, below the main citadel (Alcock *et al.* 1989, 202). Excavations in the upper citadel were very limited, but some evidence for structures and occupation was uncovered. At Clatchard Craig, Fife, a hearth and floor were identified, but few other structural traces were identified, despite the relatively large areas investigated (Close-Brooks 1986). Buildings were located within Burghead by Young in the 19th century, but these are undated and few structural details can be gleaned from his report, and few finds of the character found at more modest sites like Rhynie were identified (Young 1893). Little more than midden layers have been excavated at sites such as Craig Phadrig and Cullykhan (both Inverness-shire), and while a possible 'hall' of modest proportions and materials was revealed at the promontory fort at Portknockie, Moray, few finds or structural detail were identified to illuminate site status, function or date (Ralston 1987). The scale of excavation at these sites has admittedly been frustratingly slight and, undoubtedly, larger-scale excavations will reveal more about the internal workings of these forts. For example, at Burghead recent work has established that floor layers of late 1st-millennium AD buildings survive within the fort and will repay further excavation and study.

Elsewhere in early medieval northern Britain the evidence for the character of internal activity and the presence/absence of buildings within these enclosures has also been limited. In western Scotland, for example, at the much more extensively excavated 'royal' site of Dál Riata at Dunadd, secure traces of buildings have eluded both extensive antiquarian excavators and (more limited) modern campaigns of excavations (Lane and Campbell 2000). Clearly much more work is required to identify whether the majority of these sites were truly seats of kings or played more specialised roles (cf. Woolf 2007b, 29–30).

The documentary sources emphasise the military roles of early medieval forts rather than their residential dimensions. Hence, the Annals of Ulster in the later 7th to 8th century AD feature over 20 references to forts or strongholds in northern Britain, nearly all in connection with military action such as sieges, burnings, destruction and capture (Alcock 1988, 31). The scale of the defences of the major hillforts, the repeated textual references to their role in warfare as well as the clear archaeological evidence for the burning of defences leave us in little doubt that it was with warfare in mind that these sites were created. However, their role in a military sense would have been limited in an early medieval context – where battles are recorded, these are almost exclusively battles in the open between two armies. The effective control of a territory that forts could dictate was also curtailed by the very limited range of early medieval weaponry and tactics (Alcock 2003, 198–9). Clearly, despite their obvious military dimensions, forts would have only been one element of the control of a territory, and retreating to such a location may have been a last resort of a ruler under severe pressure and threat. Nonetheless, the visibility and defences of the fortified sites were no doubt markers of authority within contested landscapes.

As well as residence and warfare, defended sites performed other important roles. Outside of Pictland, at Dunadd, a stone footprint carved on an outcrop within the fort has been interpreted as part of inauguration rituals (Lane and Campbell 2000, 247–9). No such carved footprints are yet known at fortified sites in Pictland with the possible exception of a pair at Clickhimin in Shetland (Hamilton 1968, 75). Much better known in our study area are carved stone monuments in association with sites such as Burghead and Rhynie. At Burghead, during the 19th-century destruction of the fort, around 25–30 stones carved with bulls were recognised at the fort (Fig. 11). Sadly, only six of these survive, but they show bulls depicted in different ways – one at rest, another with head lowered, ready to charge, for example. Interpretation of the bulls has varied: some scholars (e.g. Carver 1999, 30–1; Shepherd 1986, 133) suggest that they were set into the ramparts as symbols of power; others (e.g. Foster 2014, 43–4) propose connections with a cult of fertility, with these bull stones displayed as part of a votive frieze. The idea of display as part of the ramparts is an attractive one, but it is unproven and forms part of an interpretation that only emerged in the 1990s (Ralston 2004, 38). The shape and form of the stones in fact indicate that the original forms of these monuments were kite-shaped boulders with the carvings on the upper and wider portion of the stones (Scott 2005, 217). The lower, pointed parts suggest that these were standing stones. Accordingly, it seems most likely that the bull stones were set in the ground, perhaps forming, as Alcock (2003, 197) has suggested, a processional arrangement, lining the entrance passage through the outer ramparts.

The obvious symbolism of the bull – the muscular, aggressive and dominant leader of the herd – might have formed a highly appropriate symbol of power and authority at a major hillfort of this period. In addition, the bull may have had cult dimensions (Foster 2014, 44) (see also Chapter 8). Indeed, the occurrence of later sculptural fragments of a corner post of a box-shrine at Burghead, displaying a hunt scene, points to an important and high-status early Christian site at Burghead in the later 1st millennium AD (Chapter 8) (Fig. 12). A fragment of an interlaced cross-slab with a mounted rider on the other side and other smaller fragments of early medieval carved stone monuments provide further evidence of an early church here. It is intuitive to suggest that the bulls belong to the fort's early phase (perhaps 6th–7th century) while the Christian sculpture came as part of the site's evolution in the 7th–9th centuries. Accepting this

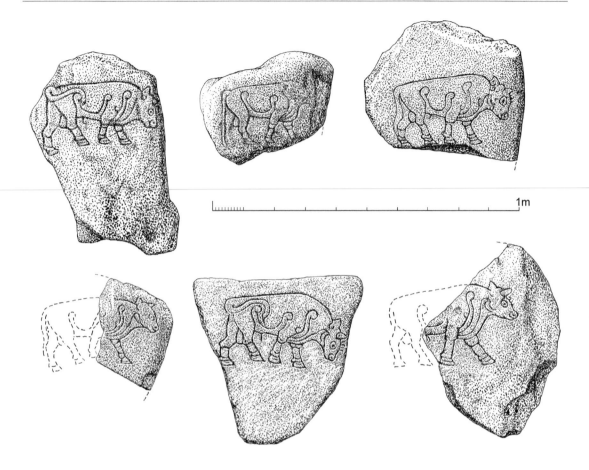

1m

chronology connects the bulls to a pre- or proto-Christian period and the overtly Christian sculpture to part of an increasing association between church and kingship from the 7th century onwards. An ideological and ritualised dimension has also been suggested for the sculptural evidence from Rhynie (Chapters 4 and 8). Thus, in a pagan as well as a Christian context, the power of fortified sites of the type outlined above did not simply rely on their military roles, nor on their role as elite residences, but as sites where the ideological dimensions of rulership were conducted, embodied and underpinned.

The fortified sites that were constructed in northern Britain in the 1st millennium AD emerged in the late Roman period and particularly in the generations after the Roman withdrawal from Britain. In many regions, these sites emerged after a major hiatus in fort building in the Roman Iron Age period. These fortified sites can perhaps be

11. The Burghead bulls © Historic Environment Scotland.

12. Early Christian
sculpture fragment from
Burghead © Historic
Environment Scotland.

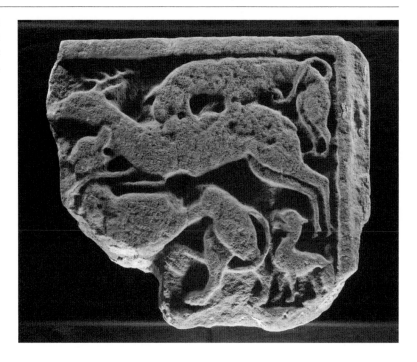

directly linked to the emergence of new forms of political authority
that emerged in the late Roman and 5th–6th centuries AD. The early
sources, although schematic and vague in places, make it clear that
these sites were deeply connected to the form and character of early
medieval society. Some sites may have played important roles as seats
or strongholds of powerful kings and sub-kings, and the sources also
make it clear that these were places of conflict and military conquest.
The ideological and cult dimension to fortified sites in northern
Britain was also clearly important and these latter characteristics are
important dimensions that can enrich our understanding of the role
of enclosed sites in the early medieval period.

The emergence and evolution of these sites is an important
research avenue, which can begin to be drawn out and one where the
evidence from northern Pictland is particularly important. The dating
evidence suggests that different kinds of fortified sites coexisted,
particularly in the 5th and 6th centuries AD. Unpicking the relationship between these different forms of site that have been identified
through recent work will be key in creating more nuanced understandings of the diverse roles that fortified sites played in the creation
of early medieval societies in northern Britain. Assessing how some of

these sites diminished in importance is also a key area for further research. The dating evidence currently signifies that a majority of these sites were largely abandoned or certainly no longer witnessed major construction events in the 9th century AD or later – hence their role in the later 1st millennium AD was clearly lessened, despite the evident rise in social unrest and political upheaval in this period. Might we envisage a nucleation of authority and defence at fewer sites in 8th- to 10th-century Pictland? However, the reference to lowland sites such as Forteviot in a 9th-century context also suggests that new forms of royal centres were important and that the structure of early medieval society and the role of fortified settlement was perhaps shifting by the end of the 1st millennium AD (Driscoll 2011, 270–4).

CHAPTER FOUR

Rhynie: A Powerful Place of Pictland

Gordon Noble, Meggen Gondek,
Ewan Campbell, Nicholas Evans,
Derek Hamilton and Simon Taylor

The nature of the power structures and the character of the power centres that filled the chasm left by the demise of the Roman Empire is of enduring interest for scholars of 1st-millennium AD Europe. In regions such as southern Britain where the Roman Empire maintained control for much of the first four centuries of the millennium, the written sources suggest political fragmentation following the demise of Roman governance (Wickham 2005). The political units that replaced the Roman Empire were smaller-scale and ruled by people called kings (*reges*) (Wickham 2005, 312). In Anglo-Saxon England, the most obvious materialisation of new power structures in the post-Roman period are the large residential hall complexes that emerged sometime in the 6th to 7th centuries AD (e.g. Brennan and Hamerow 2015; Hamerow 2012; Hope-Taylor 1977; Thomas 2013).

However, in northern Britain, fortified sites dominate our knowledge of the central places of power and governance in the early medieval period (see Chapter 3) (Alcock *et al.* 1989, 192). Unfortunately, in Pictland few fortified centres of power have been excavated on any scale, especially in the north (Carver 2011; though note Alcock's campaign of excavations; Chapter 3). Hence a fuller understanding of the character of these places often eludes us, and our understanding of these sites is generally much poorer than for the centres of power of Anglo-Saxon England. Nevertheless, important new investigations have been carried out at Rhynie, Aberdeenshire, revealing a hitherto unexplored Pictish power centre of northern Pictland. The site is undocumented in the written sources we have for this period (as is the case for much of northern Pictland) (Chapter 2), but archaeological, sculptural and place-name evidence has begun to reveal it as a previously unknown type of elite Pictish settlement with international connections.

Place-name and historical perspectives

A consideration of the significance of Rhynie can begin with the place-name. The place-name evidence from Rhynie is a crucial source for the significance of this locale, an important addition for interpreting the significance of the site in the wider political geography of Pictland. As with the majority of Scotland, the documentary evidence for the place-name and parish of Rhynie is late, occurring only from the 13th century onwards, the earliest appearance being in episcopal records which record the church of *Ryny* in 1222–42 (Innes 1837). Nonetheless, a revealing element of the place-name is that it contains the early Celtic word **rīg* 'king' (first noted by Grigg 2015, 85–6). An analogous name may be Loch Ryan in south-west Scotland, one of the earliest recorded of all Scottish place-names, appearing in Ptolemy's 'Geography' (2nd century AD) as *Rerigonios kolpos* 'bay associated with a settlement called *Rerigonion*'. W.J. Watson, the great Celtic scholar, analysed *Rerigonion* as **re-rīg-on-ion*, loosely translating as a 'very royal place' (Watson 1926, 34). This was endorsed by Rivet and Smith (1979, 447) and most recently by Graham Isaac (2005, 202), although Isaac transcribed and analysed it slightly differently, namely as *Rherigónion* and *Rherigónios kólpos*, 'place of (-*io*) the foremost (*ro*-) great/divine (-*on*-) king (-*rīg*-)'. Rhynie may contain a similar sequence of phonemes to that of Loch Ryan and a minimalist, and provisional, reconstruction of Rhynie in early Celtic might be **rīgonin* or **rīgonīn*, 'place of or associated with (-*īn*) a great/divine (-*on*-) king (*rīg*-)'.

In terms of historical sources, much of northern Pictland can be described as essentially prehistoric in the early medieval period with very few textual references available for the whole of northern Scotland until well into the 12th century or later. This is certainly true for Rhynie and its environs, which cannot be identified with any named early medieval territory or kingdom with certainty. In the Pictish period before the early 10th century, we can assume that the Rhynie area had strategic importance due to its geographical location at a cross-roads for routes between Moray and east central Scotland (Simpson 1930, 48–52). Given its position in north-east Scotland, Rhynie could have been part of the Pictish territories of Ce, Fortriu or even Fidach (see Noble *et al.* forthcoming), but the boundaries of these territories are uncertain. In the later medieval period, Rhynie was part of the Lordship of Strathbogie (Fig. 13), traditionally regarded as a royal creation of the late 12th or early 13th centuries, but the name Strathbogie was an earlier one, first appearing in Scottish king-lists as the area in which King Lulach (stepson of the famous King MacBethad), was killed in 1058 (Woolf 2007b, 260, 265). With regards to the place-name, it is interesting that it was the valley of the River Bogie, rather than the Deveron that the later caput centre Huntly is located on, which gave its name to the lordship, perhaps an indication that the smaller (at least in landscape and riverine terms) of the two straths, where Rhynie is located, had once been the most important in the region. In a 1600 rental, the market at Rhynie was recorded as being of much greater economic value than that at Huntly, indicating the long-term potential of Rhynie as a centre. In terms of wider connections, it is also important to note that Strathbogie was not only the name for a lordship, but also of a deanery of Strathbogie in the diocese of Moray, which covered a wider territory than that of the later lordship (Fig. 13). Thus, in the later medieval period the Rhynie area had connections both to the east to central Aberdeenshire and to the west with Moray, indicating a territory that has long been both at the edge of, and an important transitional area between, major polities and social and geographical boundaries.

The archaeology

Rhynie has long been known as the findspot of an important group of Class I Pictish symbol stones (Fig. 14). Eight Class I symbol stones are recorded from the village of Rhynie and its immediate environs (RCAHMS 2007, 119–22; 2008, 38–41). The Craw Stane (Rhynie No. 1) (Fig. 15) is the only one still standing in its likely original position. The stones are of a variety of different geologies and are likely to be from glacial erratics found in the environs of the modern village. The stones were carved by incision and include animal and abstract symbols of a type found widely across the corpus as well as two much rarer depictions of human (or human-like) figures – an axe carrier (No. 7) and a warrior figure (No. 3) (Fig. 16). The findspots of the stones follow a roughly north–south linear distribution, with three stones found to the south (two found by ploughing and the *in situ* Craw Stane), two from the modern churchyard and three from

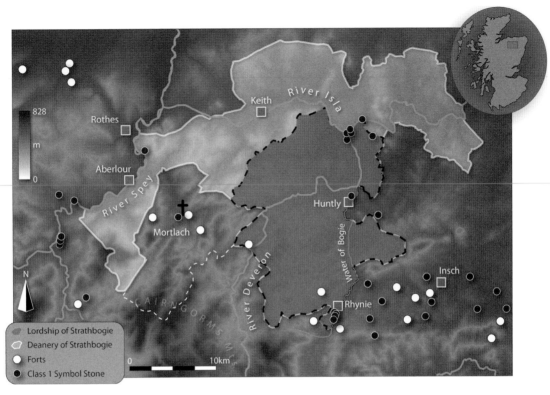

13. Map of the Lordship and Deanery of Strathbogie with the distribution of forts and Class I symbol stones.

the outskirts of the modern village. The most iconic stone is the Rhynie Man (No. 7), ploughed up by the owner of the field in 1978 (Fig. 17). The Rhynie Man stone depicts a human-like figure carrying an axe over their shoulder. The stones from Rhynie represent an unusual corpus of carved stone monuments in northern Scotland since few other sites in the region preserve significant numbers of Class I stones and there are only a few parallels for the Rhynie axe carrier (No. 7) or the warrior figure (No. 3) (Shepherd and Shepherd 1978).

After the discovery of the Rhynie Man in March 1978, aerial reconnaissance during the summer of 1978 revealed a series of circular enclosures surrounding the position of the Craw Stane, Rhynie No. 1, and the findspot of the Rhynie Man (Fig. 18). The enclosure complex identified comprised a series of enclosure boundaries surrounding the site of the still *in situ* Craw Stane symbol stone, enclosing a distinctive knoll at the end of the sand-and-gravel ridge upon which the symbol stone stands. The complex overlooks the Water of Bogie, and the ridge dramatically slopes to the east down to

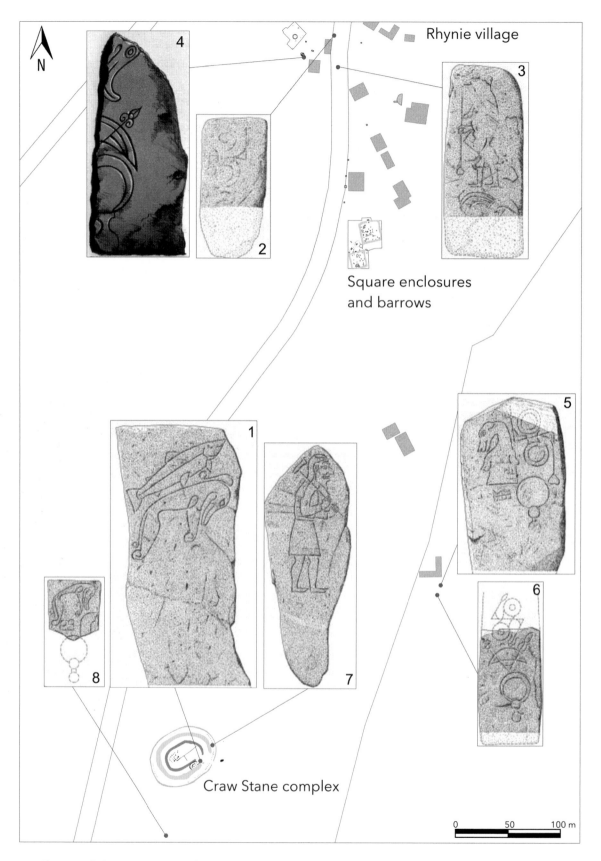

Rhynie village

Square enclosures
and barrows

N

Craw Stane complex

0   50   100 m

14. Class I symbol stones (Nos. 1–8) from Rhynie and findspots. Drawings of stones © Historic Environment Scotland.

15. Craw Stane © Cathy MacIver.

16. Rhynie No. 3 ©
Michael Sharpe.

the river. Aerial photographs suggested the enclosure complex
consisted of an inner and outer ditched enclosure and an outer palisaded boundary. The inner ditch enclosed an area 32m × 20m, and
the outer an area of circa 50m in diameter, while the outer palisade
was around 60m across (Fig. 19) (RCAHMS 2007, 122). The outer
palisade trench held evenly spaced posts that revetted an inner plank

17. Close-up of Rhynie Man showing the fierce visage of the carved figure © Aberdeenshire Council Archaeology Service.

setting, creating a continuous outer wooden boundary wall. Set back almost exactly 2m from the outer foundation trench was a series of large postholes on the interior side that may have supported a wall-walk behind the outer wall.

During the excavations a range of structures were revealed within the interior of the Craw Stane enclosures (Figs. 19, 20, 21). One structure identified consisted of a rectangular post-setting (Structure 1). The features suggest a building of at least 9m × 5m, but the presence of turf walls or non-earth-fast timbers may mean that this was a much larger building, of which the surviving remains represent only the main roof-bearing supports. A series of postholes, beam slots and burnt spreads were also found near to the Craw Stane (Structure 3). The structure would have measured approximately 6m × 9m and closely resembles the later and larger 8th-century Pictish 'bag-shaped'

18. Aerial photograph showing the cropmarks that revealed the Craw Stane early medieval enclosure complex © Aberdeenshire Council Archaeology Service.

building (S1) excavated at Portmahomack on Tarbat Ness. The excavator of S1 at Portmahomack interpreted it as a cruck frame for a large building, with the perimeter slot acting as the foundation for a turf or stone wall with a stone or plank internal revetment (Carver *et al.* 2016, 240). This seems like the most likely interpretation for Structure 3 – a timber and turf-framed building that was constructed on the hillslope. If contemporary with the Craw Stane, the Pictish stone would have stood directly next to the building's entrance. Structure 3 was built over the backfilled inner and outer ditches. Settlement associated with the complex may have also extended outside the enclosure complex. To the south-east of the entrance, a sub-circular deposit of burnt sand and charred timbers was located in 2015 and was interpreted as the vestiges of a floor layer of a building (Structure 4). Two iron buckles from horse harnesses or saddle girth straps and a late Roman amphora handle were recovered from the floor layers (Fig. 22).

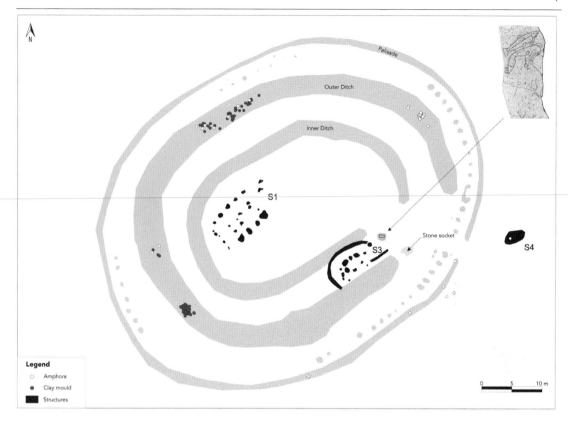

Legend
○ Amphora
● Clay mould
■ Structures

The Craw Stane was found to stand directly on the line of the entranceway of the outer enclosure and was located between the terminals of the outer and inner ditches (Fig. 19). Its current position has been recorded there since the middle of the 19th century. During the 2015 excavations, a feature found just downslope from the Craw Stane was interpreted as a socket for a standing stone. The stone socket is a strong candidate for the original position of the Rhynie Man stone, which was discovered downslope from the Craw Stane in 1979. Radiocarbon dates obtained from charcoal from basal fills of the stone socket showed that it was contemporary with the other 5th to 6th-century architectural elements of the complex.

Excavations in 2013–14 showed that the enclosure complex associated with the Craw Stane did not stand in isolation but was part of a wider landscape of contemporary features. In 1836, two of the symbol stones found in the modern village of Rhynie (Nos. 2 and 3) were removed during the construction of a turnpike road. A 'quantity' of human bone was found near the stones at this time and No. 3,

19. Ground-plan of Craw Stane enclosures showing Structures 1(S1), 3(S3) and 4(S4), the ditches and palisaded enclosure complex, along with the location of the Craw Stane symbol stone and position of the stone socket excavated in 2015.

20. Aerial view of excavations
at Rhynie in 2016 looking
towards Tap o'Noth hillfort.

21. Stripping the topsoil:
excavations at Rhynie in 2011.

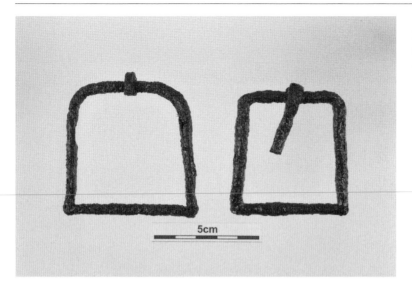

22. Two iron buckles from horse harnesses or saddle girth straps from the floor layer of a building at Rhynie.

5cm

which depicts a warrior with a spear, is said to have been found in association with a cairn (Logan 1829, 56). Antiquarian reports and local newspapers also record the discovery of east–west orientated cist burials in the same area (J.A. Henderson 1907, 163). Aerial photography in 1984 revealed the outlines of two large square enclosures near to the findspot of the stones where the cists are reported as being located (M. Greig 1994, 26). These enclosures were targeted for excavation in 2013 (Fig. 23). The two enclosures are of a very unusual type; the larger around 20m across and the smaller 16m. They are defined by ditches with a short segment of ditch projecting in front of a northwards-aligned entranceway. Immediately adjacent to these enclosures, two square barrows were found, each around 4–4.5m across. Within one of the barrows was a partially intact cist burial of an adult female that was dated to 400–570 calibrated (cal) AD, contemporary with the Craw Stane complex. The dating evidence for the larger enclosures is problematic, but radiocarbon determinations from an upper fill of the ditch of the largest suggest it was still visible in the 7th century AD, and a pit of 5th to 6th century AD date was discovered inside. Nothing was found to elucidate the function of the larger enclosures, but a similar example found at the Pictish royal centre of Forteviot, Perthshire, has been interpreted as the boundary of a shrine built on Romano-British models, and large enclosures of this kind are known from the aerial record of other barrow cemeteries in northern Pictland (Campbell and Maldonado forthcoming; Mitchell and Noble 2017) (Chapter 5).

23. Plan of the two square enclosures and square barrows found on the southern outskirts of the modern village of Rhynie. The square barrows surrounded central burials.

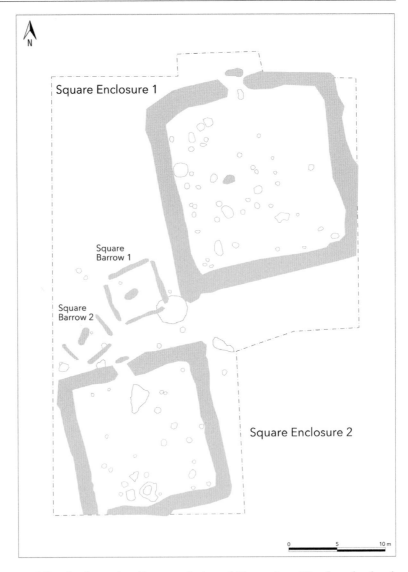

Like the later Anglian royal site of Yeavering, Northumberland, which sits in the shadow of the large Iron Age fort of Yeavering Bell, the complex at Rhynie is overlooked by one of the most impressive hillforts known in northern Britain, the site of Tap o'Noth (Plate 4). The fort(s) on Tap o'Noth comprises an upper vitrified fort and a lower stone wall that encloses an area of 21 hectares (RCAHMS 2007, 103–5). The upper fort is of a type that dates to c.400–200 cal BC (Cook 2010, 79). More than 100 house platforms survive within the lower enclosure. The scale of the defences at Tap o'Noth and the size of the settlement strongly suggest that this site and its environs were a major regional focus in the Iron Age. Two other forts lie near to Rhynie (Fig. 24). One, at Cairnmore, has been dated to the 5th to 6th centuries AD and comprises a small multivallate site enclosing an area of 64m × 48m (Cook 2011b). During small-scale excavation at Cairnmore, evidence of non-ferrous metalworking was identified, with moulds for pins and brooches recovered. The other fort, at Wheedlemont (Cnoc Cailliche in Gaelic), comprises an oval enclosure around 55m × 30m in maximum extent.

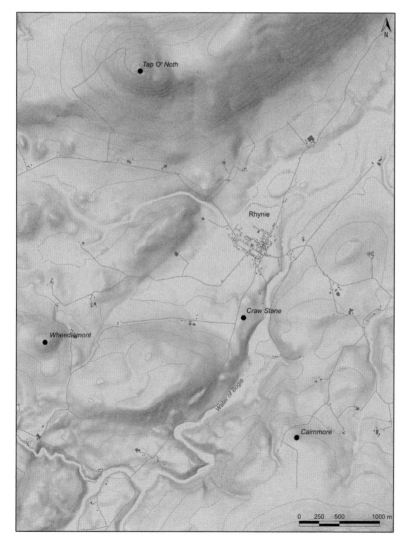

24. The landscape setting of the Craw Stane complex showing the other forts in the vicinity. Base map © Crown Copyright/database right 2018. An Ordnance Survey/ EDINA supplied service.

The artefact assemblage from Rhynie is highly unusual and gives an indication of the status of the site. Over 1,000 artefacts have been recovered over five seasons of excavation (Figs. 19, 25). The assemblage includes a large number of sherds of imported Late Roman Amphorae, alongside sherds of imported Continental glass vessels. The finds assemblage from Rhynie is exceptional, including, for example, the northernmost European examples of eastern Mediterranean late Roman amphorae imports, which lie far outside the normal Insular distribution of Mediterranean wares (Campbell 2007, Fig. 13). The other major aspect of the Rhynie finds is the evidence for large-scale production of personal jewellery, with over 300 moulds for producing pins, brooches and ingots (Fig. 26), some in precious metals. A singular feature of the mould assemblage is a series of zoomorphic figurines, which do not seem to have any parallels in surviving metalwork (Plate 5). There is also unique ironwork, such as an axe-shaped pin (Plate 6). The imports along with the presence of evidence for fine metalworking suggest that Rhynie is an extremely unusual site and illustrate a picture of long-distance contacts and a sophisticated power centre at a surprisingly early date (Campbell 1996, Table 4.1). There are also objects of more everyday significance from the site, such as small pins (Fig. 27), a complete top stone of a rotary quern, fragments of querns and coarse stone tools, spindle whorls (Fig. 28) and a small assemblage of locally made coil-built pottery, all of which attest to a residential component to the site.

25. A small selection of moulds from Rhynie for (1) a four-fingered hand-pin, (2) a hand-pin, (3) a small type H brooch, (4) an animal figurine/ornament and (5) a large barrel-shaped brooch pin. Drawing by Alice Watterson.

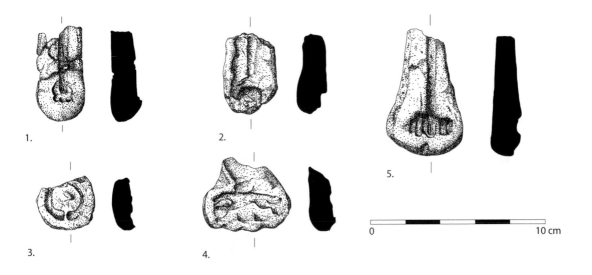

1.

2.

3.

4.

5.

0   10 cm

26. Stone ingot mould from Rhynie.

27. A bronze pin revealed during excavations at Rhynie.

28. Spindle whorl from a building next to the Craw Stane, Rhynie.

Discussion

The dating obtained from the excavations at the Craw Stane complex at Rhynie suggests that the site began to develop in the late 4th century AD and came to an end around the middle of the 6th century AD (cal AD 510–60). Prior to the excavations, our knowledge of Rhynie in the early medieval period was limited to the collection of Class I sculpture (Noble *et al.* forthcoming) (Fig. 14) – the largest number of Class I carvings surviving in any one location in Pictland. Given the limited historical evidence for much of northern Pictland, it is important to note the clues that sculptural evidence may give us to the presence of important power centres in northern Britain (see also Gondek 2006).

Various strands of evidence brought together here attest to the importance of Rhynie. The recognition that Rhynie includes the early Celtic word **rīg* 'king' provides a very illuminating area of research for considering the significance of this landscape in the Pictish period. The minimal interpretation of the name suggests the original form of Rhynie might have been a 'place of, or associated with, a great or divine king'.

With the very limited historical sources we have for northern Scotland, any historical analysis is likely to remain speculative. However, it is clear that Rhynie was situated within a landscape that has long had a strategic significance. Given the early date of the complex it may be that in the 4th–6th centuries the Craw Stane complex lay at the heart of a small polity with its core controlling the Bogie and the routes radiating from it, particularly key routes between the Moray Firth and the south of Scotland. Later Rhynie was quite close to the heart of the powerful kingdom of Fortriu centred on Moray, making it a likely target when this polity probably began to expand its territory in the 6th century. By 900, Rhynie could have been incorporated within this larger Fortriu, as the location of the deanery of Strathbogie within the diocese of Moray suggests long-term connections with Moray, but again without more detailed historical sources this is uncertain. After 900, when sub-divisions of Fortriu like Ross and Moray start to appear in our sources, Strathbogie emerges as the name for Rhynie's locality, and by the early 13th century as the name of a lordship and deanery. It is possible that the later region of Strathbogie, as well as some of its later constituent units such as its parishes, represent survivals in some form from the Pictish era, but it is difficult currently to identify any elements which are as early as the Rhynie complex.

In terms of archaeological context, we can identify that within the Strathbogie area Rhynie is the focus of a distinct concentration of archaeological sites that have direct relevance to the Pictish period. The dense concentration of symbol stones at Rhynie can be compared to the single example that survives at the later lordship caput centre at Huntly (Fig. 13). Another concentration of symbol stones occurs – that at Tillytarmont towards the northern edge of the deanery and lordship on an important crossing point of the Deveron and Isla (Gondek 2010; Mitchell and Noble 2017). There are also symbol stones at Arndilly and Mortlach, with two other major groupings in different catchments to the west and east: on the Spey to the west around Knockando and Bridge of Avon and on the east along the stretches of the Gadie and Shevock that flow into the Don. Forts are fewer than along the Don Valley to the east, but Rhynie again forms a focus of distribution, with forts clustered around Rhynie at Tap o'Noth, Cairnmore and Wheedlemont, and there is also a compara-ble cluster around Mortlach. The archaeology, like the place-name evidence, perhaps reiterates the importance of the upper stretch of the Bogie around Rhynie.

In terms of the wider context of the site, there are as yet few paral-lels for the Craw Stane complex, although until the 2011 excavations few *in situ* Class I stones had been assessed from an archaeological perspective. Only a small number of Pictish lowland enclosures are known – work on Pictish high-status sites has focused in the past on hillforts or coastal promontory forts (Chapter 3). With regards to hillforts we know that by the 7th century 'nuclear' hillforts were beginning to be constructed in Pictland and elsewhere in northern Britain, and by this stage they were generally defined by stone-faced, timber-laced ramparts (Noble *et al.* 2013) (Chapter 3). However, at sites like Dundurn, Perthshire, the early phases appear to have consisted of a palisade or timber stockade of some kind (Alcock *et al.* 1989, 200). The phase 1 palisade at Dundurn is poorly understood (Chapter 3), being interpreted from slight remains and small keyhole trenches, but it clearly utilised complex carpentry and both post and plank elements, similar to that which must have been utilised in the Rhynie outer enclosure wall (Alcock *et al.* 1989, 201). Recent work at Craig Phadrig, Inverness, has also identified that in the 5th to 6th centuries AD a palisade cut into the top of the Iron Age ramparts, defined early medieval occupation within a reused Iron Age fort (Peteranna and Birch forthcoming).

Extending the search for parallels further south, the outer wooden enclosure at Rhynie resembles some Anglo-Saxon sites, particularly those in northern England and southern Scotland. The outer enclosure at Rhynie can, for example, be compared to the 'Great Enclosure' of the Anglian royal settlement at Yeavering, albeit Rhynie was more modest in size, and the enclosure at Yeavering has been interpreted as an animal rather than a settlement enclosure (Hope-Taylor 1977). The buildings within the enclosures at Rhynie are much smaller than the impressive halls of Yeavering, but it is important to remember the early date of the Craw Stane complex with the structures at Rhynie more comparable to Anglo-Saxon buildings of the 5th and 6th centuries AD than those constructed later (Hamerow 2012, 22). The use of planks and foundation trenches for timber settings at Rhynie is paralleled in Anglo-Saxon hall architecture, but the English examples again tend to be later in date (Hamerow 2012, 24).

In a wider context, the enclosures at Rhynie have important parallels, at least in terms of scale and construction methods, with certain royal sites in Ireland. One of the close parallels is Clogher, County Tyrone, a major site of the Irish overkingdom of Airgialla. In the 6th century AD, Clogher was an enclosure, approximately 50m in diameter, defined by a massive wooden palisade, an outer ditch and bank and further palisaded elements (Warner 1988, 58; 2000). The architecture of the early phases of Clogher was also dominated by a large wooden enclosure boundary – what was in the medieval period called a *durlas* ('oak enclosure') (Warner 1988, 58), an apt name for the timber components of sites such as Clogher and Rhynie. The buildings within the Rhynie enclosures find general parallels in the Irish early medieval settlement record, with the building sizes comparable with some of the larger round and rectangular buildings known at enclosed settlements in Ireland (J. Bradley 2011, 23; O'Sullivan *et al.* 2014, 93).

In terms of the architecture of the complex itself, we can identify the complex at Rhynie as a significant material investment in a place of special significance. The outer enclosure alone would have represented a major investment in resources. The excavation has shown that some stretches of the outer plank and post wall foundation extended to 1.5m in depth, suggesting the outer wall could have stood up to 4 or 5m high. Inside the enclosures there was a series of buildings (Fig. 19; Plate 7). While the identified structures do not have entirely satisfactory ground-plans, they are among only a handful of Pictish structures yet identified in lowland Scotland. After the 3rd century AD, the domestic settlement record in mainland Scotland becomes exceptionally difficult to trace, a situation that characterises Scottish rural settlement more generally till the 18th or 19th centuries. It seems very likely that structures at Rhynie incorporated timber structural elements (not always with earth-fast elements), with plank revetting in some cases and turf or stone outer walls. At present, not much can be said about the function of the structures, but the context of the sub-oval building immediately adjacent to the Craw Stane is intriguing. The lack of preservation makes it difficult to address whether these buildings were residences, workshops or more specialised structures, but the animal bone assemblage, the metalworking evidence and the small collection of more everyday objects suggest a successful centre of production and consumption and that the site was at least an intermittent residence for powerful individuals and their followers.

One striking feature of the Rhynie finds assemblage is the evidence for the production of fine metalwork and the importation of exotic goods. The imports show that Rhynie was keyed into the Atlantic trading system of late antiquity, and the quantity and quality of the metalworking evidence suggests this was a primary centre for redistribution for the region (Campbell 2007, 123). In terms of the range and character of objects found at the site, Rhynie, with the presence of weaponry, jewellery and precious metals, has the characteristics of high-status sites located in Atlantic Britain and Ireland. The production evidence is particularly revealing with the moulds from Rhynie being one of the largest assemblages of early medieval metalworking moulds known. In Scotland, this can be compared to assemblages from Dunadd, Mote of Mark, Dumfries and Galloway and Brough of Birsay, though these are likely to be largely later in date than the Rhynie assemblage. It is likely that the brooches, pins and other objects being produced at Rhynie were redistributed by elites at the site to cement social relations with their followers, acting as a means of creating networks of affiliation and at the same time cementing social differentiation and the elite control of resources (Campbell 2007, 116).

As well as the artefact assemblage, the sculptural evidence also marks Rhynie as being a very significant Pictish site and landscape. While the assemblage of stones from Rhynie is particularly rich and striking, carved stone monuments or carvings on outcrops are not unknown from early medieval enclosed sites more generally in northern Britain. Well-known examples include the footprint and boar from Dunadd in western Scotland, Pictish-style carvings from Trusty's Hill in south-west Scotland and bull carvings from Burghead and East Lomond in northern and eastern Scotland (Gondek 2015; RCAHMS 2008, 64, 66; Toolis and Bowles 2016). In each of these cases, the sites have been interpreted as major power centres within their regional setting. In Pictland, other, as yet unexcavated, sites may provide similar evidence. The Rhynie Man, for example, is paralleled by a similar, though more modest (in terms of scale), carving from Mail (Cunningsburgh), Shetland (Turner 1994). The place-name Cunningsburgh probably derives from Old Norse *konungsborg* 'king's fort' (Stewart 1987, 48–9), hinting at the perceived high-status nature of this site in Shetland (Johnston 1999; Smith 2016, 16).

In terms of the role of the Class I stones at Rhynie, the depictions of human-like figures such as the Rhynie Man and Rhynie No. 3 are unusual, which further demonstrates the special status of Rhynie and suggests that the role of the site did not solely lie in the amassing and redistribution of wealth. Cult dimensions to the function of the Rhynie complex have recently been forwarded (Noble *et al.* 2013). The intertwining of cult and ritual with sites of residence and centres of production and consumption is a phenomenon noted widely across early medieval Europe. The evidence from Anglo-Saxon England, at high-status hall sites such as Yeavering, suggests that these settlements may have been centres of cult and ritual both in a pagan and early Christian context, though the interpretation generally relies on poorly preserved and at time ambiguous archaeological evidence (Hope-Taylor 1977, 97–102). In Ireland, cult and sacrifice have been highlighted as important dimensions of royal sites; there is for example the presence of more than 40 human skull fragments from the royal crannog at Lagore, County Meath (Gleeson and Carty 2013, 39), and the juxtaposition between royal sites and cult foci more generally is well attested (e.g. Gleeson 2012; Newman 2007; Schot *et al.* 2011). In Scandinavia too, the character of finds from a number of sites suggests that elements of ritual practice were integral to the emergence and development of important central places with a number of 'cult' buildings at major hall sites implying that ritual, and an architectural focus for such practices, formed an important element of political authority at these locations (e.g. Ringtved 1999, 50; Watt 1999). A concentration of sacred place-names has been shown to occur in the vicinity of Scandinavian central places; at the high-status centre at Gudme, for example, an Odin cult has been suggested to have been directly connected with the sacral kings that ruled there (e.g. Hedeager 2011, 152; Ringtved 1999; Sundqvist 2002). Novel forms of cult and ritual more generally seem to have underpinned the new sociopolitical identities that emerged across north-west Europe in a late and post-Roman context, and at elite centres these dimensions of power were deeply interwoven with the secular trappings of power and rulership (e.g. Hedeager 2011; Ringtved 1999; Sundqvist 2002). The practices and beliefs portrayed on monuments such as the Rhynie Man stone may have been much more widespread across Britain and Ireland. For example, axe hammers of the type depicted on the Rhynie Man stone have been found at sites such as Cadbury Castle, Somerset, and Lagore, Ireland (Alcock 1972, 80–1; Hencken 1950, Fig. 40a), both high-status sites in their regional settings.

In Pictland, the alignment of sacred and secular power is emphasised in Adomnán's account of the 6th-century Pictish King Bridei's fortress near Loch Ness, where the presence of *magi* within the king's court is vividly highlighted in one of the vignettes of Columba's life and miracles (*VSC* II.33; see also Kelly 1988, 59–60). The material culture from Rhynie suggests similar blurred divisions between secular power and the supernatural. The iconography of the Rhynie Man – perhaps part-human, part-animal or mythical creature – suggests that the stones with human-like figures related to pagan religious practices (Chapter 7). Other examples of axe-bearing individuals in Pictland suggest similarly blurred lines between human and animal and perhaps underlined the connections between rulership and spiritually ordained power. Other important monuments from Rhynie can be highlighted. The warrior figure, No. 3, came from near the northern extent of the cemetery and near to two large square enclosures of a type that have been interpreted as shrines at Forteviot with parallels with similar features at Anglo-Saxon cemeteries (Blair 1995; Campbell and Maldonado forthcoming). This suggests that other foci, perhaps also with cult dimensions, existed in the Rhynie landscape. At the cemetery, the presence of the Rhynie No. 3 stone (Fig. 16), carved with a figure with spear and shield, suggests that a warrior ideology was also intertwined with the ideology of rulership at Rhynie. Clearly the power of sites such as Rhynie drew on ritualised, spiritual and martial dimensions, with these concepts embodied and materialised through the sculpture that stood within the enclosures and in the surrounding landscape.

Bringing the evidence together, we would suggest that Rhynie was a high-status centre of the northern Picts from the 4th to the early 6th century AD, the first major non-hillfort secular elite site identified in Pictland so far. The place-name as well as the archaeological evidence indicates that this was a site associated with a northern Pictish ruler. The Mediterranean imports are the first of their kind in Pictland and the northernmost examples yet identified in Britain and Ireland. The evidence for metalworking from Rhynie shows that this was a major centre for production and trade, while the presence of buildings and the artefact and faunal assemblage suggest that at least at times the site acted as a residence for powerful individuals and their followers. It was also located next to an extensive cemetery and other fortified sites existed in the landscape overlooking the upper Strathbogie river valley, indicating that it was part of a wider social and political landscape; Rhynie was clearly embedded in a landscape of power that was polyfocal and multifunctional in nature. The sculptural evidence provides unique insights into the cult and martial dimensions of the orchestration of power. Overall, the evidence from Rhynie with its rich sculptural, architectural and material evidence can now begin to more fully contribute to international debates and dialogue on the emergence of sites that materialised the various pathways to power more generally followed by rulers in northern Pictland and early medieval northern Europe.

CHAPTER FIVE

The monumental cemeteries of northern Pictland

Juliette Mitchell and Gordon Noble

The emergence of formal cemeteries is one of the most significant transformations in the landscapes of 1st-millennium AD Britain. In Pictland, from around the 4th century onwards, square and circular burial monuments were constructed to commemorate a small proportion of the population – perhaps a newly emerging elite in the post-Roman centuries. This chapter outlines the evidence for monumental cemeteries of the northern Picts in the areas of Fortriu and Ce. A number of factors that seem to have been important to their siting are assessed, including their landscape location, relation to Pictish symbol stones, fortified sites and settlement sites of the 1st millennium AD. In terms of the architecture, two particular elements of the monumental burial tradition of northern Pictland can be highlighted: barrow enlargement and the linking of barrows through the sharing of barrow/cairn ditches. Both of these practices may have been implicated in the creation of genealogies of the living and the dead during an important transitional period in early medieval northern Europe when hereditary aristocracies became more prominent.

The cemeteries of northern Pictland

In Wainwright's classic 1955 edited volume, *The Problem of the Picts*, the lack of any conclusively Pictish examples of cemeteries meant that the discussion of burial traditions was limited (Wainwright 1955b, 94–6). Nonetheless, in the same decade, the identification of long cist cemeteries in southern Pictland in the Lothians and Fife led to the first characterisation of early medieval burial traditions in eastern Scotland (Henshall 1956). Recognition of monumental cemeteries of this period followed in the 1960s with the excavations of long cist burials in association with square and round cairns at Lundin Links, Fife (Greig *et al.* 2000; Ritchie 2011). However, the biggest advances in our knowledge of burial traditions in Pictland came with the onset of the aerial survey programme by the RCAHMS in 1976 (Maxwell 1978), alongside more geographically focused survey programmes by local government SMR teams. Aerial reconnaissance during the hot summers of the mid 1970s revealed hundreds of previously unknown sites as cropmarks, especially in the rich arable zones along the coastlines of eastern and northern Scotland (Plate 8). These surveys identified an entirely new burial type: the square-ditched barrow with central grave (RCAHMS 1978, 9–10). Upstanding monuments were also recorded, and small-scale excavation provided further characterisation of a monumental Pictish cemetery tradition.

This chapter focuses on the Pictish cemeteries of Aberdeenshire, Moray and Inverness-shire. These areas loosely cover the heartlands of the regions of Fortriu and Ce (Chapter 2). Figure 29 shows the distribution of cemeteries in these areas. The cemeteries of Aberdeenshire are relatively few in number, but this may be due to the generally poorer definition of cropmarks in Aberdeenshire (Fraser and Halliday 2011, 312). Here, the cropmark barrow sites range from a single barrow at Boynds to medium-sized cemeteries such as Hills of Boyndie (Fig. 30). There are few cairn sites, but a small number of possible examples were identified in the 1970s at Tillytarmont. The only excavated examples of Pictish barrows in Aberdeenshire were recently identified at Rhynie, Aberdeenshire. The barrows are located less than 0.5km to the north of the settlement at Rhynie (Chapter 3) (Noble *et al.* 2013). The two square barrows excavated were found a short distance to the south of where the two symbol stones and reports of human remains and cist burials have been identified (J.A. Henderson 1907, 163). The barrow cemeteries of Moray include single barrows at sites such as Kinloss Airfield and North Alves and small cemeteries at Lower Auchenreath, Wester Coltfield and Midtown. Greshop Farm, near the River Findhorn, had square barrows to the south-east of the lower stretch of the river and settlement remains and/or further barrows to the south-west. Three of the square barrows at Greshop have been excavated during development-led archaeology projects, including one barrow that was more than twice the size of the others (Fig. 31) (Dunbar 2012). The largest and most complex cemetery identified in Moray is Pitgaveny, located close to the former Spynie Loch (Figs. 32, 33). Here the remains of at least ten square barrows and around five circular barrows are arranged in linear alignment. The barrows were very large, up to 20m across, and at least four of the barrows appear to enclose smaller square-ditched features, probably barrows.

29. Distribution of monumental cemeteries in Aberdeenshire, Moray and Inverness-shire. Base map © Crown Copyright/ database right 2018. An Ordnance Survey/ EDINA supplied service.

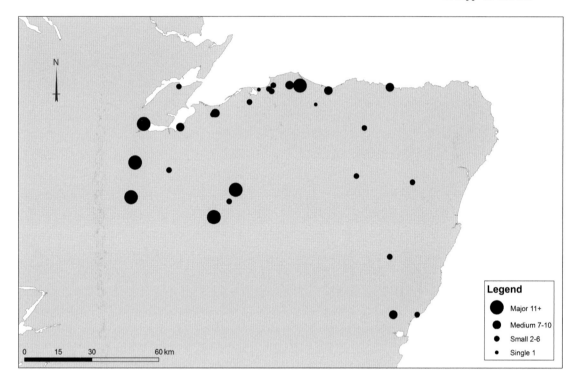

Legend

● Major 11+
● Medium 7-10
● Small 2-6
• Single 1

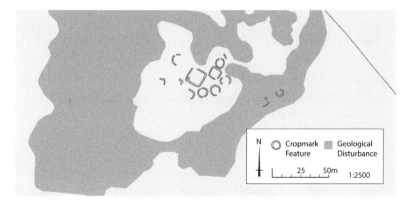

30. Hills of Boyndie, Aberdeenshire. Transcription of aerial photograph showing the square and round barrows clustered on a high plateau. The plateau overlooks the Bay of Boyndie on the Moray coast. Base map © Crown Copyright/database right 2018. An Ordnance Survey/ EDINA supplied service.

31. Transcription of Greshop Farm (Pilmuir), Moray, showing the square and round barrows near the River Findhorn. Base map © Crown Copyright/database right 2018. An Ordnance Survey/ EDINA supplied service.

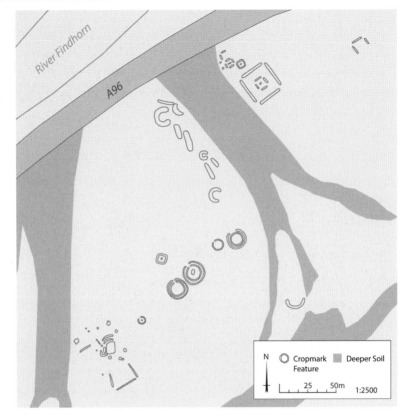

In Inverness-shire, the smaller cemeteries known from cropmarks include sites such as Kerrowaid with two barrows and Allanfearn with seven. An intriguing example is Kinchyle, where a large double-ditched square enclosure with central, possible grave, pit, is clearly visible as a cropmark alongside a dense array of features, many of which may be prehistoric settlement features (Fig. 34). Slightly larger cemeteries in Inverness-shire are represented by sites such as Mains of Garten, located at a bend in the River Spey, comprising a cemetery of around 20 round and square barrows (Fig. 35). At Poyntzfield on the Black Isle, a barrow cemetery of perhaps six barrows is evident, including round and square examples, running in a linear arrangement along a low terrace. The most impressive cropmark sites in this area are Croftgowan and Tarradale. The cemetery at Croftgowan comprises a linear setting of around 27 circular and square barrows located on the slope of Tor Alvie (Fig. 36). Tarradale House is located on a terrace overlooking the Beauly Firth (Fig. 37). Around 18

32. Pitgaveny cemetery cropmarks as identified from the air © Aberdeenshire Council Archaeology Service.

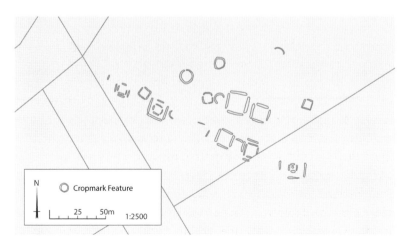

N

○ Cropmark Feature

25 50m 1:2500

33. Transcription of the Pitgaveny (Pitairlie), Moray, cemetery. A linear barrow cemetery with an exceptional number of large square barrows, some with multiple enclosing ditches. Base map © Crown Copyright/database right 2018. An Ordnance Survey/ EDINA supplied service.

34. Kinchyle, Inverness-shire. An extensive group of cropmarks recorded by RCAHMS in the 1970s. These include a double-ditched square enclosure or barrow with a central feature, possibly a gravecut. There are also a number of circular ditch features measuring 5m to 9m in diameter. Some of these may be barrows, but others appear to be later prehistoric houses. Base map © Crown Copyright/database right 2018. An Ordnance Survey/EDINA supplied service.

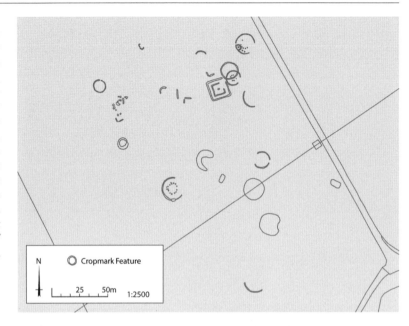

35. Mains of Garten, Inverness-shire. At a bend of the River Spey, the cropmarks of a barrow cemetery of at least 20 round and square barrows are visible on aerial photographs. Base map © Crown Copyright/database right 2018. An Ordnance Survey/EDINA supplied service.

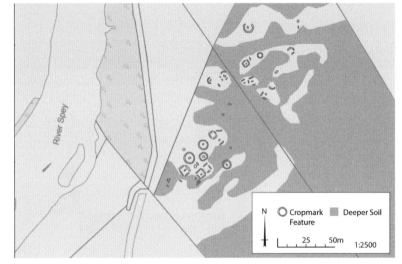

circular barrows, the largest 10–12m in diameter, and eight square barrows each measuring around 5–6m across, are evident, with two larger enclosures and a trackway (Fig. 38).

In addition, we are fortunate in Inverness-shire that a small number of upstanding cemeteries have also survived. The largest is Garbeg, where a total of 26 upstanding barrows have been recorded, 14 square or sub-rectangular and 10 circular (Figs. 39, 40) (Wedderburn and

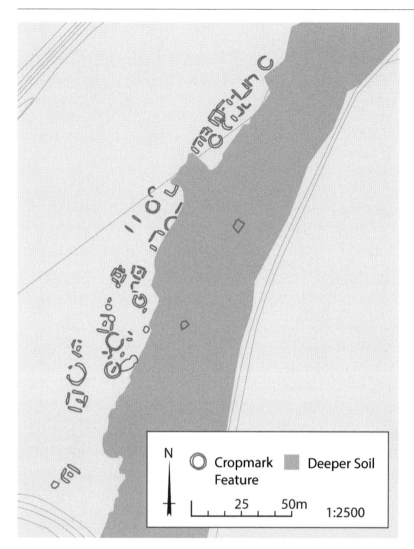

36. Croftgowan (Kinrara Farm), Inverness-shire. A linear cemetery of 27 circular and square barrows sits on an area of higher ground on the slope of Tor Alvie. Base map © Crown Copyright/database right 2018. An Ordnance Survey/ EDINA supplied service.

Grime 1984). The square barrows range from 3.5m to 5.5m across, and the round mounds are up to 10m in diameter and nearly all have surrounding ditches. Four barrows were excavated in 1979 following the discovery of a fragment of a Pictish symbol stone associated with one of the round barrows, although no relationship was conclusively proven between the stone and the burial monuments (J.B. Stevenson 1984; Wedderburn and Grime 1984). All examples overlay central inhumations, though the human remains were very badly preserved or non-existent in some cases. The second largest upstanding cemetery in Inverness-shire is at Whitebridge, situated on a ridge at the

37. Tarradale House, Inverness-shire. Aerial photographic survey has identified the remains of an extensive barrow cemetery 1km north-west of the mouth of the Beauly River. © Crown Copyright/database right 2018. An Ordnance Survey/ EDINA supplied service.

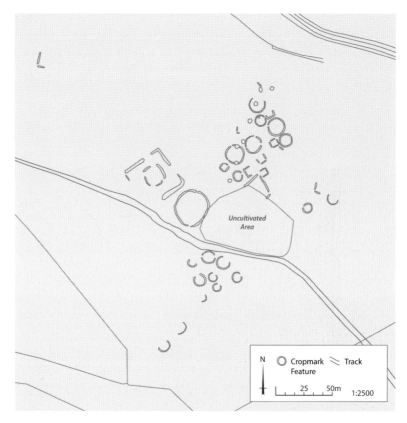

38 Aerial view of cropmarks of the barrow cemetery at Tarradale © Andy Hickie.

confluence of the River Foyers and Allt an Lòin. The cemetery consists
of at least seven burial mounds and five small round cairns. One of
the mounds has been excavated, but no human remains survived
(Alexander 2000; J.B. Stevenson 1984). Two smaller upstanding
cemeteries also survive: Brin School and Pityoulish. Brin School sits
on the eastern bank of the River Nairn on a low ridge and comprises
five barrows. These two cemeteries contain both square and circular

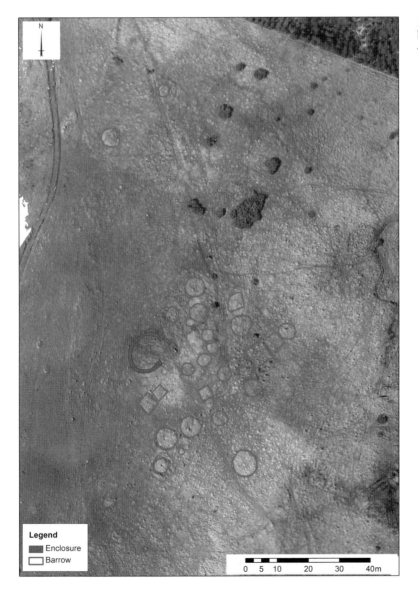

39. Garbeg, Inverness-shire,
barrow cemetery. Drone image
with barrows outlined.

40. The low mounds of
Pictish square barrows
as they survive today at
Garbeg © Juliette Mitchell.

mounds up to 10m in diameter. At Pityoulish, monoliths project from
three of the barrows. At this cemetery, one barrow was excavated in
1953 and human remains were recovered from a pit adjacent to the
standing stone (Rae and Rae 1953).

General characteristics of the cemeteries

The aerial photographic evidence shows that most monumental
cemeteries identified in Aberdeenshire, Moray and Inverness-shire
were relatively small in scale: over half of the probable or confirmed
examples contain six or fewer monuments. This corresponds to both
Winlow's and Henshall's studies of cemeteries further south in
Pictland, which suggest that many cemeteries were composed of one
to six burials (Henshall 1956; Winlow 2011, 341). The general trend,
north of the Forth, is for small clusters of graves rather than extensive
cemeteries (e.g. Dunbar and Maldonado 2012; Maldonado 2013,
9–11). The larger cemeteries (Garbeg, Pitgaveny, Croftgowan, Mains
of Garten, Tarradale) all have upwards of 11 barrows. They display
more variety in their size, shape and architectural construction, which
could be suggestive of their importance, their longevity or both.

As well as the number of monuments, other characteristics mark
some cemeteries out. The majority of barrows and cairns conform to

the sizes and types known elsewhere. The barrows are 4–12m in diameter, and most lie towards the smaller end of that spectrum. Yet some sites contain barrows that are much larger than the norm, including examples of square and round barrows up to 25m across. Examples of cemeteries with large barrows include Greshop, Pitgaveny, Wester Buthill (all Moray), Kinchyle, Inverness-shire, and Hills of Boyndie, Aberdeenshire. In three of these cases oversized square monuments appear to have been enlargements or elaborations of smaller monuments (Greshop, Pitgaveny, Kinchyle). Tarradale (Inverness-shire) also has larger circular barrows of 20m diameter, but with as yet no evidence of multiphased development.

Long cist cemeteries may represent another aspect of Pictish burial tradition in northern Pictland. However, although in Tayside and Fife around 90 examples are now known (Winlow 2011, 344), in the area of Fortriu and Ce long cist cemeteries are rare: examples are restricted to a handful of sketchy antiquarian accounts and a small number found during development, but all are undated and unpublished. They are largely restricted to the southernmost part of Aberdeenshire and include five long cists found at two different locations in Stonehaven (RCAHMS 1984, 17, nos. 82 and 83), another two at Johnshaven, Kincardineshire (RCHAMS 1984, 19, no. 135), and a single inhumation at Inverbervie. The lack of long cist cemeteries in the area may represent a real difference in the burial traditions of northern Pictland, or it could reflect a lack of defined detail in the cropmark evidence. Certainly nothing comparable to the long cist cemetery of Hallow Hill, Fife, where at least 150 inhumations were found, has been identified in the study area, though Hallow Hill is also exceptional. In Tayside and Fife over half of the identified long cist cemeteries contain fewer than five graves (Winlow 2011, 344–6). This is comparable to the size of most monumental cemeteries in the study area under discussion here.

Landscape location

Examining the aerial photographic record shows that the cemeteries often formed linear distributions that followed topographical features. These include areas of higher ground and rivers, similar to patterns observed in Tayside and Fife (Winlow 2011). It is possible that these linear distributions may reflect routeways through the landscape. At Croftgowan (Inverness-shire) for example, a major cemetery of 27 barrows follows a distinctive linear arrangement, which runs almost parallel to the route north from Stirling to Inverness where the traversable land narrows through the Cairngorm mountains. Likewise, at Whitebridge, Inverness-shire, the cemetery is located just north of the routeway that leads from Fort Augustus to Inverness and adjacent to a number of 18th-century and modern river crossings that include a natural ford. Dalbreck, Aberdeenshire, is close to a ford across the Water of Feugh, and the site is also located at the northern end of the route that leads across the Cairn o' Mount, a strategic mountainous pass through the Mounth, an eastward projection of the Cairngorms (Small 1974). At Pitgaveny, Moray, the linear layout again leads to a ford (NMRS: NJ26NW 51). Garbeg, Inverness-shire, may also sit on an old route through the highlands that leads from the mouth of River Enrick at Loch Ness northwards to Beauly and Inverness. Greshop, Moray, is located just off the main routeway depicted on the earliest detailed maps for the area. Mains of Garten, Inverness-shire, may also sit at a river crossing, in this case over the River Spey, near the crossing at Boat of Garten where a ferry crossing, now replaced by a bridge, was located. On the other side of the river from the Mains of Garten cemetery is a Pictish Class I symbol stone, found at Lynchurn (RCAHMS 2008, 74). Other examples of cemeteries show a more clustered layout, but some of these too may also relate to important land routes. The large barrow cemetery at Tarradale, Inverness-shire, for example, is dissected by a hollow way that leads southwards to a landing place on the Beauly Firth (Fig. 37) (Gregory and Jones 2001, illus. 1; Yeoman 1988, 131, no. 92).

Likely contemporary sites in the surrounding landscape include settlements and fortified enclosures. Unfortunately, evidence for Pictish settlement is still rare across much of mainland Scotland. As noted in Chapter 4, in the lowlands there is an absence of settlement remains after the 2nd or 3rd centuries AD (Hunter 2007a, 49). In Fortriu and Ce, virtually no unenclosed Pictish settlement evidence is known. The majority of the area is fertile, but intensively cultivated land and major agricultural improvements over the past 200 years have levelled upstanding features (RCAHMS 2007, 17–24). Excavations at Granton, Moray (Cook 2003), near Greshop cemetery and Dalladies, Aberdeenshire (Watkins 1981), near Balmakewan cemetery, have identified ephemeral remains dating from the mid 1st millennium AD, broadly contemporary with the cemeteries, and at Kintore,

Aberdeenshire, pits and other structural remains indicate domestic and metalworking activity from later in the 1st millennium AD (Cook and Dunbar 2008, 149–59). However, even these very ephemeral traces of possible Pictish settlement are rare in the lowlands of eastern and northern Scotland. Thus, it is difficult at present to situate the cemeteries within the settlement landscapes of the same period. However, in the upland landscapes towards the Great Glen in Inverness-shire, better preservation exists, presenting opportunities to study landscapes that have escaped the agricultural improvements and modern settlement expansion of the last few centuries. Three upstanding cemeteries are found along the Great Glen. The landscape in the wider environs preserves upstanding archaeological sites, including hut circles and platforms, hillforts and cairns. While none of the settlement remains are dated and many undoubtedly date to the Bronze or Iron Age, their distribution demonstrates that the cemeteries were located in areas that were densely settled in prehistory. Barrow cemeteries were, it seems, located in good agricultural areas, with some degree of importance placed on their accessibility to main routes across the landscape (Evans 2014, 33–7; Reynolds 2002, 186; Taylor 2011).

More fortified sites in the study region have been dated to the 1st millennium AD than settlements, though the numbers are still small. The promontory fort at Burghead, Moray (Chapter 2), is within 5km of Wester Buthill cemetery, a site with a large square enclosure and three possible barrows. The cemetery is located near to one of the modern routes into Burghead from inland areas to the south. Garbeg, Inverness-shire, is located around 4km north-east of Urquhart Castle. Urquhart Castle, excavated by Leslie Alcock, lies at the head of the Great Glen (Alcock and Alcock 1992). Here a medieval masonry castle overlays a site that Alcock suggested could have been the 6th-century fort (*munitio*) of Bridei son of Mailcon referenced in Adomnán's 'Life of Columba' (Alcock 1981, 159–61; Alcock and Alcock 1992, 260). All other forts within the vicinity of cemeteries are undated, but some examples where cemeteries and forts are closely juxtaposed are worthy of further investigation. Brin School, Inverness-shire, for example, is overlooked by the hillfort, Creagan An Tuirc, 'the boar's rock' (Taylor with Márkus 2012, 342, 520). The old route adjacent to the cemetery also leads northwards towards Inverness where the spectacular boar stone at Knocknagael and another possible barrow cemetery were located. Croftgowan cemetery is located on the south-west slope of Tor Alvie, which has an undated fort on the summit. Other fortified sites may exist in the vicinity of Pictish barrow and cairn cemeteries. As outlined above and in Chapter 4, the barrows at Rhynie, Aberdeenshire, were located near to a contemporary fortified settlement and at Tarradale, Inverness-shire, excavations in 1991–93 found a large ditched enclosure, palisade and internal features at a site located just to the north-east of the barrow cemetery (Gregory and Jones 2001). Pottery from one of the internal pits has been suggested to be early medieval in date, but the enclosure itself remains undated (McGill 2001, 255–8).

Even before Pictish burial traditions were fully identified, Wainwright postulated a landscape and site-based relationship between symbol stones and burial (Wainwright 1955b, 87–96). Since then, the relationship of Pictish symbol stones to burial has been widely discussed (e.g. Clarke 2007, 27–31; Close-Brooks 1980; Foster 2014, 64–5; A. Ritchie 2011, 133–4). Of the confirmed or probable cemetery sites in the study area, few show close relationships with symbol stones. Fragments of a Class I symbol stone were found in 1974 at Garbeg, Inverness-shire, in association with one of the round cairns (Cairn 1) (Wedderburn and Grime 1984, 151–2). However, the stone is incomplete and no direct relationship with the cairn could be conclusively demonstrated. At Tillytarmont, symbol stones have also been found in the close vicinity of potential burial monuments (Gondek 2010). In 1975, Tony Woodham excavated a small square cairn made up of large waterworn boulders with evidence for a large central quartz monolith and identified two stone spreads that may have been other cairns. These were found in the same general area as five Pictish Class I symbol stones located on the haughland at Tillytarmont (Woodham 1975, 6). However, no burial was found at the cairn and no direct association can again be demonstrated. Relationships at other sites are suggestive. At Mains of Garten, for example, a symbol stone was ploughed up in a field near to the cemetery, but in this case the stone was located on the opposite side of the river.

Only the barrows at Rhynie have been radiocarbon dated, representing the only scientific dates available for Pictish burial monuments in the study area. Two radiocarbon dates for the individual in the central cist burial indicate that the square barrow dates to cal AD 400–570. This corresponds well with the dating for the cairns and mounds of the two largest Pictish cemeteries excavated: Redcastle, Angus, and Lundin

Links, Fife, both in southern Pictland. Square and round cairns may have been constructed earlier in the 1st millennium AD (e.g. Murray and Ralston 1997; Neighbour *et al.* 2000), but the floruit of this tradition can be placed in the 5th–6th centuries AD and the tradition appears to have largely ceased by the 7th century AD (Maldonado 2013).

The monumental cemeteries of northern Pictland in context

The 5th–6th centuries AD, when the monumental cemeteries of Pictland flourished, are increasingly seen as a critical period in the formation of the early kingdoms of northern Britain and north-western Europe more generally. While there are examples of burial monuments and even small cemeteries in the earlier centuries of the 1st millennium AD, the establishment of monumental cemeteries marks an important transition in the visibility of the dead in the archaeological record (Maldonado 2011; 2013). Across northern and eastern Scotland, from Shetland to the Firth of Forth, very similar burial monuments were constructed, suggesting strong links between the dispersed communities of Pictland (Bigelow 1984, 127; O'Brien 2009). In Scotland generally, burial becomes much more visible in the 5th and 6th centuries (Maldonado 2013, 1). The emergence of monumental cemeteries from the 5th century and the dwindling occurrence of such monuments by the 7th century mirrors patterns of change evident elsewhere in Britain and Ireland in this period.

The square and round barrows of Pictland can be paralleled with similar traditions of monumental graves across Britain and Ireland (Longley 2009, 112–15; Maldonado 2013, 17). In Ireland, enclosed cemeteries were established for the first time in the 5th–6th centuries AD, marking a change from the sparser burial evidence of the Iron Age (O'Brien 2009, 136–8). Some monumental or enclosed cemeteries were also created, including the construction of 'settlement-cemeteries' defined by ditches, ring ditches and cairns (O'Sullivan *et al.* 2014, 283–99). However, while monumental cemeteries and mounds occurred in Ireland, the focus on individuals, which is common to Pictish barrows, remains rare. In Ireland, the enclosing of groups of burials within mounds, cairns or enclosures was more common. Nonetheless, there are examples in Ireland of cemeteries that appear to cluster around founder barrows or graves, and a very small number were furnished

with grave goods (Bhreathnach 2014, 125–6). In Wales, the most typical burials from the 5th century onwards were east–west orientated and
unenclosed, but enclosed graves are also known, including square
enclosures that were probably barrows (Longley 2009, 113). The Pictish
monumental cemeteries emerged prior to the elaborate princely burials
of the late 6th and 7th centuries in Anglo-Saxon England, but over-
lapped with the practice of a more modest barrow-building tradition
(Carver 2005; Dickinson 2011, 230; Geake 1992; Welch 2011, 269).
Early Anglo-Saxon barrows are not generally associated with rich
assemblages of grave goods; it is the investment in construction, time
and material that demonstrates wealth or status (Scull 2009, 277).

In Anglo-Saxon England, the building of mounds has been
connected with the emergence of powerful hereditary aristocracies
(Carver 2002, 136). In Ireland, like Scotland, the lack of grave goods
has meant that questions of status or elite practice have not been
addressed to the same level. Nonetheless, occasional grave goods such
as neck or toe rings, found in early medieval burials in Ireland, do tend
to be associated with barrow traditions (Gleeson 2014, 672–3;
O'Brien 2009, 142–3; O'Sullivan *et al.* 2014, 293). In Ireland, it has
been suggested that examples of central grave mounds within unenclosed cemeteries may also represent high-status burials (Bhreathnach
2014, 125–6), and multiple burials found in a small number of Irish
barrows (as occasionally found within Pictish mounds and cairns)
have been claimed to have been the burial monuments of kindred
heads of ruling lineages (Gleeson 2014, 162). In Wales, references in
the early praise poem *Englynion y Beddau* suggest that burial in
mounds was an elite practice (Longley 2009, 115).

In Pictland, the small number of mounds or cairns found at most
sites suggests that this was not a common rite. They were instead acts
of selective remembrance, perhaps commemorating only certain individuals. The presence of barrow monuments at sites such as Rhynie
(Fig. 41, 42), implies that at least some of these monuments were part
of high-status cemeteries, the mounds and cairns built for the few
rather than the many. The chronological spread of mounds and cairns
within individual cemeteries, with perhaps only a half-dozen or so
constructed over two or three centuries, also suggests a restricted,
probably elite practice (Alexander 2005, 110) – episodes of intense
construction that would have been memorable, creating powerful
statements within the landscape (cf. Mizoguchi 1993).

41. The square barrows at Rhynie under excavation in 2013.

While similar forms of burial architecture are found throughout Pictland, generally there are no grave goods distinguishing individual burials. Nonetheless, some monuments were made more prominent through the scale of the mounds or cairns constructed. At Tarradale, Inverness-shire, for example, a series of round barrows was built on a much grander scale than the others, and the cemetery also contains an even larger circular enclosure, 36m across its widest point – whether this too was a barrow, albeit greatly enlarged, remains to be seen (Fig. 37). Likewise, at Hills of Boyndie, Aberdeenshire, a cluster of barrows was centred around a large square barrow 14m across (Fig. 30). The other very revealing phenomenon, laid bare by the plough-truncated form of most examples, is the occurrence of more than one set of enclosing ditches, suggesting barrow elaboration or perhaps enlargement. At Greshop, Moray, a square barrow 10m across was enclosed by a set of additional ditches, creating a monument 28m in length/width. The more elaborate monument at Greshop was the largest of three excavated at the site. The others measured 7m and 8m across and the inclusion of additional ditches greatly increased the size differential. Thus, from the outset or through time, one of monuments at Greshop was made to stand out through a greater investment in labour and was more monumental in form. Once complete, it was around four times the size of the other barrows

42 Long cist grave
found within a square
barrow, Rhynie.

in the cemetery and would have required approximately 16 times the volume of soil in its creation. At Kinchyle (Fig. 34), Inverness-shire, a square barrow appears to have been enlarged and elaborated, an average-sized barrow around 8–10m across seemingly encased within an additional ditch extending to around 20m in length/width. The larger square enclosures at Rhynie have been suggested to be some form of shrine (Chapter 4) but, given that other cemeteries in northern Pictland have greatly enlarged monuments, it is possible that these too were large burial monuments. If this is the case, then these were four times the size of the smaller barrows identified at Rhynie. The phenomenon of creating monumental barrows on this scale or enlarging barrows, cairns or enclosures is a little recognised tradition in Pictland. A handful of larger barrows are known in southern Pictland in Tayside and Fife, such as Hallhole, Perthshire, but there has been little discussion of their significance (Winlow 2011, 337, Fig. 10.4). The monumental and/or enlarged barrows are evenly spread across the study area, suggesting they may have been regionally significant monuments and/or cemeteries.

Within cemeteries such as Greshop, only a single barrow seems to have been emphasised through the construction of a much larger monument, but at others such as Pitgaveny, four barrows were emphasised or enlarged and the majority of the barrows in the cemetery were changed into large monuments up to 20m across. The larger barrows are predominately found within the likely bounds of Fortriu (Fig. 29). Barrow enlargement or aggrandisement suggests that the burial places of some individuals were elaborated and perhaps increasingly venerated through time. At Pitgaveny, the whole cemetery population was marked as important through investment in the construction of the additional earthen mounds and ditches that enclosed the burials. While individuals buried in certain enlarged barrows may have been particularly influential in life, what perhaps mattered more were the ways in which the living community manipulated the status of the dead and the architecture of the cemetery for their own needs (Barrett 1994, 51; Ó Corráin 1998). The aggrandisement of particular barrows and cemeteries was an act that would have been socially and politically charged. The elaboration or enlargement of existing barrows may have happened during the creation of other monuments or as part of other important social events, perhaps when social relations were being established, reworked or maintained. In this respect, social structure was not simply reflected in architecture of this kind; it was actively forged and manipulated through the creation of cemeteries of this kind (Maldonado 2013, 8; Williams 2007). Each mound or cairn constructed altered the form of the landscape through a process of accretion, each adding to an evolving narrative that embodied the community of both the living and dead (Barrett 1994, 113, 123; Bradley 2007, 165).

As well as barrow enlargement, Pitgaveny cemetery is also an excellent example of another phenomenon found in Pictish barrow cemeteries: the conjoining of barrows or cairns to create elaborate linked monuments. At Pitgaveny, the barrows were arranged in two main rows, aligned ESE–WNW. The southern row had at least seven barrows, but nine may have been joined together in total. The conjoining and elaboration of certain barrows may be related phenomena. Both developments suggest the importance of particular members of society and imply that the creation of lineages of the dead (whether real or fictive) may have comprised an important element in the establishment and maintenance of cemeteries (Williams 2007). One of the major transformations of the early medieval period was the instigation of a hereditary aristocracy and the emergence of individuals with sufficient power and authority to call themselves kings. The occurrence of elaborate fortified enclosures from at least the 5th century onwards also implies an increase in social differentiation (Chapter 3). At the same time, monumental cemeteries proliferated and their architecture suggests that these monuments may also have been implicated in the establishment and maintenance of hierarchy.

The transition towards hereditary aristocracy relied on the creation and maintenance of lineage and the linking of leadership to a powerful past where ancestry was critical (Gleeson 2012, 9). In early Irish literature, burial places were seen as nodal points through which the Otherworld and the world of the dead could be accessed and cemeteries were one means by which lineages were materialised and forged (Gleeson 2012, 23–4). Pictish barrows and cairns may have acted in similar ways – through these places, claims of lineage and kinship may have been highlighted and genealogies created that were instrumental in establishing hierarchical social relations. The establishment of monumental cemeteries in Pictland is commensurate to the first references to kings in northern Britain, while the decline of the tradition in the 7th century coincides with the references to an overking of the Picts (Evans 2008, 9). Thus, the creation of the first large formal cemeteries since the Bronze Age in north-east Scotland may have gone hand in hand with the establishment of regional hegemonies across Pictland. Their demise, or the cessation of such rites, was perhaps prompted by increasingly centralised forms of authority (Evans 2008, 7–9; J.E. Fraser 2011, 27).

How these cemeteries were situated within the early medieval landscape is also important. While some of these barrows and cairns could reach proportions of up to 25m in diameter or more, they were not generally located in highly conspicuous locations that would have been visible for kilometres around. The siting of the barrows of northern Pictland suggests they were located on more locally visible terraces and knolls. In addition, a number were situated in areas tied into the geographies of routine movement in the landscape: on routeways, at fording points and on general lines of movement through the landscape. Some cemeteries were also located at key transitional points in the landscape. The cairns at Tillytarmont, Aberdeenshire, for example, were located at the confluence of two rivers and a boundary location between two old counties, the division between three later medieval parishes and the site of a number of fords and crossing places. The place-name itself derives from *tulach* – a term often associated with assembly (O'Grady 2014, 114–19; Taylor with Márkus 2012, 519–20). Tillytarmont is the find-spot of five Class I symbol stones found since the 19th century, suggesting the cemetery was a component in wider landscape of Pictish power. In Anglo-Saxon England, some field cemeteries seem to have later become important assembly places (Brookes and Reynolds 2011, 235–40), and in Ireland 'cemetery-settlements' may have played roles in assembly practices too (Fitzpatrick 2004; Gleeson 2015, 45). The location of Tillytarmont on an important natural and cultural boundary and its place-name evidence may similarly suggest the cemetery was located in an area that functioned as a place of assembly. This particular cemetery also shares characteristics with the burial places in Ireland known as *ferta,* which acted as places of legal assembly and as boundary markers and protectors of the land and territory of particular kin groups (O'Brien and Bhreathnach 2011, 54–5; see also Charles-Edwards 1993, 259–61). The second element of the Tillytarmont place-name derives from *an tearmainn* 'sanctuary', which implies that in a later period there was also an important church nearby. Tillytarmont may represent an important site of assembly and burial that originated in a pagan context, but continued as an important place in a Christian milieu (Brookes and Reynolds 2011, 88).

The landscape setting of these monumental cemeteries also reveals something of the wider geographies of northern Pictland. With the exception of Rhynie, there are no known close juxtapositions between confirmed Pictish fortified sites and cemeteries in the study area. The cemeteries thus may offer important clues to additional important nodes in the Pictish landscape and may signal elements of an emerging multifocal landholding system that formed the basis of power of high-status Pictish communities (Ross 2006). What is also notable is the lack of a clear relationship between monumental cemeteries and Pictish stones. Symbol stones have been found in close proximity to monumental cemetery sites in only a small handful of cases (Rae and Rae 1953). It seems that a direct relationship existed between Pictish cemeteries and symbol stones only in exceptional cases. The lack of a relationship between symbol stones and cemeteries except in a few cases suggests that they had more varied purposes than just grave markers. In this respect, they can perhaps be directly compared to the ogham stones of Ireland. Most ogham stones in Ireland appear to have been used to express genealogies of elite members of society. In the past these have been interpreted as burial markers, but like Pictish symbol stones there are very few examples of stones found in direct association with graves (see also Chapter 6). Some may be memorials, but others had a legal function concerned with boundaries and landholding, acting as 'visible, physical declarations of land possession' (Bhreathnach 2014, 42–4). Thus, ogham stones may have acted in similar ways to barrows, proclaiming the rights and genealogies of particular elite lineages. The Pictish Class I symbol stones appear, like the Irish ogham stones, to have been markers of elite identities (Forsyth 1997b; Samson 1992). They may have complemented the role of cemeteries in marking important landscapes of power and perhaps directly indicated land ownership and rights. There are similarities here in the ways symbol stones and barrows expressed ideas about identity: symbol stones, like barrows, on occasion appear to have symbol sets added and, in a smaller number of cases, symbols were overwritten by new carvings (Clarke 2007). This implies the identities expressed on symbol stones were cumulative, and the overwriting of symbols might demonstrate that these identities were reworked or even directly contested.

Monument building often occurs at horizons of social change and centralisation, with the greatest labour inputs occurring in transitional periods in the establishment of elites (Cherry 1978; Whittle 1997, 145). Emulation, competition and a desire for power within an emerging early medieval society may have been strong motivating factors in the construction of monumental cemeteries in Pictland (Whittle 1997, 167). In this chapter, the increasingly rich aerial photographic record available for north-east Scotland has been used to review the evidence for burial traditions in an area of Pictland that was central to the establishment of the Pictish kingdoms of northern Britain. While few sites have been excavated, the cemeteries of northern Pictland are an important resource in assessing how burial architecture may have been deeply implicated in the creation of new forms of society in northern Europe in the 1st millennium AD. In this area of northern Europe, the appearance of formal cemeteries and the creation of the Pictish monumental cemeteries can be seen to go hand in hand with the establishment of a more hierarchical form of lineage-based society (Barrett 1988). The end of this tradition can be linked to changes within the social and political order, with the dead becoming a less prominent source of power as superregional polities emerged.

CHAPTER SIX

(Re)discovering the Gaulcross hoard

Gordon Noble, Martin Goldberg, Alistair McPherson and Oskar Sveinbjarnarson

During the 18th and 19th centuries, many antiquities were both discovered and destroyed through agricultural improvement and expansion. In northern and eastern Scotland this included the discovery of some of the most famous pieces of metalwork and hoards dating to the Pictish period. In 1838 the Gaulcross hoard was found during the process of removal of two Bronze Age stone circles just outside of the village of Fordyce in northern Aberdeenshire. The hoard included a range of items, but only three have survived to the present day. The hoard has been discussed in many previous accounts of Pictish metalwork and has often been the subject of art-historical analysis, but very little was known of the true composition of the hoard until new fieldwork at the site of discovery in 2013. This chapter outlines the (re)discovery of one of the major metalwork hoards of northern Pictland and what it can tell us about early medieval society in northern Scotland and beyond.

The original discovery of the hoard

The Gaulcross hoard was discovered in 1838 at Ley Farm, Aberdeenshire, in a field that contained two stone circles of likely Bronze Age date (Fig. 43). In 1837 a man called James Lawtie gained the tenancy of the farm at Gaulcross and began improving the land soon after. The stone circles were ruthlessly removed with some of the stones blown up with explosives. Only one monolith of the northern circle was still standing at the time of the first account of the hoard by John Stuart (Stuart 1867, 74–5). He suggested that the silver hoard was found on the southern side of the northern circle among the boulders of the ring cairn that the standing stones were set into. Stuart confirmed that other 'pins and brooches' were found, but only illustrated three objects. A few decades later, the Revd William

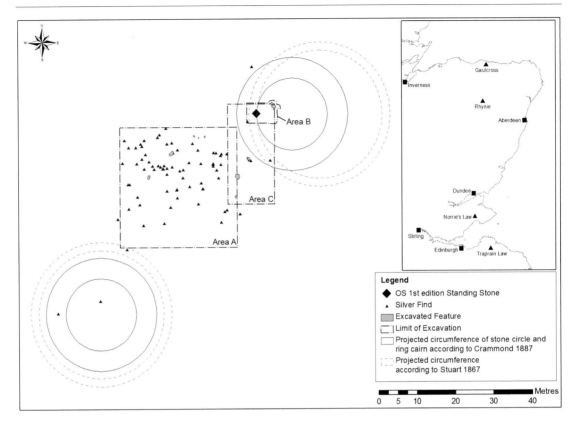

Cramond also reported that the hoard was found to the south of the remaining monolith of the northern stone circle. Like Stuart, Cramond suggested the hoard included other pins, buckles and brooches (Cramond 1887, 92). However, only three objects survive from the original discovery and include a hand-pin (so-called because of its resemblance to a clenched fist), a spiral bracelet and a length of silver chain (Plate 9). These were given by the landowner, Sir Robert Abercromby, to Banff museum, and subsequently have been on loan and display at the National Museum of Scotland (Stevenson and Emery 1964).

43. Location map of the findspot (inset) and the projected position of the two stone circles at Gaulcross North and the location of the silver finds at the site.

Revisiting the Gaulcross hoard

Gaulcross is now an intensively farmed arable field in rural Aberdeenshire and nothing is now evident of the stone circles. In Spring 2013, the Northern Picts project and the National Museum of Scotland teamed up to investigate the findspot of the Gaulcross hoard. The initial aim of this joint venture was to investigate whether new contextual information could be provided for the important antiquarian find at Gaulcross. Fieldwork began with a geophysical survey. Metal-detecting was also planned with the aim of addressing the level of antiquarian recovery of the hoard and to identify any additional small fragments of the hoard that may have been missed by the original finders. On the second day of the project, Alistair McPherson, a local metal-detectorist working with the project, found three late Roman silver siliquae, pieces of folded hack-silver, a silver strap-end and part of a silver bracelet.

With these early successes, the project stepped up a gear – the arable field was due to be ploughed and planted imminently. Geophysical survey was extended over a large part of the field, but revealed little, so the project quickly focused on metal-detecting (Figs. 44, 45). Finds were plotted to provide an accurate three-dimensional record, and over the next three days metal-detecting allowed the finds scatter to be plotted with a large trench opened over the most concentrated area (Fig. 46). Careful excavation demonstrated that all of the finds were located in the modern agricultural plough-soil (Fig. 43: Area A). A smaller trench was also opened at the recorded position of the last standing stone of Gaulcross North stone circle (Fig. 43: Area B), but only a scatter of prehistoric features were identified and none that could be linked directly with the silver finds. Boulders found in one area may have been part of the ring cairn of the stone circle, but all of the identified features were highly truncated – the agricultural improvement of Lawtie and his labourers had been comprehensive.

44. Metal-detecting at Gaulcross.

45. One of the Roman coins uncovered by metal-detecting by Ali McPherson at Gaulcross.

46. The excavation underway. The topsoil was stripped back by machine in spits to allow detecting at different levels of the topsoil. The subsoil was also detected, cleaned and features recorded and excavated.

Antiquarian reports suggest the hoard was only a slight depth below the surface 'found between two stones' (Stuart 1867, 75), and the new finds were all within the plough-soil. It seems likely that dispersal of the fragments of hacksilver began during the extensive improvements to the field in 1838 that led to the initial discovery, and subsequent ploughing dispersed the silver further. The lack of remaining evidence for the stone circle and the dynamiting of the stones of the circles are testament to the vigour of improvement and the intensive ploughing carried out since that time. Many small fragments of hacksilver and other objects had clearly been missed or dispersed before the hoard was discovered by the original finders.

Character and composition of the hoard

The new fieldwork at Gaulcross entirely changes our knowledge of the scale and character of the hoard. Over 100 new silver items were recovered, mostly small fragments of sheet silver, hacked fragments of objects and occasionally more diagnostic and intact objects (Plate 10). The three surviving items were part of a larger hacksilver hoard similar to the only other comparable Pictish hoard known in Scotland – the Norrie's Law hoard in Fife (Fig. 47). Large silver hand-pins found in both had always linked the two hoards (Youngs 2013), but

47. The Norrie's Law hoard, Fife, central Scotland © National Museums Scotland.

within the new finds from Gaulcross there were more recognisable late Roman objects than in the Norrie's Law hoard, such as hacked dish fragments, spoon handles and a strap-end or belt fitting. There were also clipped siliquae – during the 4th to early 5th century the edges of Roman silver coins were removed in order to stretch out increasingly diminishing supplies of silver (Guest 2013). Not all objects from Gaulcross have been hacked. Intact ornaments included a lunate/crescent shaped pendant (Plate 11) with two double-loops at either end perhaps for suspension from a small-gauge double link chain and two hemispheres that may have originally formed one ornament, perhaps a hollow spherical bead or pinhead (Fig. 48).

48. The silver hemispheres from Gaulcross © National Museums Scotland.

A number of the finds were unique or very rare – for example, only one confirmed silver ingot was previously known from Pictland, from excavations at the hillfort of Clatchard Craig in Fife (Close-Brooks 1986). The Gaulcross hoard includes at least two distinct types of ingots: D-sectioned and rectangular-sectioned comparable to those found in other hacksilver hoards from Britain and Ireland such as that from Coleraine, Northern Ireland (Marzinzik 2013). Fragments of two penannular brooches in the Gaulcross hoard are object types with a wide currency in late Roman and early medieval Britain and Ireland, but these objects span that historical transition. One is a flattened terminal of a penannular brooch with a twisted hoop of a type only otherwise found in the Norrie's Law hoard (top left in Fig. 47). The other is a substantial portion of a smaller zoomorphic penannular brooch (Fig. 49). Both are rare in both form and material: before the Gaulcross (re)discovery the Norrie's Law twisted

49. A small zoomorphic penannular brooch from Gaulcross © National Museums Scotland.

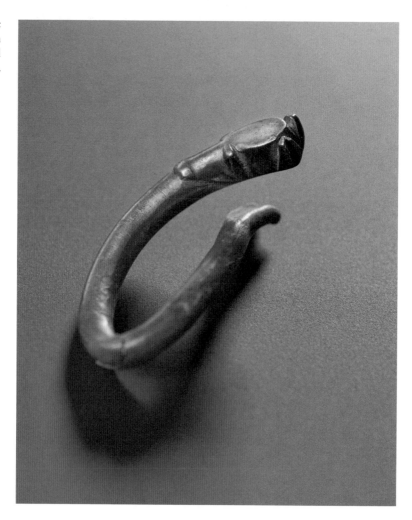

penannular hoops were unique; and although the zoomorphic penannular brooch is much more widely distributed in bronze across
Britain and Ireland, it is very unusual in silver. A large proportion of
the hacksilver came from bracelets. They are a variety of shapes,
widths and diameters, chopped up, folded and sometimes bundled
into packages, and provide a further parallel to the many similar
fragments found in the Norrie's Law hoard. Two of the Gaulcross
bracelet packages had late Roman siliquae pinched between the
terminal and a fold (Fig. 50).

50. One of the bracelet
fragments from Gaulcross
with a late Roman siliquae
pinched inside © National
Museums Scotland.

The hoard in context

The Gaulcross hoard can now be studied alongside two other pre-Viking Age hacksilver hoards from Scotland – Traprain Law, East Lothian, containing only late Roman items, and Norrie's Law, Fife, a mix of late Roman and non-Roman objects. Traprain Law is the largest hoard of late Roman hacksilver known, buried at some point in the 5th century AD inside a large hillfort in East Lothian (Curle 1923). It weighs *c.*22kg and is dominated by fragments of dishes, flagons and platters, their composition typical of high purity late Roman silver (Hunter and Painter 2013). The closest comparison for the contents of the Gaulcross hoard is the Norrie's Law hoard (Plate 10; Fig. 47), discovered around 1819 by a labourer digging for sand at the base of a large prehistoric cairn in Fife. Like Gaulcross, only a fraction of the Norrie's Law hoard survives – 750g whereas over 12kg of silver is estimated to have been found originally (Graham-Campbell 1991). The majority of the silver was immediately dispersed, sold and melted down. The hoard now consists of around 170 pieces and includes two hand-pins, a plaque decorated with Pictish symbols, two penannular brooches with twisted hoops, a complete spiral finger-ring and fragments of others, chain fragments, decorated fittings, many fragments of bracelets and hacksilver, including an inscribed late Roman spoon bowl (Blackwell and Goldberg in press; R.B.K. Stevenson 1955). As at Gaulcross, Roman coins were also found, and although they are now lost, three late 4th-century Roman siliquae have been identified from an early drawing of the hoard (Blackwell and Goldberg in press; Bland *et al.* 2013, 132). The most remarkable object from the Norrie's Law find is the plaque decorated with Pictish symbols.

Dating the hoard(s)

The dating of both the Gaulcross objects and the Norrie's Law hoard has been much debated. The Gaulcross hoard has generally been seen as earlier than Norrie's Law, perhaps dating to the 6th to 7th century AD (Graham-Campbell 1991, 241; Stevenson and Emery 1964; Youngs 1989, 26). The dating of the Norrie's Law hoard has seen more discussion, ranging from the late 4th or 5th century (Laing 1990, 41) to the 8th century AD (R.B.K. Stevenson 1955, 110). There are more late Roman items in the new finds from Gaulcross, but it is also uncertain how many Roman objects were lost from Norrie's Law due to its dispersal. The similarities between the two hoards mean that discussion of their date has often been intertwined.

A date in the 7th to 8th-century range for the deposition of the Norrie's Law hoard has been generally accepted, based primarily on art-historical analysis of the symbols on the silver plaque (Fig. 47) (Graham-Campbell 1991, 255; I. Henderson 1989, 211; Henderson and Henderson 2004, 88), and on one of the hand-pins. Graham-Campbell, for example, compared the juxtaposition of the Z-rod on the back of the hand-pin and a small cross detail on the front of the hand-pin with Class II Pictish cross-slabs dating to the 7th century or later. However, recent research has shown this hand-pin is a 19th-century copy of the other large Norrie's Law hand-pin, with the addition of a Z-rod on the back (Goldberg and Blackwell 2013). This object cannot therefore be used to date the hoard. One of the two plaques has also been shown to be a 19th-century copy.

The symbols on the remaining plaque from Norrie's Law consist of a double-disc and Z-rod and a 'beast-head' shown in profile. R.B.K. Stevenson (1955, 110; Stevenson and Emery 1964, 208), Graham-Campbell (1991, 255) and Henderson (1989, 211; Henderson and Henderson 2004, 88) have compared the latter symbol to a dog motif in the Lindisfarne Gospels. A closer comparison for the plaque is on a Pictish symbol stone from Rhynie (No. 5), Aberdeenshire, which depicts the same two symbols of a beast-head, double-disc and Z-rod, but with the addition of a mirror and comb symbol (Fig. 51). Indeed, the art-historical comparison to the Lindisfarne Gospels is misleading. The beast on the Norrie's Law plaque and on Rhynie No. 5 is not a dog – both clearly have flippers and are more readily identifiable as some form of sea- or water-creature.

As with so many Pictish symbol stones, the context of Rhynie No. 5 is uncertain, having been found in the foundations of the later parish church. However, excavations of the high-status settlement at Rhynie and associated dating all point to a 4th to 6th-century AD date for this complex (Chapter 4). Clay moulds for the production of hand-pins have also been recovered from Rhynie, providing further material links to the two silver hoards. The Pictish symbol stone Rhynie No. 5 is one of the best parallels for the symbols on the Norrie's Law plaque. The number of Roman finds in the Gaulcross

51. Rhynie No. 5 symbol stone showing the 'beast' head, similar to that shown on the silver plaque from Norrie's Law © Michael Sharpe.

hoard (and increasingly recognised in Norrie's Law) also suggests an earlier date for both hoards should be considered. An earlier date would place the hoards within a wider north European context of hoards from Denmark of 5th- or 6th-century date that also contain a mixture of Roman and non-Roman objects (Blackwell and Goldberg forthcoming; Painter 2013, 226).

Europe's northernmost pre-Viking Age hacksilver hoard

As well as re-examining the dating of the hoards the discovery of a much larger range of objects at Gaulcross also allows us to address the biography of these hoards. Some of the objects within these hoards in Pictland had long histories – fragments of vessels from Roman silver dining sets and objects with late Roman military associations. Alongside these objects were fragments of objects such as penannular brooches, made locally and found across Britain and Ireland. Silver was not mined in Scotland in this period. All silver used in the post-Roman period in Scotland had its origins in the hacksilver from the late Roman world, as exemplified by the Traprain Law hoard. The differing compositions of individual objects in the three Scottish hacksilver hoards can show how, through time, late Roman silver was recycled and re-cast into high-status objects that underpinned the development of elite society in the post-Roman period. During the process of recycling, the Roman silver was remade into new objects, but its origin may not have been entirely forgotten. Some of these later objects may have also directly referenced the late Antique world, with items such as hand-pins showing the adaptation of late Roman military styles both in terms of design and in decorative techniques (Gavin 2013, 430; see also Youngs 2013, 415). As Gavin notes, the use of Roman models may have been to invoke military prowess and ostentation among elites in early medieval Britain and Ireland (Gavin 2013, 433).

As for the ultimate origins of the Roman items in these hoards, interpretations of the distribution of silver into non-Roman hands has ranged from looting, trade and bribes to natives, to military pay for native groups in contact with the Romans. Hunter (2007a, b), has argued for the deliberate use of bribes and subsidies by the Romans in Scotland to both build up and destabilise native society. Recent scholarship, however, has focused on hacksilver as evidence of indigenous individuals or groups serving in the late Roman military (e.g. Guggisberg 2013, 213). The 'parcels' of silver from Gaulcross, including coins clasped between bracelet fragments, certainly suggest that standardised weights of silver could have been used as a means of payment. However, whether this was from direct payment for military service in the late Roman army, or as bribes to leaders of native warbands in the late 4th or early 5th century AD, raiding, or due to exchange between indigenous elites themselves remains a moot point (Painter 2013, 230). Through time, this silver made its way into hacksilver hoards.

The northern Picts

Looking at the more regional context in Pictland, this new discovery adds to the growing evidence for the importance of northern Pictland in the post-Roman period (Woolf 2006, 2007b). The iconic Pictish Class I symbol stones are more common in northern Pictland, and the distribution of massive silver chains shows a distinctive scatter in this region, but they are absent from southern Pictland (I. Henderson 1958; Youngs 2013, illus. 26.1). A whole series of Pictish fortifications have also been identified along the Moray coastline, including the largest Pictish fort known at Burghead in Moray (Chapter 3). The identification of the settlement at Rhynie, Aberdeenshire, and a series of ringforts recently dated to the 5th and 6th centuries AD also suggest the importance of northern Pictland, an area that at times has been thought to be peripheral to the major social and political developments in northern Britain (Noble *et al.* 2013) (Chapter 4).

Nonetheless, in the immediate area around the Gaulcross hoard there are few identified contemporary Pictish sites – and the region has a notable absence of symbol stones. Two forts are located nearby, but radiocarbon dating evidence suggests these are Iron Age in date. The nearest confirmed Pictish fort is 7km along the coast at Green Castle, Portknockie, which has been partly excavated and dated to the 7th to 9th centuries cal AD (Ralston 1987). However, one curious object has been found less than 5km from the hoard site: an object known as the Portsoy whetstone (Plate 12). The object is a small cylindrical stone of phyllite carved with human heads on either end, one apparently displayed on the end of a sword, with carvings of a fish, three crescents, an arch and tongs set between the two heads. The object is unique, but the symbols resemble those found on Pictish symbol stones. The Portsoy object has been compared to the whetstone or sceptre from the Sutton Hoo burial mound and interpreted by Enright and others as a symbol of sacral kingship (Enright 1982, 130). Although much simpler and less refined than the Sutton Hoo example, the Portsoy whetstone shows similar opposed human heads and perhaps one of the most revealing elements of the carving is the set of tongs – an obvious reference to metalworking. At Rhynie and other Pictish sites, metalworking evidence is interpreted as an indicator of high-status activity, the products of which were used to create and support elite identities in the post-Roman period.

Some of the objects in the Gaulcross hoard themselves were almost certainly connected to elites. Items like silver hand-pins and silver bracelets found in Gaulcross and Norrie's Law are uncommon finds – these were clearly high-status objects that would have belonged to some of the most powerful members of post-Roman society (Youngs 2013, 421). Some hoards in Denmark and Germany have been interpreted as the family treasures of emerging elites in post-Roman northern Europe (e.g. Collins 2013, 38; Painter 2013, 228; Rau 2013, 345). Like Gaulcross, the hoards of hacksilver from Denmark include Roman and non-Roman objects, but in contrast many of the new finds from Denmark are found in close association with high-status central places with evidence for imported goods and working of precious metals (Dyhrfjeld-Johnsen 2013, 321). At Gaulcross and Norrie's Law there is as yet no evidence of high-status settlements at the site or in the near vicinity.

In contrast to the Danish hoards, a striking feature of Gaulcross and Norrie's Law is the sense of isolation of the findspot. Like Gaulcross, there are no known Pictish settlements, forts or symbol stones in close vicinity to the Norrie's Law hoard (although a Class II Christian cross-slab was discovered on the same estate). Both of the hoards are in similar topographic positions on elevated ground with views towards the coast. If the hoards were connected to wealthy post-Roman communities, then that wealth was accumulated and buried, but never reclaimed. Some hoards in the Roman Iron Age, such as the two silver *denarii* hoards at Birnie, Moray, buried in between a series of roundhouses, have been interpreted as gifts to the gods (Hunter 2009, 13). Gaulcross is also on a hill less than 1.5km to the east of Deskford where a boar-headed carnyx (war trumpet) was votively deposited in a pit dug into a bog sometime in the 1st to 3rd century AD (Hunter 2001, 100). The Gaulcross hoard can perhaps be seen as part of a long-standing tradition of votive deposition in this area.

The Gaulcross and Norrie's Law hoards were both deposited at what were already ancient monuments in the Pictish period. An association with the prehistoric past as a way of bolstering the power and legitimacy of contemporary lineages is a well-known phenomenon in the early medieval period in Britain and Ireland (R. Bradley 1987;

Driscoll 1998a; see also Clarke 2007; Gleeson 2012). The appropriation of ancient places through an act of ritualised deposition could be one way in which an emerging elite connected the present with a deep ancestral past through places associated with otherworldly powers (Driscoll 1998a, 143, 155). The act of deposition might also imply a rejection of the more recent past through the sacrifice of the silver objects – we need to consider the processes of accumulation, curation and deposition of the hoards as potentially embodying differing motivations, appropriate in vastly different social circumstances. Of course, these hoards could have also had much more prosaic origins. We cannot rule out the possibilities that these hoards were the accumulated wealth of a powerful northern Pictish dynasty that hid their valuable stash of raw materials for safekeeping and never returned. Nonetheless, whether a gift to the gods, the raw materials of a smith or unrecovered wealth, it seems likely that the landscape location was not fortuitous or without significance (Needham 2001). For what better location to place one's valuables than under the protection of the ancestors or the gods?

The (re)discovery of the Gaulcross hoard has uncovered a remarkable range of important new objects, some never seen before in Scotland. The composition of the Gaulcross hoard and the close comparanda from Norrie's Law embody both the material resources of the late Roman Empire and fragments of objects that became central to the power and status of early medieval elite identities. The objects the hoard contains span what is traditionally seen as a historical transition from late antiquity to the new forms of society emerging in the post-Roman period. In tandem with the new work on settlement, burial and carved stone monuments, the work on metalwork finds can help illuminate the rise of new forms of society in northern Britain in the early medieval world, emphasising the importance of northern Pictland and its elites in forging the new social, political and economic frameworks of power of the post-Roman period. Prior to its rediscovery the focus of discussion of Pictish metalworking hoards had concentrated on Norrie's Law and the evidence from southern Pictland. The Gaulcross hoard shows that powerful and valuable materials ultimately sourced from the Roman Empire circulated in north-east Scotland at an early date and would have undoubtedly contributed to the creation of the powerful Pictish polities of this region.

CHAPTER SEVEN

The development of the Pictish symbol system: Inscribing identity beyond the edges of empire

Gordon Noble, Martin Goldberg and Derek Hamilton

The evolution of writing was one of the most critical developments in world history, with a range of dramatic transformations in human society ascribed to literacy (Innes 1998, 3). Writing can instigate a revolution in the forms and possibilities of communication and has been directly linked to state formation in many social contexts and time periods across the world (Baines 1995, 471; Goody 1968, 4; Papadopoulos 2016, 1252; Postgate *et al.* 1995, 459). In northern Europe, the alphabetic systems of the Greeks and Etruscan and Roman derivatives in the west inspired new forms of writing with vernacular scripts developing on the fringes of the Roman Empire in the 1st millennium AD. These included the runic system of Scandinavia and north Germany and the ogham alphabet of Ireland and western Britain (e.g. Barnes 2012; Findell 2014; Swift 1997). Both of these scripts were used across early medieval Britain and Ireland, but the most common and monumental form of communication that survives from northern Britain is the lesser understood Pictish symbol system. Strong arguments have been made in recent years for the symbol system being a script, albeit undeciphered (Samson 1992; Forsyth 1997b; Lee *et al.* 2010). Debates on its origins and dating have taken place for over a century, and this chapter outlines new dating on a range of sites and objects from northern Pictland that have produced a new and more robust chronology for the development of the symbol system, with an earlier origin proposed than many scholars had previously countenanced.

Symbols of the Picts

The Pictish symbol stones represent an iconic element of the archaeological record – sculptured stones carved with a distinctive group of symbols, some abstract, others naturalistic, for example the striking animal designs or recognisable objects, such as mirrors and combs (Henderson and Henderson 2004, 167). The symbol stones have long been identified as Pictish because their distribution closely matches the extent of the Pictish kingdoms as reconstructed from the limited historical sources and from place-names (Wainwright 1955c, 43).

There are over 200 stone monuments with symbols known from eastern and northern Scotland (RCAHMS 2008) – approximately two-thirds are incised symbol stones and the other third are Christian cross-slabs (Fig. 52). The symbols also occasionally appear on metalwork, bone and other portable objects. There has been little agreement about the number and range of symbols, but around 30 core symbols have been suggested (Forsyth 1997b, 87; Samson 1992, 37). There have been repeated attempts to decipher the meaning of the symbols since the 19th century, with wide-ranging interpretations, including icons of pagan or Christian religion (e.g. Allen and Anderson 1903; Earl of Southesk 1893), symbols of rank or tribal identity (Diack 1944; Henderson 1967; Thomas 1963), symbols of marriage alliances (Jackson 1984), memorials to the dead (Driscoll 1988; Laing and Laing 1984; Mack 2007), as well as countless 'fringe' ideas and speculation.

52. Examples of Pictish symbols (after RCAHMS 2007).

Current consensus suggests that the symbol system was a form of script, albeit undeciphered, and part of broader northern European trends of experimentation with writing at the fringes of the Roman Empire. The roots of this research lie with Samson (1992) who saw the common pairing of symbols as key to interpretation, arguing that the symbols did not work in isolation, but that the recurrent symbol pairs worked together to represent personal names – perhaps two elements of a di-thematic name, i.e. the symbols represented a written version of a language rather than abstract ideas. Forsyth (1997b) also identified symbol pairs as 'the fundamental syntax' of the Pictish symbol system, and more recent work applying statistical analysis has supported the interpretation of the symbols as a written language (Lee 2010; Lee *et al.* 2010; though see Sproat 2010). A naming system is also suggested by some specific monuments, for example, on the back of a cross-slab from Dunfallandy, Perthshire, two seated figures and a mounted individual are shown with symbol pairs directly next to them, and the close juxtaposition of symbols with human figures can also be identified on other monuments (Plate 13) (Allen and Anderson 1903, 38; Stevenson 1955, 123). While the symbols are likely to have communicated names, as is common in the runic and ogham systems, the Pictish symbols were not an alphabetic script, and this has perhaps contributed to the 'othering' of the Picts (See Alcock 2003, 373 for latter point).

Dating the symbol tradition

The dating of the symbol system has been a matter of debate for more than a century. The seminal volume *The Early Christian Monuments of Scotland* set out a typological classification commonly used to the present day (Allen and Anderson 1903). The relative dates of the 7th–8th centuries AD were given for Class I monuments (incised symbols usually on unshaped boulders) and the 9th and 10th centuries for the Christianised Class II monuments (where symbols appear with a much broader repertoire of ornament, narrative scenes and a Christian cross), a chronology that remained popular throughout the 20th century. Charles Thomas related certain symbols to late Iron Age art styles and consequently suggested a 5th-century start date for the simpler Class I designs (Thomas 1961), a scheme followed by Laing and Laing (1984, 1993). Nonetheless, dating has remained controversial and there has been no direct dating that conclusively showed the symbol system dated earlier than the late 6th or early 7th century (Clarke and Heald 2008). The suggestions of earlier dating were based entirely on art-historical analysis as opposed to absolute or closely contextualised dating.

Establishing a new chronology

The major problem in establishing a definitive chronology has been the difficulty in obtaining absolute dates. Stone monuments are problematic to date and it has been necessary to rely on contextual dating, such as dates from human remains found in association with the Class I symbol stone at Dairy Park, Dunrobin, Sutherland (Close-Brooks 1980). This was found during ploughing in 1977, directly above a burial cairn covering an extended inhumation (Close-Brooks 1980, 328). Two radiocarbon dates were obtained at the time of the excavation, suggesting a later 1st-millennium AD date for the burial, but the determinations were of low precision.

One symbol-bearing object has been directly dated previously: an ox phalange bearing two symbols, a crescent and V-rod and a mirror-case, from the Broch of Burrian, Orkney which provided a radiocarbon date of AD 570–655 for the bone upon which the carvings were made (Clarke and Heald 2008). Few other organic objects are available for direct dating, but an ox phalange decorated with a crescent and V-rod and rectangular symbol was found at the multiperiod settlement at Pool, Sanday, Orkney (Hunter *et al.* 2007, 509), and was sampled for radiocarbon dating as part of the Northern Picts project (Fig. 53).

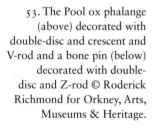

53. The Pool ox phalange (above) decorated with double-disc and crescent and V-rod and a bone pin (below) decorated with double-disc and Z-rod © Roderick Richmond for Orkney, Arts, Museums & Heritage.

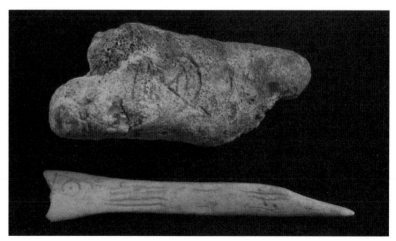

Given the lack of absolute dates, any opportunity to add to the corpus of dated examples is important, and new fieldwork by the Northern Picts project has also targeted sites in eastern Scotland where contextual dating evidence for the symbol system was possible. The fairly simple designs found in caves and occasionally in other contexts, such as the stone 'plaques' found at a coastal site at Dunnicaer, Aberdeenshire, have been suggested as the earliest examples of the symbol system (e.g. Alcock 1996; 2003, 372; Henderson and Henderson 2004, 171) (Fig. 54). Recent fieldwork at Dunnicaer by the Northern Picts project explored the context of the symbol stones found there. Dunnicaer is located on a precipitous sea stack near another stack site at Dunnottar, which appears in a 7th-century annalistic account as the site of a siege, suggesting an important power centre (Fraser 2009a, 214). The symbol stones were discovered from 1819 onwards when stone was removed from the stack for building material. In 1832 a group of youths found a low stone wall

54. Symbol stones from Dunnicaer © Crown Copyright: Historic Environment Scotland.

on the stack and threw a number of stones into the sea (Thomas 1858). Few people had visited Dunnicaer since the 19th century, but three seasons of fieldwork in 2015–17 have identified the remains of this wall as a rampart, which survives on the southern and western edges of the stack (Plate 14). Few stones survived from the rampart, but excavation identified a number of facing stones and slots dug for timber beams. The fieldwork has demonstrated that Dunnicaer was a promontory fort (and this was Thomas's interpretation in 1858) with a timber-laced rampart and other enclosing works of the kind known from the Iron Age and 1st millennium AD around the coasts of Scotland. Alcock (1996) had interpreted the site as the focus of a pre-Christian cult, but without any excavation of the site. The recent work has shown that the stack was in fact much larger, with most of the site lost to erosion. Inside the rampart, contemporary buildings and hearths, many partly falling into the sea have been identified (Fig. 55). Finds included Roman Samian (Fig. 56) and coarseware, glass and a lead weight – all rare imports this far north of the frontier – along with burnishing stones for metalworking (Fig. 57).

Other contextual excavations have been carried out from 2012 to 2017 at Rhynie, also in Aberdeenshire as outlined in Chapter 4. The excavations at Rhynie focused on an enclosure complex surrounding the *in situ* Pictish symbol stone, the Craw Stane, and the findspots of

55. Pole camera shot of hearths and floor layers within the upper terrace at Dunnicaer.

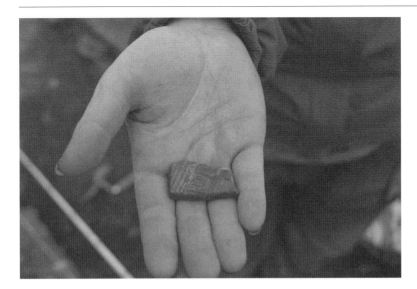

56. Sherd of Roman Samian ware found at Dunnicaer.

57. A burnishing stone for metalworking from Dunnicaer.

two others (Noble *et al.* 2013). The excavations showed that the Craw Stane stood at the entrance of a high-status fortified site with imports from the Mediterranean and Continental Europe (Noble *et al.* 2013). A few metres from the Craw Stane, a stone socket, likely to be for another Pictish stone, was identified during excavations in 2015. This may have been the socket for the Rhynie Man stone found downslope during ploughing in 1978.

Radiocarbon dating and chronological modelling

Radiocarbon dating and Bayesian modelling can provide refined and robust chronologies for the sites and objects highlighted above and can also help provide clearer chronologies for previously investigated sites or samples (Bronk Ramsey 1995; 1998; 2001; 2009; Buck *et al.* 1996; Hamilton and Kenney 2015; Reimer *et al.* 2013; Stuiver and Reimer 1993). Bayesian modelling has revolutionised the world of radiocarbon dating and is a way of modelling more refined probabilities, providing more accurate dating for sites and objects. Analysis of the sites and objects highlighted above took place as part of the Northern Picts project (for full analysis see Noble *et al.* 2018). From Pool, Orkney, the ox phalange decorated with symbols returned a date of 420–540 AD (68% probability) (Fig. 53). Bayesian modelling helped to refine the older dates from Pool and helped contextualise another bone artefact with symbols from the site. In this case, the dates from settlement layers in which a bone pin incised with a double-disc and Z-rod was found were shown to most likely date to the 5th or 6th centuries AD, broadly contemporary with the directly dated ox phalange. The Northern Picts project, with the help of the National Museum of Scotland, also relocated the human remains from Dairy Park, Dunrobin. The previous dates were so divergent that issues with the original dating were suspected. The dates also seemed very late for a square cairn of this type (Maldonado 2013, Fig. 3; Mitchell and Noble 2017, 22). From a sample of human bone, a high precision date of 575–625 AD (68% probability) was obtained.

Through the extensive excavations at Dunnicaer many radiocarbon dates were available, and the number allowed accurate models of the dating of the fort to be ascertained. In particular, single-entity, short-lived roundwood charcoal was targeted for dating the rampart and settlement features of the promontory fort to provide precise dating evidence. The modelling produced an estimated start date of AD 130–220 for the settlement and fort and an end date for activity of cal AD 345–425 (68% probability). This broad chronology was supported by the artefactual evidence, which indicated a 2nd–4th-century AD date for the use of the site. There were four dates that could be specifically related to the rampart with which the symbol stones were associated. The modelling produced an estimate for wall construction of AD 285–350. The extensive excavations at Rhynie also allowed for precise dating with a total of 35 radiocarbon dates from the excavations of the enclosure complex at Rhynie available for Bayesian modelling. The samples were from all phases and major structural components including the feature interpreted as the socket for a Pictish stone. The modelling estimated that activity at Rhynie began in AD 355–80 and ended AD 510–60 (68% probability). The material culture typologies again strongly supported the radiocarbon ranges, with no evidence for use of the site after the mid 6th century AD.

Pictish symbols: the origins of the system?

Of course, none of the dates that were modelled for the sites and objects outlined above directly dated the act of carving of symbols, simply the associated settlement layers, materials and possible contexts for the erection of monuments with symbols such as the interment of a burial at Dairy Park. The dates from Dunnicaer, for example, cannot directly date the carved stones that were found on the stack, but the antiquarian accounts make it clear that they were found in association with a wall built along the edge of the stack. Indeed, several of the Dunnicaer symbol stones have been interpreted as 'plaques' that were suitable for being set into a rampart (e.g. Alcock and Alcock 1992, 282; Alcock 1996, 2003). The stone wall mentioned during discovery, and into which plaques are likely to have been set at Dunnicaer, was re-identified during the recent fieldwork and its construction dated to AD 285–350. None of the other dated activity on the stack significantly diverges from the construction date for the rampart, and the material culture comfortably fits into that bracket. While the symbol stones have been damaged by the 19th-century circumstances of discovery and reuse, they appear to be largely intact. Dunnicaer No. 5 has carvings on both sides that may belong to different phases of carving, but there was also extensive remodelling of the site and settlement with multiple overlapping dwellings. However, none of the dates or the stratigraphy suggests later activity unconnected to the fortified settlement. There is thus a strong argument for the symbol stones being contemporary with the promontory fort, which provides the best evidence to date that the carving of symbols originates in a Roman Iron Age context, in this case in association with a high-status promontory settlement.

The early dating from Dunnicaer sheds new light on other sites with similar styles of carving, such as cave sites. Carvings from Sculptor's Cave, Covesea, Moray, with simple, small-scale designs (including a fish, crescents and V-rods, mirror-cases, a triple-oval and a 'flower' symbol) are similar in style to the Dunnicaer carvings (Fig. 58). From inside the cave, other than modern finds, none of the material culture suggests activity later than the 4th century AD. There is a collection of human remains that provides evidence for decapitation in the period AD 220–335 (Armit *et al.* 2011, 276), and there is also an important assemblage of Roman coins, metalwork and pottery, with the latest coin dated AD 365 (Armit *et al.* 2011, 259). These dates are broadly contemporary with the construction of the wall at Dunnicaer. There are also Pictish symbols carved in a number of caves at East Wemyss, Fife. Very few *in situ* deposits have been found during excavations at the caves, but one cave, the Sliding Cave (which has carvings of a double-disc, serpents and a comb case) was found to have an intact floor layer (with no evidence of later use) dated to AD 240–390, again broadly contemporary with the dates from Dunnicaer (Gibson and Stevens 2007).

58. The fish and crescent and V-rod symbols at the Sculptor's Cave, Covesea © The Sculptor's Cave Publication Project, University of Bradford.

0 ———— 10cm

Individually, and because they are associated and not direct dates, any one of these sites would not be considered sufficient evidence to support the early dating for these simple examples of the Pictish symbol system. However, when taken together, the fact that the symbols at all three sites had previously been stylistically linked and that all three have since produced very similar chronological ranges for activities during the 3rd to 4th century AD increases confidence in these early associated dates from the Scottish mainland. Forsyth (1997b, 93) suggested that the Dunnicaer and cave symbols were 'cursive' and thus their form may not relate to date, but the available dating evidence suggests they are indeed early examples.

An outline chronology and a complementary typology for Pictish symbols

Using the range of associated and direct dates obtained through the fieldwork of the Northern Picts project, we can suggest a new and more robust outline chronology for the Pictish symbols: the evidence from Dunnicaer and cave sites suggests that unelaborated carvings, generally of a smaller size and less standardised compared to the later standing stone monuments, probably originated in the 3rd to 4th centuries AD. The larger standing stone monuments in eastern Scotland were being set up in the period from the late 4th to the early 6th century AD and the dated evidence includes a detailed chronology for Rhynie that includes dates from a probable stone socket. The dated examples from settlements in Orkney show symbol use in the most northerly parts of Pictland from as early as the 5th century AD and certainly by the early 6th century. At Dairy Park, Dunrobin, doubt has been cast over the association between the symbol stone and cairn (Clarke 2007, 27), but the stone was found directly over the cairn when the field was ploughed for the first time in 1977 (Close-Brooks 1980, 330). The burial has now been precisely dated to AD 575–625.

This outline chronology also supports a new typology (see Goldberg forthcoming). Examining the style of the symbols from the dated sites shows that relatively plain, small-scale symbols were present at Dunnicaer, Pool and the cave sites. A relatively plain, but clear, linear style is also consistent across the cluster of symbol stones at Rhynie. This contrasts with the more elaborate symbols at Dairy Park, and at a minute scale the carefully depicted internal elaboration of the crescent and V-rod found on the ox phalange from Broch of Burrian, Orkney, both of which have dates from the late 6th or early 7th century. The typology proposes changing conventions in symbol form that may be chronologically sensitive, that are largely confirmed in light of this new dating evidence. For example, single-sided combs are only shown on Class I stones and tend to be depicted in plain linear style, whereas only double-sided combs are shown on (Class II) Christian monuments. Class I stones with double-sided combs, like Dairy Park, often accompany more elaborate carving techniques and are suggested to date closer to the Christian monuments of the 7th to 8th centuries (Goldberg forthcoming).

There also appears to be a general trend towards larger monuments through time. The double-disc symbols from Dunnicaer, for example, are among the smallest in the symbol stone corpus. The symbol stones from Rhynie, which only have conventional mirrors and single-sided combs, include a stone, Rhynie No. 8, that although it has been cut down shows symbols of a scale that indicates it was always a more modest monument of a similar character to the Dunnicaer plaques. Tellingly this stone has a symbol that only appears at the Sculptor's Cave, Covesea, Moray. With the cave symbols likely to be of early date, these connections in form, size and style of symbol use on Rhynie No. 8 bring together many of the strands of evidence used here.

Previous art-historical analysis had suggested that the most complex designs were the earliest based on the idea that there was a 'master' carver and symbol and that these designs tended to simplify or break down through time (Stevenson 1955, 102–3). However, the complementary absolute dating and typological scheme outlined here suggest that symbols without significant internal elaboration, of the style found on the Dunnicaer 'plaques' and the caves and some of the Rhynie monuments, are likely to be early, while monuments with symbols that show elaborate internal decoration are likely to be later, probably of 6th to early 7th century AD based on the complementary dating of the Broch of Burrian ox phalange and the burial at Dairy Park (Fig. 59). Almost all of the symbols on Class II cross-slabs are elaborated using an international repertoire of decoration shared widely in the early Christian world, but with a particular 'Insular' style that shares similarities with contemporary monuments across Britain and Ireland (Goldberg 2015; Henderson and Henderson 2004). An 8th-century high point for the larger cross-slabs is likely, such as those with prominent relief-carved symbols from the monastery at Portmahomack (Carver *et al.* 2016, 167) and the Tarbat

Plate 1. Aerial photograph of Mither Tap, Bennachie. The fort consists of an upper and lower citadel surrounding a spectacular granite tor.

Plate 2. Aerial photograph of Portknockie promontory fort under excavation in 1977.
© Aberdeenshire Council Archaeology Service.

Plate 3. *Right*. The 2012 excavation trench at Rhynie, showing the Craw Stane (mid left), traces of the inner and outer ditches and the outer box-rampart (top); the rectangular outline of one of the internal buildings can also be identified (bottom right).

Plate 4. *Below*. Tap o'Noth. This impressive Iron Age fort overlooks Rhynie. The image shows trial excavations by the Northern Picts project in 2017.

Plate 5. Mould from Rhynie for making an animal figurine. © AOC Archaeology.

Plate 6. The head of the iron axe-pin from the Craw Stane complex.

Plate 7. Digital reconstruction of the enclosure complex at Rhynie. © Alice Watterson.

Plate 8. The 'ghostly' outlines of the Pictish barrow cemetery at Hill of Boyndie as revealed by aerial reconnaissance. © Aberdeenshire Council Archaeology Service. Images like this are used to create the maps of the barrow cemeteries used in Chapter 5.

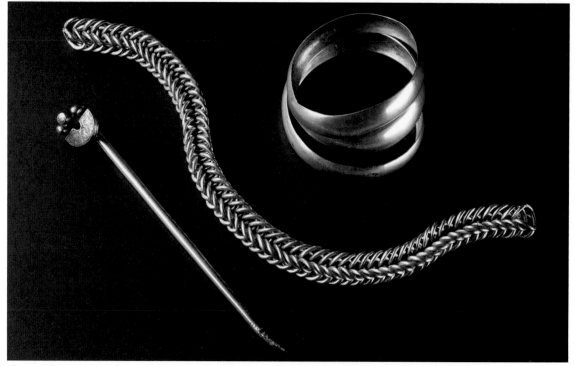

Plate 9. The surviving objects from the nineteenth-century Gaulcross hoard find. © National Museums Scotland.

Plate 10. The Gaulcross silver hoard including a silver ingot, hacksilver and folded bracelets. © National Museums Scotland.

Plate 11. *Left*. The lunate/crescent shaped pendant with two double-loops. © National Museums Scotland.

Plate 12. *Below left*. The Portsoy whetstone. © Trustees of the British Museum.

Plate 13. *Below*. The Dunfallandy stone, Perthshire. The people depicted are 'labelled' with symbols: the figure upper left has a single symbol only (though note the stone surface here is unfinished perhaps leaving space for a second symbol). © Historic Environment Scotland.

Plate 14. Excavations at Dunnicaer 2017.

Plate 15. Mail figure, Cunningsburgh, Shetland (left) Complete stone (right) Close-up of axe-wielder. © Shetland museum.

Plate 16. Tullich, Aberdeenshire. The modern cemetery from the air. © Aberdeenshire Council Archaeology Service.

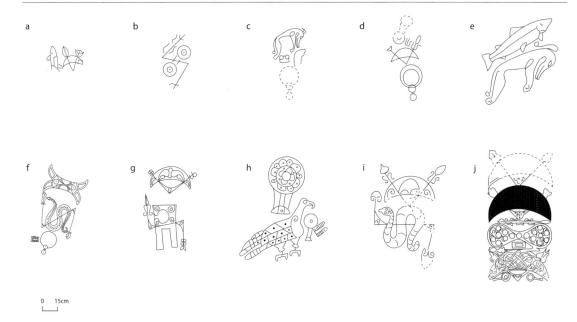

0   15cm

peninsula. A probable end date for the symbol system is during the 9th–10th-century AD ascendancy of the kingdom of Alba when a new language and new lineages began to dominate elite power in eastern and northern Scotland (Woolf 2007b, 312).

Interpreting the symbols

The new dates strongly suggest that the symbols originated earlier than often countenanced and did so in a context that makes contact with the Roman world a likely factor in their origin. In the 3rd and 4th century AD, raiding, trading and diplomatic gifts and bribes shaped imperial contact and social change in eastern Scotland (Blackwell *et al.* 2017; Hunter 2007a), and it is in this context that the idea of a written script may have emerged. In this respect, the symbols are likely to have appeared in a similar context and chronological horizon to other epigraphic systems in north-west Europe. In Scandinavia, the use of runes has been traced back to the 2nd century AD, with their use likely influenced by the Greek alphabet and its Etruscan and Roman derivatives in the west, created by people with experience of Mediterranean language, reading and writing traditions (Barnes 2012, 10–11; Findell 2014, 15; Odenstedt 1990, 169). The dating of ogham in Ireland has been based largely on linguistic

59. Symbol typology. The earlier examples, (a) Sculptor's Cave, Covesea; (b) Dunnicaer; (c) Rhynie 8; and (d) Rhynie 6, show symbols only in outline with single-sided combs. The larger examples may be later such as (e) the Craw Stane (Rhynie 1). The Dairy Park, Dunrobin example (f) is likely to be late 6th to early 7th century in date and broadly contemporaneous with other examples showing decorative elaboration to the symbols, e.g. (g, h, i) Ballintomb, Inveravon, Brandsbutt. The last phase of symbols are on Class II monuments with obvious references to manuscript art, e.g. (j) Rosemarkie.

archaisms and innovations, with few inscribed objects directly dated (Swift 1997, 54). Traditional dating schemes based on epigraphic styles have suggested a 5th-century start date (Jackson 1950, 1953; Nash-Williams 1950), but earlier origins in the 2nd or 3rd century AD have also been forwarded (Ahlqvist 1982, 8–10; Harvey 1987, 9). An ogham inscription among the votive offerings from the later phases of deposition at Newgrange, including a medallion of Constantine II, may be as early as the 4th century (Charles-Edwards 2013, 119). Recent radiocarbon dating of an ogham-inscribed knife-handle from the Broch of Gurness in Orkney shows that ogham was also known in the far north of Scotland by cal AD 340–540, in a phase that also includes small unelaborated symbol stones, like those from Pool. An ogham inscription from Silchester in southern England has also been dated to the 4th or 5th century in a context in which Roman inspiration is highly likely (Fulford *et al.* 2000, 17; see also Swift 1997, 49). Like runes and ogham, the Pictish symbols are also likely to have been created beyond the frontier in response to Roman influence, but just like Irish- and Germanic-speaking groups, the Picts did not directly adopt the alphabet – they invented their own system, albeit non-alphabetic in origin. Nonetheless, in all three cases the script innovators imitated the literate cultures of Rome, but in ways that at least partly 'proclaimed an independence' from the Mediterranean world (Barnes 2012, 11).

Whatever the origins of these epigraphic systems, the roles of runic, ogham and Pictish symbols were clearly multiple. A number of ogham inscriptions expressed lineage and others may have been memorials, but others were concerned with boundaries and landholding, and early forms of runes appear to have had a similar variety of roles (Barnes 2012, 11; Bhreathnach 2014, 42–4; Swift 1997, 44). The main purpose of Pictish symbols seems to be to communicate identities, most likely names, and where well contextualised they often appear in high-status contexts, like Rhynie, or on elite objects such as the massive silver chains or the silver plaque from Norrie's Law (Blackwell *et al.* 2017, 101). The Dunnicaer site includes extremely rare Roman imports for north-east Scotland and enclosed sites are very unusual for this period. While at first glance the cave sites seem difficult to reconcile with high-status activity, the Roman material from this site is also exceptional for this period and region, and the contemporary human remains have been interpreted as the beheadings in Roman style of what may have been native elites (Armit *et al.* 2011, 276). Given the context of use for these early dated symbols, it may be that Pictish symbols operated like early hieroglyphs in Egypt, which evolved as a public form of display concerned with prestige and high-status identities and activities (Baines 1995, 471).

Recent scholarship has suggested that Pictish ethnogenesis was brief and late, a phenomenon of the 7th century AD (Fraser 2009a, 43–67; Woolf 2017; see also Chapter 2). However, writing has long been linked to the development of more complex societies in a variety of contexts around the world (Postgate *et al.* 1995, 459), and the development of the Pictish symbols from possibly as early as the 3rd century coincides with the new social and political identities evident in late Roman sources and with broad archaeological changes evident in the same period (Hunter 2007a, 42–4; and see Chapter 2). The shared use of this symbolic script across eastern and northern Scotland by the 5th century is in precisely the areas that 7th- and 8th-century historical sources locate the Pictish kingdoms. Once introduced, the symbol system would have had important social consequences, allowing names and perhaps lineages to be transmitted across space and time (Driscoll 1988; Goody 1968, 4; Innes 1998, 3) and communicated within a distinct social milieu. This would have had particular implications for long-term memory transmission with the recording in stone of elite names perhaps helping to underscore intergenerational rights and wider group identities.

Previous dating of the Pictish symbol system has largely relied on art-historical analysis, but it is only through scientific dating that more robust chronologies can be constructed. The dating and typology outlined here suggests that interaction with the Roman world is likely to have been the context for the development of the symbol system. Establishing an outline chronology through a combination of direct dating, Bayesian modelling of associated dates from archaeological excavation, and combining typological and contextual methods can help us rewrite the history of these symbolic traditions of northern Europe and understand more clearly the context of their development and use. Here the work of the Northern Picts project and sites and objects from northern Pictland have proved instrumental in establishing a new chronology for the long-studied Pictish symbol system.

CHAPTER EIGHT

The early Church in northern Pictland

Nicholas Evans and Gordon Noble

One of the most important changes of 1st-millennium AD Britain and Ireland was the adoption of Christianity. In Scotland, iconic sites and monuments such as 'Celtic' crosses and monasteries like Iona, and religious figures including Columba, Cuthbert and Kentigern have become symbols of the wider religious transformation that took place across the country in the 1st millennium AD. These early Christian sites and monuments are often placed in contrast to the 'paganism' and 'mysteriousness' of Iron Age religious practices. In a modern context where the participation in formal religion is in decline, it can be difficult to understand the significance of embracing a new religion in the 1st millennium AD. As Driscoll (2011, 253, 267–70) has commented, scholarly attention on this subject has also at times not been as directed as it could be. Nonetheless, research utilising different strands of evidence and more integrated approaches are gradually producing advances which enable us to build a more substantial and accurate picture of the practices, beliefs and social structures of this period, and how the societies of the northern Picts moved from paganism to Christianity.

Pre-Christian belief in northern Pictland

In order to situate the coming of Christianity to Pictland it is important to consider the evidence for pre-Christian beliefs, a task that is by no means straightforward. The study of pre-Christian religion has, for example, been hampered by a tendency to draw on broad narratives of 'Celtic' religion that have at times created generalising, timeless and occasionally fanciful narratives about non-Christian belief systems (A. Fitzpatrick 2007, 288; Goldberg 2015, 212). We are of course also curtailed by the lack of historical sources and the limited archaeological record, a situation that is pertinent for most of Europe. In terms of written sources that do exist, we also have to rely on external viewpoints. In the earlier 1st millennium AD, those include classical writers such as Caesar and Tacitus, who give us hints about the structure and form of religion in northern Europe in a pre-Christian context. In these sources, religious leaders are referred to, highlighting the presence of religious specialists during the Roman Iron Age, but few sources give any detail for northern Britain (A. Fitzpatrick 2007, 290). In our Insular sources, reliable written evidence for pre-Christian belief and practices in northern Britain is also meagre. Most of our sources, predominantly hagiographical texts, were also written much later in the Christian period, reflecting later priorities (Evans 2014, 23), with the result that paganism was predominantly depicted negatively. The portrayal of pre-Christian religion was distorted and potentially even created anew in order to depict dramatic confrontations with usually saintly Christian missionaries which demonstrated the superiority of Christianity. Without independent evidential support, this makes it difficult to determine what elements in any account of paganism are authentic.

For the Picts, our main source for paganism is Adomnán's 'Life of St Columba' (VSC), written c.697, which contains a small number of episodes in which Columba in the late 6th century confronts and confounds pagan *magi* (for the term, see VSC, Sharpe 1995, 334), sometimes converting people to Christianity. Pagans are depicted in VSC (II.11; cf. Sharpe 1995, 322–3), at Chapter II.32 as believing in multiple gods. One god was thought to reside in a well (VSC II.11), but Columba converted it from a malevolent place inhabited by demons to a blessed source of healing. The *magi* are generally portrayed as malicious, not only taunting and opposing Columba and other Christians (VSC I.37, II.11, II.32, II.33), but also able to perform 'magical' feats through demons, such as controlling the weather on Loch Ness (VSC II.34). The references in Adomnán's 'Life' seem to reflect the continuation of pre-Christian beliefs in a modified form in Pictland, but given that Adomnán was writing a century after Columba's death, it is unclear whether he was simply projecting Gaelic superstitions and perceptions of paganism onto the Picts. However, while we need to be sceptical, where Adomnán attempted to explain away or denigrate beliefs by associating them with demons, the text probably reflects some real pre-Christian concepts.

In the areas that encompassed the provinces of Fortriu and Ce in a Roman Iron Age and early medieval context, archaeological evidence for non-Christian belief is limited as is the case across Scotland (see A. Ritchie 2003 for a review focusing on the Northern Isles). Indeed, the possibilities of tracing an archaeological record associated with pagan belief in the late Roman Iron Age and early medieval period is challenging given the generally non-furnished nature of burial and the more limited settlement and artefactual record from the later 1st millennium AD in northern Scotland. In terms of architecture, there are few settlement sites after the 2nd century AD, though there is clear potential for exploring orientation, cosmology and the presence or absence of foundation and closing deposits in a later 1st-millennium AD context as has been done for Iron Age settlements (e.g. Armit and Ginn 2007), but this has not been explored to any great extent (though see Brundle *et al.* 2003, 95 for the Northern Isles). Armit and Ginn (2007, 116) have shown that the deposition of human remains within settlement contexts continued in the Northern and Western Isles at least into the later 1st millennium AD, and a detailed consideration of these practices in their wider context would repay further study.

Some of the evidence from the later 1st millennium AD in northern Scotland may suggest a belief in the significance of particular landscape features. Gildas, in his early 6th-century *De Excidio Britanniae*, chapter 4 (Winterbottom 1978, 17), implies that British pagans believed in the sanctity of natural places. In addition, his statement that these locations were 'now useful for human needs' indicates that these special spaces had in pagan times been excluded from full human exploitation. At the Sculptor's Cave, Covesea, Moray, redating of skeletal material has shown evidence for the decapitation and other violent treatments of certain individuals in a cave-setting in a late Roman Iron Age context (Armit *et al.* 2011) (Fig. 60). As well as the human remains, the specialness of the cave at Covesea was marked in other ways, including the deposition of late Roman material (Hunter 2007a, 50) and the carving of symbols on the cave walls. The quantity of late Roman objects is beyond the norm of settlement sites of the period and again suggests a specialised role for the cave in the late Roman Iron Age.

Another element of pagan practice may have been an interest in springs, wells and other places associated with water (see *VSC* II.11). The best-known well in a Pictish context is that at Burghead, which has attracted endless speculation since its discovery in 1809 in the

60. The entrance of the Sculptor's Cave, Covesea © The Sculptor's Cave Publication Project, University of Bradford.

lower citadel of the Pictish fort (see summary in Oram 2007, 251–2) (Fig. 61). The well is certainly one of the most elaborate features of its type known from an early medieval fortified settlement in Britain. The well is a rectangular rock-cut chamber with a paved walkway around, with a curved pedestal and a stone basin surviving in adjacent corners of the chamber. Due to its elaborate nature, the well was initially interpreted as being of Roman construction. In the 20th century, the well was reinterpreted as a Pictish pagan water shrine and a location where ritualised drownings may have occurred (Laing and Laing 1993, 23; A. Ritchie 1989, 15). A ritualised function for the well was followed by later authors (e.g. Carver 1999, 30; Foster 1996, 44). The well has also been interpreted from a Christian perspective as a baptistery, supported by the presence of early Christian sculpture from Burghead, including part of a shrine (Alcock 2003, 197) (see below). However, without further contextual information the role of the well is debatable and there is little specific evidence to suggest it was anything other than a functional water supply for the fort, although of course there may have been a ritualised as well as a functional element to its significance (Bell 1992).

61. The well at Burghead fort © Joan Megson.

In an early medieval context in northern Pictland, it is perhaps the sculpture that gives us the best window into possible pagan practices and imagery. At Burghead, only six bull carvings survive from a possible 1805–09 total of 25–30, but their number and character have supplied a rich vein for interpreting their significance and the character of the fort (Oram 2007, 250). Foster (1996, 44) associated the carvings with a pagan fertility cult, but they could be regarded more broadly as ritualised symbols of power and authority at a key fortified settlement of northern Pictland. Unusual carved stones at other sites can also perhaps give us insights into the character of pre-Christian belief. At Rhynie, the carving of the Rhynie Man has been linked with pagan animal sacrifice (Noble *et al.* 2013). The Rhynie Man carries an axe-hammer, with a very distinctive double-ended blade and extremely thin shaft. Its morphology is strongly paralleled by the axe-hammer found in the Sutton Hoo Mound 1 ship burial (dated to the 7th century), which has been interpreted as an implement for sacrificing cattle (Dobat 2006). Dobat highlights comparative imagery and textual associations that suggest strong links between cattle, animal sacrifice and a cultic ritual role that supported the status and position of early Germanic kings and chieftains (Dobat 2006, 889). The abnormal facial features of the Rhynie Man may also be intentionally creating a distorted or 'shocking visage' designed to convey the otherworldly aspects of the figure and his actions (cf. Aldhouse-Green 2004, 182). Indeed, a shamanic quality or role has been linked to other depictions of figures with exaggerated features or part-human, part-animal figures, such as the one at Mail and the two at Papil, both from Shetland (A. Ritchie 2003, 4; Turner 1994) (Plate 15). Perhaps the Rhynie Man and the depiction of bulls at sites like Burghead referred to practices of sacrifice, and potential parallels can be found across early medieval Britain – Bede in his 'Ecclesiastical History' (*HE*) refers to the English pagan practice of sacrificing 'many oxen to devils' (*HE* I.30). Similarly, early medieval evidence for pole-axed bulls and cattle has been found at Irish royal sites, such as Lagore and Moynagh Lough, both County Meath.

As in the Iron Age, we can consider the reuse of ancient sites as specialised locations for ritual practice (Hingley 1996). In southern Pictland, such appropriation was highlighted in the 1990s with Driscoll's work on Forteviot and Scone (e.g. Driscoll 1998a, 2011). Northern Pictland has been considered less. Certainly, some prehistoric stones were reused in an early medieval context, and they have been interpreted by some as a way of legitimising the present or even reacting against the new Christian religion (Clarke 2007; but for a counter-argument, see Forsyth 2008b, 406–7). First-millennium dates have also occasionally been obtained from prehistoric monuments. In the far north, during excavations, a pit was found at the centre of the Stones of Stenness, Orkney that has been dated to the 1st millennium AD (J.N.G. Ritchie 1976, 44). The date has a wide error margin but centres on the period 420–770 cal AD (68 per cent probability [SRR-352]; 1430±35 BP). The pit contained charred barley and a range of other plant species. From Inverness-shire there are also mid to later 1st-millennium dates from a spread of charcoal and cremated bone associated with the central ring cairn of the Bronze Age cemetery of Balnuaran of Clava (Bradley 2000, 115).

Early Christianity

Conversion to a new religion can be a long process that may be archaeologically invisible for significant periods of that change (Lane 2001;
Maldonado 2011, 42). Indeed, from a historical perspective we can
identify cases where pagan practices continued alongside Christian
ones in the wider early medieval world – Bede for example notes that
the Anglo-Saxon King Rædwald had altars for both Christian and
pagan worship. There were also clearly periods when conversion was
not irreversible. After the death of Æthelberht, King of Kent, in AD
616, the kingdom reverted back to paganism as his son Eadbald was
not a Christian (*HE* II.5). As regards the conversion process itself,
secular elites may have had an important role in Christianisation in
terms of the donation of land and the protection of missionaries, and
in some cases it was clearly important that elites converted. Indeed, the
king's conversion could result in the conversion of the kingdom as the
responsibility of a ruler was to ensure the spiritual and physical welfare
of his people (Cusack 1999, 104). However, this was not always the
case; regarding Eadbald, Bede (*HE* II.5) specifically states that he
refused Christianity even though his father had converted. Indeed, we
need to be wary of accepting Bede's elite-focused account too readily.
While the king and secular (and religious) elites were clearly important, it is possible that conversion could have begun more gradually, by
individual conversions at any level of society (J.E. Fraser 2009a, 84–7).
In Ireland, the 6th–7th-century text 'The Synod of the Bishops' envis-
ages a society in which there were both Christians and pagans, with
the Church trying to ostracise and marginalise pagans and stop
Christians lapsing back into pagan ways. In many cases, Christianity
won by a longer, more piecemeal process of conversion.

Turning to the Picts specifically, traditional accounts about their
conversion have centred around saints Ninian and Columba. In
northern Pictland, following Bede, the focus has been on the
'Columban Church', but it is likely that the conversion process was
much more complex and drawn out (Clancy 2008, 363; J.E. Fraser
2009a, 68–115). The written evidence for the date and nature of the
conversion of the Picts is uncertain due to limited and contradictory
sources, but that does not mean that Kathleen Hughes (1970) was
correct to argue that the Picts became Christian only late in the 7th
century. The only conversion narrative occurs in Bede's *HE*, III.3–4,

where he states that Columba (d.597) converted the northern Picts, with his island foundation on Iona important not only as a monastic foundation with daughter houses, but also significant in the wider Pictish Church. In the same account, Bede wrote that a Briton, Ninian, had previously converted the southern Picts from a base in Whithorn in Galloway. Somewhat confusingly Bede then follows this by implying that Columba converted all of the Picts, so it seems likely that multiple perceptions of the conversion influenced Bede's account. J.E. Fraser (2009a, 71, 97–115) argues that the different views reflect the political and ecclesiastical situation at various stages in the late 7th and early 8th centuries, but that none of them accurately portrays the reality of the conversion process, which is likely to have involved many now unknown early ecclesiastical figures of different backgrounds active over a long time period.

As Adomnán's 'Life', written *c.*697, indicates, Columba was involved in some missionary activity, and place-names and dedications in Pictland demonstrate that his immediate successors were also active south of the Mounth, but much of this evidence may not relate to conversion, and the Columban community cannot have been responsible for the entirety of the conversion process (J.E. Fraser 2009a, 97–9, 103–5; S. Taylor 1996). The numerous episodes demonstrating Columba's holiness and miraculous power in Adomnán's 'Life' present Pictland in the period 563–97 as primarily pagan with some Gaelic Christians present. These encounters sometimes resulted in conversions, but Adomnán does not stress this aspect of Columba's activity among the Picts. Indeed, Columba's influence in northern Pictland can be questioned: a poem written soon after Columba's death, the *Amra Coluimb Chille*, states that he was active among 'the peoples of the Tay', but does not mention the northern Picts (J.E. Fraser 2009a, 99).

When other textual evidence is considered, it is clear that by the 670s there is no indication in any sources that the Picts were not Christian; if they were still pagan, this would have been mentioned in texts such as Eddius Stephanus's 'Life of Wilfrid' (Webb 2004) and Bede's *HE*. The Irish chronicles *c.*623 include the death of a *Uineus*, abbot of Ner, which Clancy (2008, 367–71) has argued persuasively was close to Fetternear in Aberdeenshire (see below). If so, then this indicates that not only was this area already Christian, at least in terms of its elite, but Christianity was also established to the extent that it could afford to have a monastery there (cf. Dumville *et al.*

1993, 188–9, for similar arguments about Iona's foundation), placing the conversion period some time prior to the 620s. The Pictish king-lists may also provide similar evidence, albeit for the southern Picts, for they suggest that the foundation of the monastery of Abernethy by the Tay took place in the early 7th century (J.E. Fraser 2009a, 134).

How early Christianity came to Pictland is difficult to determine. In his 'Letter to Coroticus', St Patrick in the 5th century railed against those who had seized his followers in Ireland and were about to sell them to *apostatae* identified as *Picti* (Hood 1978, 37, 58). Dumville (Dumville *et al.* 1993, 129–31) has argued that this does not neces-sarily mean 'apostate' in the modern sense, simply that the Picts shared the crimes of Coroticus and his rebels against Christ. However, in order for them to be partly culpable, it does indicate that some of the Picts may have had knowledge of Christianity by this time (J.E. Fraser 2009a, 112). If so, then according to Patrick, most had clearly not accepted it, as in §14 he states (Hood 1978, 37, 57) that Coroticus was selling Christians to outside peoples not knowing God (*illos genti exterae ignoranti Deum*). Christianity was certainly established in Pictland by the late 7th century, with monasticism already appear-ing by the early 7th century. The spread of Christianity in Pictland by the 7th century perhaps conflicts with Adomnán's portrayal of Pictland as primarily a pagan territory during the lifetime of Columba in the late 6th century, but it has been suspected that the depiction in *VSC* was intended to emphasise the major role of Columba in the foundation of Pictish Christianity (J.E. Fraser 2009a, 98–100). To achieve this, Adomnán could have presented the Picts as more pagan than they actually were in the late 6th century, although it may be a mistake to reject the depiction completely.

In terms of the mechanics of conversion, our picture of early Christianity in northern Scotland is difficult to disentangle from later historical processes that have clouded the picture. The later Gaelicisation of eastern and northern Scotland, for example, some-times promoted Gaelic over more local religious figures in the origin-legends and dedications of ecclesiastical centres. For example, in 12th-century notes added to the Book of Deer, it is stated that Deer was founded by Saint Drostan, foster son/pupil of Columba (Forsyth, Brown and Clancy, 2008, 137). However, in a following text by the same scribe, reference to Columba is omitted. Clancy (2008, 363–4) suggests that the Columba connection was a later addition designed to attract patronage from the Gaelic nobility, which consolidated itself in north-east Scotland in the late 1st millennium AD. Therefore, we should be cautious in accepting the antiquity of any Columban dedications in northern Scotland: it is likely that these were often appended to ecclesiastical sites centuries after their initial foundation (Clancy 2008, 365). Likewise, even if Gaelic clerics did play a significant role in the conversion process, some of the Gaelic attributions in our study area may be late: the association of Rosemarkie with Moluag, for example, is likely to relate to the later cult of an Argyll saint again due to late 1st-millennium and early 2nd-millennium AD Gaelic expansionism (MacDonald 1994, 28–9) or the later popularity of these cults. The original dedication of Rosemarkie was to the probably Pictish Saint Curetán, perhaps also called by the universal Christian name of Boniface (A. MacDonald 1994).

More local clergy and saints, some at least of Pictish descent, are likely to have had strong roles in the conversion of northern Pictland, albeit many of them may have been trained in the west (Clancy 2008, 387). Other dedications suggest that Christian clergy from Fortriu and Ce may have been converting areas further north. For example, Drostan and Fergus, important saints in north-east Scotland, also have dedications in Caithness – these may indicate missions from north-east Scotland to northern Scotland in the 8th century (Clancy 2008, 384). Likewise, it has been suggested that Curetán was responsible for the spread of Christianity in the Northern Isles (Veitch 1997, 638). However, we should be wary of seeing clear patterns through such dedications as their dates are questionable without the support of other evidence.

The early medieval Church of the Picts did have bishops and presumably clergy ministering at a local level to the people, but the nature of parochial and episcopal systems, and the contribution of monasticism to them, is difficult to establish. The parochial structure of the later medieval period evolved mainly during the 12th century (S. Taylor 2008, 275), but a number of strands of evidence such as the location of early medieval carved stones on later parish boundaries or at parish churches suggest that the later parochial structure's roots lay in the early medieval period (Forsyth 2008a, 407, 409; RCAHMS 2007, 118–19, 124, 128). Contemporary historical sources that refer to any sense of Church organisation in Pictland are extremely limited. Curetán in the later 7th century is one of the few Christian figures referred to in Pictland. Curetán was one of the guarantors of *Cáin*

Adomnáin in AD 697 (A. MacDonald 1994, 5; Woolf 2007a, 315).
He is called a bishop and the dedication of Rosemarkie to Curetán
suggests that Rosemarkie may have been his seat (Veitch 1997, 637);
clearly by the early 9th century he was associated with a place including the element *ros* (J.E. Fraser 2009b, 15–16; MacDonald 1994,
5–7), either meaning the place (Rosemarkie) or region (Ross). An
obituary notice is recorded in the 'Annals of Ulster' (AU) in 865 on
the death of Tuathal, son of Artgus, styled *prím-epscop Fortrenn*,
'chief bishop of Fortriu', as well as abbot of Dunkeld, indicating that
there were superior and lesser bishops, but no further details regarding the lives or roles of this bishop, and his possible subordinates, are
known (Woolf 2007b, 56). Woolf states that the death of a further
bishop of Fortriu is recorded in AU 725.7, although, as the text only
has *Brecc Fortrend*, 'Brecc of Fortriu', his exact status is uncertain.

Insular sources suggest that episcopal organisation tended to coincide with the extent of secular kingdoms, thus it is probable that from
the 7th century onwards Pictland had at least two bishoprics, one in
the north and another in the south (Woolf 2007a, 316). However,
there may have been more if Church organisation coincided with the
regions of Pictland, such as those mentioned in the Pictish king-lists
(in northern Pictland Ce, Fortriu, Cat and possibly Fidach) or other
units, like the Orkneys (J.E. Fraser 2009a, 254–9). It is also possible
that there were no clear equations between secular polities and Church
organisation with bishops having looser jurisdictions depending upon
the dispersal of churches and the extent to which monasticism had
impacted on the form and spread of particular forms of Christianity
(Clancy 2008, 390; Woolf 2007a, 317). For Ireland, Etchingham
(1999) has argued for the importance of bishops and that, while their
seats often changed, their jurisdictions did correspond to those of
secular units (e.g. the *túath*). It is possible that in Pictland bishops
were connected more to a people than a particular place.

Other evidence for the early Church in northern Pictland has to
rely on the archaeology, but physical evidence for the Church in
Pictland and Scotland has traditionally been difficult to identify and
characterise (Foster 2015). However, in northern Pictland the
evidence has been hugely boosted with the publication of the extensive campaigns of survey and excavation at Portmahomack, Easter
Ross (Carver *et al.* 2016). In northern Pictland, the physical evidence
for the early Church includes evidence for enclosures around

churches, cross-marked stones and architectural fragments, and at sites like Portmahomack, rich artefactual and structural evidence for the production of fine metalwork and other craft activities. The physical evidence can at times be correlated with the limited historical sources, place-names, saints' dedications and hagiography to identify some of the key early Christian centres of northern Pictland. Evidence for a diverse range of relief-carved sculpture, for example, can help identify some of the important centres of Moray and Easter Ross, which can occasionally be tallied with historical evidence for important ecclesiastical centres in later sources (e.g. Henderson and Henderson 2004, 196, map 6). Direct archaeological investigation is also increasingly helping to increase our knowledge of the character, dating and morphology of early ecclesiastical sites. The evidence discovered to date suggests that within the provinces of Fortriu and Ce, the most important ecclesiastical establishments were in Easter Ross and Moray. A number of major sites important for any study of the early Church in northern Pictland can be highlighted, and the tour must begin with the rich evidence uncovered at the site of Portmahomack in Easter Ross. The survey of evidence below is far from exhaustive but highlights some of the major sites where future investigation is likely to be fruitful.

The archaeology of the early Church in northern Pictland

Portmahomack, Easter Ross

Any consideration of the physical evidence for the Church in northern Pictland has to start with the investigations at Portmahomack, which have greatly enriched our understanding of ecclesiastical centres in Pictland (Fig. 62). The name Portmahomack, which includes the name Mo Cholmóc, may reflect a dedication to a Colmán venerated north of the Mounth by the late 12th century (Macquarrie 2012, 336–7; Ó Riain 2011, 463; Stokes 1905, 76). One possibility is that he was the bishop who left Lindisfarne after the Synod of Whitby in 664 (Carver et al. 2016, 337), the Anglo-Saxon connection potentially representing a parallel with Burghead where there is an Aethan dedication, which may be to the evangelising Columban bishop of Lindisfarne who died in 651 (see below). However, there were many saints called Colmán (and the related name Colum) and Áedán (Macquarrie 2012, xxii–iv, 322, 336–7; Ó Riain 2011, 71–5,

62. Portmahomack: the early medieval road leading to the early church with workshops on either side © FAS Heritage.

183–208), so definite identification is not possible. Whatever the attribution, these Gaelic dedications are likely to have been made before the Anglicisation of these areas in the later Middle Ages.

At Portmahomack, investigation at the site was prompted by aerial photographs that showed three sides of a vallum enclosure around the modern churchyard. The visible area enclosed by the vallum is at least 2.3 hectares, but the enclosure could have been much larger with the seaward northern side not currently traceable. The site has been interpreted as having origins as an elite settlement in the 5th to 7th centuries AD based on a small number of structural remains and finds, some early cist burials and the possible presence of a barrow cemetery (Carver 2016a, 89; Carver *et al.* 2016). The monastic settlement began sometime in the late 7th to early 8th century AD. Within the vallum, on either side of a road heading towards the church (Fig. 62), evidence for craftworking was found with the production of precious metalwork, glass and vellum being undertaken to the south of the church. The vellum working evidence is particularly striking, showing that the production of illuminated books was occurring at Portmahomack during the life of the monastery. Large timber and turf-built 'bag-shaped' buildings were also identified. One of these, Structure S1, may have played a role in metalworking in its first incarnation and was later converted into a kiln-barn. There was also evidence for the management of water with a dam, bridge and pool and other structural remains associated with a densely populated site. During the excavations, hundreds of fragments of sculpture were found with different types of monument identifiable. These included simple cross-marked stones, grave markers, a sarcophagus lid, a possible panelled shrine, a corbel for a stone church and fragments of four monumental cross-slabs. At the church, 58 burials from the second phase were identified, the vast majority mature males, strongly suggestive of a monastic population (Fig. 63).

63. Cist grave under excavation at Portmahomack © FAS Heritage.

Rosemarkie, Easter Ross

Rosemarkie, based on its dedication, sculpture and limited historical evidence, may have been an episcopal centre for Fortriu (Woolf 2007b, 56). By the end of the Middle Ages, the body of Moluag, an important Gaelic saint, was believed to lie at Rosemarkie (A. MacDonald 1994, 28–9), but its principal association was with Curetán (Woolf 2007a, 311). As noted earlier, a Curetán listed in Irish sources as the head of *Ros Mind Bairend* or *Ros Meinn* probably refers to the same figure (J.E. Fraser 2009b, 15), and there was also a popular local cult to Curetán in the vicinity of Rosemarkie with place-names and a well named after the saint (A. MacDonald 1994, 5–7, 38–41; Veitch 1997, 637). The urban area around Rosemarkie is significantly built up, making identification of any kind of enclosing vallum (if one existed) difficult. Nonetheless, from the site, a large body of early Christian sculpture survives of a sufficiently diverse character to suggest a very important early church existed at Rosemarkie. The sculptural assemblage includes a magnificent cross-slab boldly decorated with key-patterning and vine-scroll on the cross-face and a series of profusely decorated Pictish symbols on the back (Fig. 64). Also on the back of the slab is a square cross-carpet page displaying a design resembling pages from the Book of Durrow (Henderson and Henderson 2004, 66). From Rosemarkie there are also a number of large decorated panels that may be from shrines or may have been panels mounted on the walls of the church. The collection also includes what may be other architectural fragments from a stone-built church such as an equal-armed cross on a small boulder which was possibly placed on the wall behind an altar (Henderson and Henderson 2004, 211).

Parc-an-caipel, Congash, Inverness-shire

Heading south-east in Fortriu, what may have been a smaller ecclesiastical establishment is located at Parc-an-caipel, Congash, Inverness-shire. The footings of a rectangular building up to 15m × 8m in maximum dimensions lie within a sub-rectangular or square enclosure, which measures around 35m × 31m, defined by a stony bank up to 3m wide (NMRS NJ02NE 1) (Fig. 65). Two Class I Pictish symbol stones flank an entrance to the banked enclosure on the south-west side. Aerial photographs have identified a larger ditched enclosure that surrounds the inner enclosure and chapel. This measures 96m

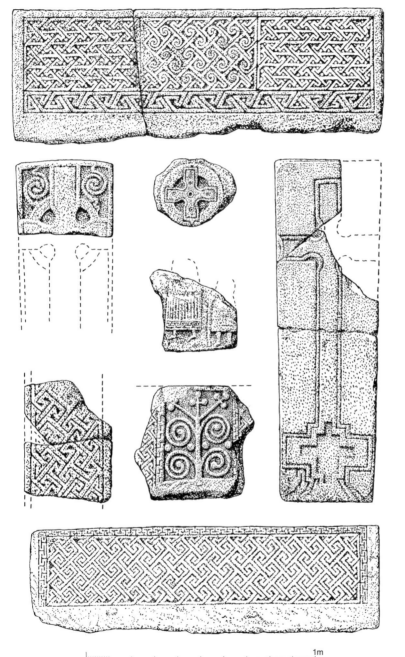

64. A small selection of the early medieval sculpture from Rosemarkie including shrine panels and fragments of cross-slabs © Historic Environment Scotland.

1m

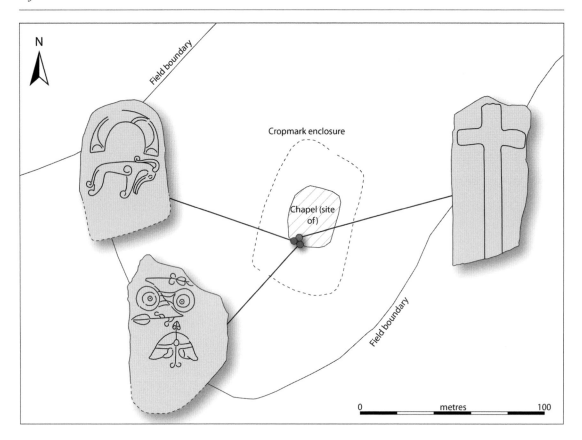

65. Parc-an-caipel plan of chapel and enclosures with sculpture findspots.

NE–SW by 67m NW–SE with two entrances on the two shorter sides of the enclosure. The place-name is strongly suggestive of a chapel, and in 2011 a cross-slab was found within the banked enclosure. The cross is a simple pecked design on a large flat slab which was located near the entranceway to the banked enclosure.

Kinneddar, Moray

Kinneddar stood at the edge of the former sea loch of Spynie on a raised ridge of land. During the later medieval period, Kinneddar was one of the seats of the bishops of Moray (Dransart 2016, 59). Earlier origins to the site are suggested by an extensive collection of early medieval sculpture and its dedication to (or establishment by) Gartnait, a royal name in the Pictish king-lists (Clancy 2008, 378). The sculptural evidence from the site includes fragments of a Class I symbol stone, of composite box-shrines, of cross-slabs and of a free-standing cross, along with other sculptural fragments (Fig. 66). The

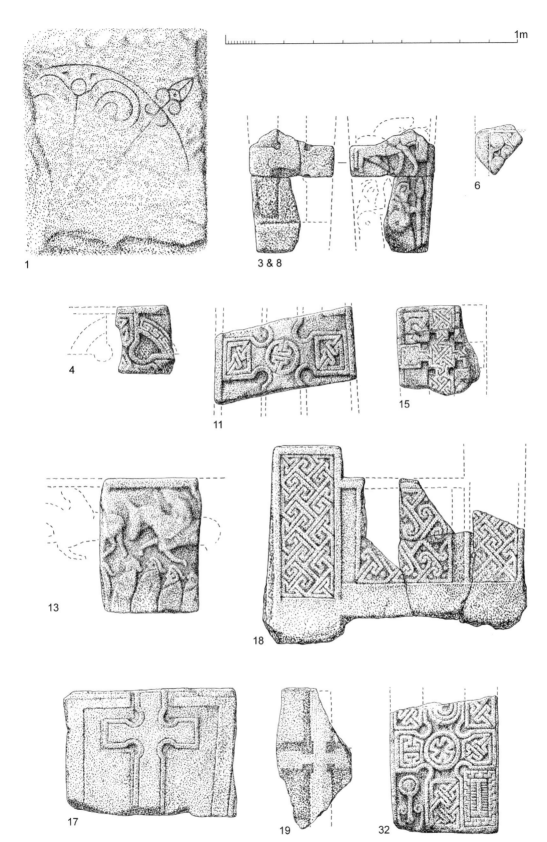

66. A selection of sculpture from Kinneddar including a Class I symbol stone (1), fragments of cross-slabs and fragments of shrine/sarcophagus (18) © Historic Environment Scotland.

sculpture at Kinneddar is diverse and of the highest quality with the closest parallels being from Burghead, Rosemarkie, St. Andrews and Portmahomack. One sculptural fragment is worthy of particular mention: a box-shrine fragment showing David wrenching apart the jaws of a lion (Fig. 67). This can be directly compared with the St Andrews Sarcophagus, which Henderson dates to the 8th century and the reign of the powerful Pictish king Onuist son of Uurguist (Henderson 1998), although that precise attribution is uncertain.

67. Drawing of David rending the jaws of a lion, Kinneddar No. 16 © Historic Environment Scotland.

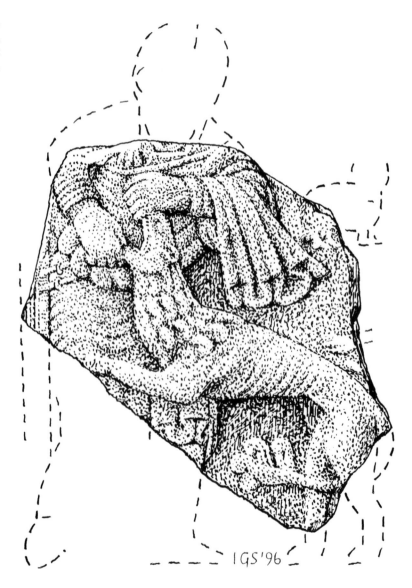

Previous archaeological work at Kinneddar had been limited (Cameron 1995; Dransart 2016, 73), but in 2015 geophysical survey was carried out at Kinneddar by team members of the Northern Picts project with the aim of trying to identify signs of an outer enclosure system around the modern graveyard (Fig. 68). The most impressive results of this survey were the identification of traces of a vallum to the west and south. The projected line of the vallum would enclose an area of 8.6 hectares. The enclosure complex was particularly complicated

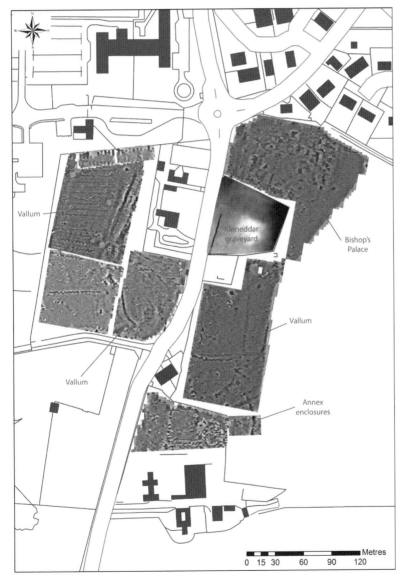

68. Results of the geophysical survey at Kinneddar showing the monastic vallum around the modern graveyard © Crown Copyright/database right 2018. An Ordnance Survey/ EDINA supplied service.

on the west side in the area just outside the glebe field around the old church manse. The area north of the cemetery revealed a diverse range of anomalies that confirm the presence of the later Bishop's Palace in this area. The full layout of the vallum at Kinneddar remains unknown due to urban development to the north and east of the site, but the emerging plan has some striking resemblances to that of Iona (Fig. 69). In particular, the doubling of the ditch on the west side is identical to that at Iona, and the Kinneddar results to date suggest the possible presence of subsections to the enclosure on the south side, again very much like that at Iona. The identification of the monastic vallum and its parallels to Iona underline the importance of Kinneddar, long hinted at by the surviving sculptural evidence. Recent excavations by the Northern Picts project suggest that the vallum enclosure was created in the 7th or early 8th century and was maintained into the 12th century or later. The excavations also showed that settlement evidence survives around the modern graveyard, though more extensive programmes of investigation will be needed to outline the full significance and survival of elements of the early medieval ecclesiastical establishment at Kinneddar.

69. Kinneddar: comparison of the ground-plan to that at Iona © Crown Copyright/database right 2018. An Ordnance Survey/ EDINA supplied service.

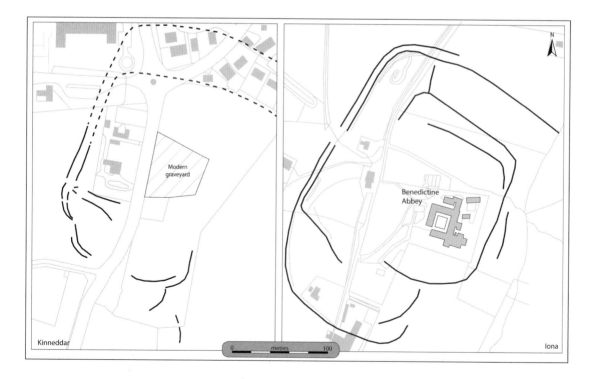

Burghead, Moray

The impressive northern Pictish fort at Burghead also preserves examples of early Christian sculpture. These appear to be associated with an early chapel within the fort depicted on General Roy's 18th-century map as a level area adjacent to the entrance causeway through the outer defences of the fort (Oram 2007, 256). In the 18th century, it is recorded that the chapel at Burghead was dependent on the parish church of Duffus, which local tradition says (Walker and Woodworth 2015, 552) was founded after Burghead was destroyed by the 'Danes' in the 9th century, a 'historical' nugget that we should approach with caution! The chapel at Burghead and a nearby well is dedicated to St Aethan. The sculpture from Burghead includes fragments bearing interlace and key-pattern that may be from a cross-slab or series of cross-slabs, a slotted corner slab, and a fragment of a panel with a carving of a stag being brought down by hounds (Henderson and Henderson 2004, 203) (Fig. 70). The latter two fragments suggest the presence of composite shrine monuments of the type found at nearby Kinneddar. There is also a fragment from a small cross-slab with a relief-carved cross on the front and a mounted warrior on the back. The sculptural evidence hints that an important early Christian site was a key feature of the fortified settlement at Burghead in the later 1st millennium AD.

Cross-slabs from Easter Ross to Moray

A few other, more isolated findspots of early Christian sculpture are worth mentioning in areas that are likely to equate to the province of Fortriu. Now in Sutherland, but formerly part of Easter Ross, is Kincardine parish church, which preserves a recumbent grave marker with a miniaturised version of the St Andrews and Kinneddar shrine panel scenes (Henderson and Henderson 2004, 203). The recumbent grave marker shows David rending the jaws of the lion, and the link with Kinneddar and St Andrews may suggest some royal patronage at Kincardine. A fine cross-slab carved with crosses on both sides is found at Edderton, Ross and Cromarty, and shows a mounted figure on one side. Further south, an unusual stone lies in the grounds of Glenferness House, Inverness-shire (Fig. 71). The stone, known as the 'Princess Stone', would have perhaps rivalled those of the Tarbat peninsula in terms of fineness of carving, but the monument survives

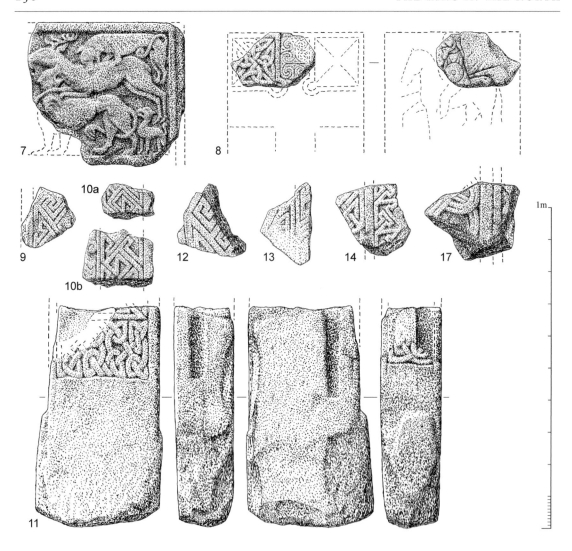

70. Early medieval sculpture from Burghead including a shrine panel fragment (7), cross-slab fragment with mounted warrior (8) and shrine corner post (11) © Historic Environment Scotland.

in a fairly poor state. The findspot is on a bend of the River Findhorn, and the location may be a good bet for an undocumented early monastery. There are also fine Class II cross-slabs at Rodney's Stone, Brodie, Moray, originally found in the old churchyard at nearby Dyke; the Kebbuck Stone to the west of Nairn (which may mark a cemetery); and a granite example at Elgin Cathedral, which on the back depicts a hunt scene accompanied by Pictish symbols and on the front has an interlaced cross and the four evangelists (Allen and Anderson 1903, 135–6). The Altyre cross-slab is also worth highlighting – this 3.3m-high sandstone pillar is said to have come from

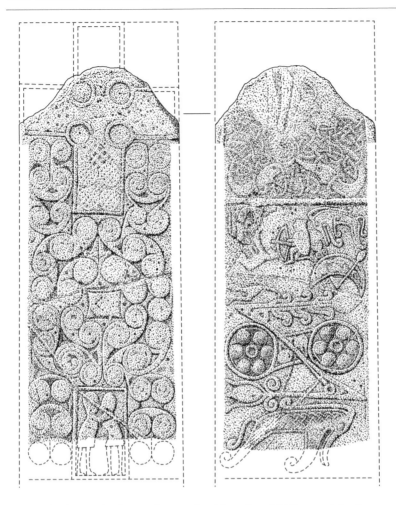

71. The magnificent cross-slab at Glenferness House © Historic Environment Scotland.

Rose Isle, located a few miles south of Burghead (Allen and Anderson 1903, 136). The stone is a relief-carved cross with a long ogham inscription on the undressed left side of the monument.

The early Church in Aberdeenshire

In Aberdeenshire there are no sites that rival the richness of early Christian sculpture from the likes of Portmahomack, Rosemarkie or Kinneddar. Overall, in contrast to its impressive collection of Class I sculpture, the lack of Class II sculpture from Aberdeenshire is noteworthy (e.g. RCAHMS 2007, 126). However, there are sites with important collections of early Christian sculpture and some important recent survey and excavations of early ecclesiastical sites that can add to the discussion. Historical sources are particularly limited for Aberdeenshire, with few sites referenced in early texts, even if there are many little-known saints likely to have Pictish origins who appear in the early 16th-century 'Aberdeen Breviary', such as St Mayoc, associated with Dalmaik on the Dee, St Caran, linked to Fetteresso and Premnay, and St Voloc, to whom Dumeath and Logie (Ruthven) in Mar were dedicated (Clancy 2008, 377; Macquarrie 2012, 10–15, 44–8). However, Clancy (2008, 367–8) notes that the deaths of two people linked to a place called *Nér* in *c.*623 and 678 may relate to Fetternear in Aberdeenshire, which contains the Gaelic element *foithir* plus *Ner*. The later death was of a certain Nechtan, perhaps the saint to whom, in the hypocoristic form Mo Nithoc, the nearby Abersnithock, originally Eglismonithoc, was dedicated. This church was also dedicated to St Finnan, probably the same person as the *Uineus* abbot of Nér who died *c.*623 (Clancy 2008, 368–71). This site is near Braehead Farm, 2.5km north of Monymusk, the church to which Abersnithock belonged in the early 13th century. Ruins of a small rectangular chapel and rectangular enclosure overlooking the River Don survive at the site (RCAHMS 2007, 129). Abersnithock or somewhere nearby may be the earliest historically documented ecclesiastical centre in north-east Scotland (Clancy 2008, 371), but it remains unexplored archaeologically.

Mortlach, Aberdeenshire

The earliest episcopal seat for Aberdeenshire is said to have been founded at Mortlach in the 11th century before being transferred to Aberdeen. Mortlach has a dedication to Moluag, and there are both Class I and II Pictish monuments at Mortlach, which could suggest an earlier origin for the church. In June 2016, a magnetometry survey was conducted by a Northern Picts team in the glebe field west of Mortlach's church and in fields to the east and north. The survey in the fields to the west and north failed to identify any anthropogenic features. In a small area just east of the burial ground, a possible structure was located, but no traces of an enclosure were identified. The lack of an identifiable vallum or further features may support the idea that Mortlach's wider importance emerged only in the later 1st millennium AD or even in the 11th century when King Malcolm II (perhaps correctly Malcolm III) is said to have granted the church to Bean, bishop of Aberdeen, to build the episcopal seat (Woolf 2007a,

313–15). Both Woolf (2007a, 322) and Clancy (2008, 388–9) have suggested that Mortlach was a late establishment or its association with Moluag was late and that many of the Moluag dedications in north-east Scotland were associated with the expansion of Mortlach's influence after its 11th-century establishment or re-establishment. There is an unusual Class I symbol stone from Mortlach and the 'Battle Stone', a similarly unusual Class II cross-slab, stands to the south of the modern parish church. The cross-slab has a relief cross on one side with two poorly executed hippocamps above and a centaur-like creature below. On the back there is an incised eagle, serpent, bull's head and a mounted figure with a hound. The carving style is basic and there is little comparison between this monument and those of the Tarbat peninsula, Rosemarkie or Kinneddar.

Tullich, Aberdeenshire

The largest concentration of early Christian sculpture in Aberdeenshire is found at Tullich, a site near the east end of the Pass of Ballater, an important routeway (Geddes *et al.* 2015, 229) (Plate 16). The early 16th-century 'Aberdeen Breviary' (Macquarrie 2012, 20–3, 401–2) states that the church of Tullich, along with those at Bethelnie near Oldmeldrum and Cowie near Stonehaven, were built by St Nathalan, who died at Tullich, where his relics continued to heal the sick. Nathalan probably is the same Pictish saint as the Nechtan at Abersnithock (Clancy 2008, 368, n.5, 371). Recent survey and excavation have identified two different enclosing features around the modern church – an inner one measuring around 58m × 55m and an outer one of at least 95m × 64m. The monuments from the site include a Pictish Class I symbol stone and 16 incised crosses. These monuments may have demarcated entrances or areas of special sanctity within a relatively modest ecclesiastical enclosure (Geddes *et al.* 2015, 261). On the basis of the archaeological and textual evidence, Clancy (2008, 371–4, 392) has suggested that Tullich was a mother church or a monastic centre, though in terms of its size and the range of sculpture there, it seems much more modest than sites such as Kinneddar, Portmahomack or Rosemarkie.

Dyce and other cross-marked monuments

As well as the collection at Tullich, there is also a significant collection of early Christian sculpture at Dyce. In the later medieval period,

the parish of Dyce was one of the components of the thanage of
Kintore, one of three thanages in Donside (RCAHMS 2007, 134–5,
145). It has been argued by Geoffrey Barrow and Alexander Grant
that thanages reflect royal landholding links that could extend back
into the early medieval period before 1100 (Evans 2014, 49–51), but
Dauvit Broun (2008, 322, 325–6, 354–5) has been more sceptical.
Dyce was later a dependent church of Kinkell, Inverurie, a powerful
ecclesiastical centre in the Garioch (RCAHMS 2008, 130). The stones
at Dyce include a magnificent cross-slab with Pictish symbols on the
front and an ogham inscription on the side, four smaller cross-incised
stones and a fragment of a possible cross-shaft. In Aberdeenshire,
there are also fine cross-slabs at the Maiden Stone (Chapel of
Garioch), Monymusk, Fordoun, Formaston and Migvie and potentially a relatively late cross-slab at Kinord opposite a crannog on
Loch Kinord that has 9th–11th-century dates (Stratigos and Noble
2014). Some of the cross-slabs are isolated monuments, but others
are found in association with small numbers of simple cross-incised
stones, as occurs at Monymusk and Migvie (Clancy 2008, 373–4).

The early Church in a long-term perspective

Understanding pre-Christian belief from an archaeological perspective (cf. Andrén *et al.* 2006, 11) and from a few, later Christian texts
is always going to be challenging. How humans relate to the trans-
cendent even with the benefit of richer historical records is something
that will prove difficult to approach, particularly in the context of
non-book-based religions. In the case of pre-Christian beliefs in western Europe, it is important to recognise that our written sources were
produced from the perspective of the converted, who would not
necessarily accurately recount how and why such an important transition took place (Wickham 2016, 20–2). Our knowledge of pre-
Christian religion and belief in northern Scotland in late Iron Age and
early medieval contexts is restricted to a few remarks in *VSC* and a
small range of difficult to interpret archaeological sites and material
culture. Our limited sources suggest an interest in natural places like
caves for transformative acts and the use of human remains within
acts of deliberate marking of time or place in settlement contexts.
There is little obvious sense of a systematic or standardised set of
beliefs or a unifying cosmology, but, given the diversity of religious

practices and ideologies in the Roman Empire, as well as in pagan Celtic- and Germanic-speaking societies, we should expect diversity rather than uniformity anyway.

The conversion process in northern Pictland is similarly vague, for the Pictish Church barely featured in either Irish or Northumbrian chronicles (Woolf 2007a, 56). Nonetheless, a slim body of historical sources, place-names and dedications and now increasing archaeological evidence provide the framework for beginning to evaluate the timings and tempos of the introduction of a new religion to northern Scotland. Clancy (2008, 392) suggests that the establishment of churches began to occur from the 7th century in north-east Scotland, and the recent dating from Portmahomack and Kinneddar would not disagree with Clancy's narrative for northern Pictland more generally. Clancy proposed that the early establishments were small churches that initially served restricted territories defined by the geography and structure of secular land divisions and polities. However, it should be acknowledged that the near total lack of references to Pictish ecclesiastics before the late 7th century means that the names of important early Church figures of the conversion period, perhaps before many of the more substantial church buildings and institutions were established, are probably lost to us, making it difficult to link dedications and churches to that period.

Adomnán's 'Life of St Columba' shows that Gaelic ecclesiastical figures were trying to garner influence among Pictish elites in northern Scotland from the late 6th century onwards, and elsewhere in northern Britain in the 7th century we know from sources like Bede's 'Ecclesiastical History' (*HE* III.3) that the Gaelic Church was playing an important role in conversion and the establishment of an ecclesiastical structure. The monastic tradition that flourished across Christian Europe from the 6th to 8th centuries AD would have been another important influence on the development of the Church in northern Pictland (Carver *et al.* 2016, 339). Whatever the exact process that conversion and establishment of the Church followed, we can see that it had perhaps differing impacts across northern Pictland. If we look at sculpture and the patronage networks that lay behind the commissioning of sculpture, we can see that Aberdeenshire shows less evidence for the commissioning of elaborate cross-slabs, church furnishings and Christian grave markers than areas to the west that are likely to have been part of Fortriu. Henderson (1972,

172) interpreted this as due to a lack of royal activity in the north-
east and/or the power of secular elites in this area (See also Forsyth
2008a, 429–30), but it is also possible that the Church had less of an
impact in north-east Scotland and/or the conversion process was a
longer drawn-out one in an area further away from the influence of
the Gaelic Church.

In terms of the organisation of the Church in northern Pictland,
basic facts about the episcopal organisation remain unknown – did
episcopal organisation mirror the developing structure of the Pictish
kingdom or provinces or did it follow its own developing logic and
organisation? In the later medieval period, northern Scotland was
controlled by bishoprics in Caithness (based at Dornoch), Ross
(Rosemarkie), Moray (Birnie then Kinneddar then Spynie and finally
Elgin from the 1220s) and Aberdeenshire (Mortlach then Old
Aberdeen) (Evans 2014, 51). The extent to which this pattern had
earlier roots is unknown. The historical sources hint at the pre-
eminence of Rosemarkie as a major centre of religion in the north
and that its bishop, Curetán, in the late 7th century may have been
one of the most important religious figures in Pictland. The archaeology certainly suggests an important early medieval Christian community at Rosemarkie, but excavation has also revealed significant early
Christian establishments at completely undocumented early medieval
sites such as Portmahomack. The sculptural evidence at certain sites
may suggest royal patronage was concentrated at particular locations. The David imagery at Nigg, Kincardine and Kinneddar, for
example, has been used to suggest royal patronage at these establishments, and James Fraser (2009a, 360) argues that the use of David
highlighted the imperial pretensions of powerful Pictish kings of the
8th century.

Judging by the quality of the sculpture at Kinneddar, it may well
have been a royal foundation and perhaps the residence of an early
bishop (Dransart 2001, 233; J.E. Fraser 2009a, 366; Henderson and
Henderson 2004, 49). As well as sculpture, there are perhaps other
clues to the importance and character of particular centres of early
Christianity. There tend to be direct correlations with the size of
vallum enclosures and the importance of particular Church sites in
Ireland, for example (O'Sullivan *et al.* 2014, 147). Thus the identification of the vallum at Kinneddar is a key development: its size is on
a par with the larger ecclesiastical enclosures found in Ireland, and it

is the largest yet identified in northern Pictland. The structural parallels between the enclosure at Kinneddar and that at Iona are also intriguing and perhaps suggest very direct connections between the Columban Church and the establishment of Kinneddar. The location of Kinneddar within Moray and its proximity to Burghead may also again indicate royal patronage in its establishment. Kinneddar is not far from the River Spey and thus likely to have been located towards the edge of Fortriu. Its location makes for an interesting juxtaposition with Portmahomack, which may conceivably have been located towards the northern edge of the kingdom. The place-name Kinneddar derives from Gaelic *cenn*, 'head, end' (either in terms of promontory or a chief place), plus *foithir*, probably derived from a Pictish word meaning something like 'district, region', thus it means 'end of the *foithir* (district)' (S. Taylor 2008, 277–8, esp. n. 11; S. Taylor 2011, 107; Taylor with Márkus 2012, 325). It, therefore, relates to a centre or a subordinate focus of a Pictish administrative unit in the area that presumably included Burghead. The place-name and sculptural evidence alongside the evidence for the vallum and connections to, or emulation of, Iona help to identify Kinneddar as a key target for future work that attempts to more fully understand the ecclesiastical organisation of the early Church in northern Pictland and the character of one of its major churches.

In the provinces of Fortriu and Ce, the archaeological evidence indicates large ecclesiastical establishments at sites such as Portmahomack, Rosemarkie and Kinneddar, but it is likely that there was a patchwork of Church sites of different sizes and form (Clancy 2008, 391). Here smaller assemblages of early Christian sculpture than that found at the larger centres may provide an important correlate for sites below the top tier of the major ecclesiastical centres. In Inverness-shire, the evidence at Congash may be a good example of an important, but smaller-scale church establishment. At Congash, the aerial evidence suggests that a more modest series of enclosure boundaries defined the church and to date a single cross-slab has been found in association with the likely chapel enclosure. The scale of the enclosures at Congash is similar to those found at Tullich, Aberdeenshire. The occurrence of small numbers of cross-marked slabs and the relatively modest character of the carving at sites such as Congash and Tullich may indicate a developing network of early Christian sites with the smaller establishments part of an expansion of pastoral services from leading churches, a process that was perhaps underway in the later 7th and 8th centuries (Clancy 2008, 392). The substantial sculptural corpus (Woolf 2013), combined increasingly with excavation evidence, renders unlikely Martin Carver's claim (2016b, 315–16) that Christianity was only really influential in Pictland in the 8th century.

At the ecclesiastical sites themselves, we have a growing body of evidence with which to interpret the character of the early Church. The evidence from Kinneddar, Congash and now Tullich suggests the importance of enclosure in association with at least some ecclesiastical centres. The early 8th-century collection of canon law, the *Collectio Canonum Hibernensis*, states that a holy place should be surrounded by two or three enclosures of increasing sacredness (O'Sullivan *et al.* 2014, 145). The geophysical, aerial and excavation evidence from sites such as Kinneddar, Tullich and Congash suggest at least two enclosures at these sites, one marking the immediate area around each church and a larger outer enclosure. At Portmahomack the outer enclosure appears to have enclosed different zones of activity with an industrial quarter found to the south of the church and the main burial ground around the church itself (Carver *et al.* 2016, 194). In Ireland, ecclesiastical sites tend to have two enclosing boundaries, very occasionally three, and these also show evidence of zoning of activities with craftworking often confined to the outer enclosures (O'Sullivan *et al.* 2014, 147).

The *Collectio Canonum Hibernensis* also states that holy places should be marked by signs of the cross, and the elaborate cross-slabs that survive at sites across northern Pictland show that monumental versions of the cross were located prominently at Christian centres (Henderson and Henderson 2004, map 5). These monuments were huge investments in time, labour and craft and speak of high-status patronage being concentrated at particular Church sites in the later 1st millennium AD. However, the exact role of these monuments remains uncertain – they may have been high-status burial markers in some cases, but they may have also marked the sacred geography of a holy place. They might have been in some cases associated with specific saints or events in the life of that saint, acting as the focus for prayer (Blackwell 2012, 33). The property notes in the Book of Deer also suggest that stones may have been used as estate boundaries of early churches (Forsyth 2008a, 406). The presence of box-shrines indicates that relics of saints were kept at the more important sites, and it is likely that the location of the most sacred relics were Church centres that became famous places of pilgrimage and sanctuary (Blackwell 2012, 43). Certainly, some ecclesiastical sites were in landscape locations that were extremely accessible whether by design or chance – at Portmahomack the monastery was established in an area that was well connected, the peninsula itself being a porterage between two major firths. Indeed, the magnificent cross-slabs on the peninsula may have been important waymarkers for travel by boat and perhaps essential waymarkers for pilgrims to navigate to the cult centre (Carver *et al.* 2016, 255).

What was the character of the churches at these early Christian centres? That is a difficult question to answer given current evidence. Work on known early sites has tended to be small-scale and piecemeal, hampered by the presence of later churches on top of earlier sites (Foster 2015, 74). The historical sources suggest the presence of stone churches, but few traces of such structures have been found with the exception of a possible, but disputed, wall at Portmahomack (Carver *et al.* 2016, 168; Foster 2015, 74). As noted above, some of the sculptural evidence indicates the presence of stone churches or stone elements to churches such as the corbel from Portmahomack. The cross-slab at Hilton of Cadboll on the Tarbat peninsula originally had tenons on the sides, suggesting it could have been part of a screen in a large stone building (Clarke 2012, 97). Timber construction is also likely for some sites and wooden buildings have been excavated at major ecclesiastical sites in Scotland such as at Whithorn, south-west Scotland, and there are European parallels too (Ó Carragáin 2010, 15). Most of the identified wooden churches in Ireland suggest modest buildings, but the historical record suggests much larger buildings in timber also existed (O'Sullivan *et al.* 2014, 152). The presence of probable altar screens and other church fittings in the sculptural record gives clues to the internal fittings, but otherwise few pieces of church metalwork survive in the study area other than a very large example of a hand bell from Birnie, Moray (Bourke 1983).

The archaeological evidence also highlights sites like Portmahomack as important centres of production and dense areas of settlement and industry. Indeed, the role of the largest ecclesiastical sites is open to debate. In Ireland and elsewhere, there has been a long-running debate about the potential proto-urban role of the largest monastic sites. The idea of 'monastic towns' was developed by Doherty (1985), who suggested that some of the most influential sites were large religio-economic complexes incorporating social, religious, administrative and commercial functions. Doherty's writings have generated a fierce debate that remains unresolved (e.g. Etchingham 1999; Graham 1987; Sullivan *et al.* 2014, 175–8; Swift 1998; Valante 1998). Certainly, some of the larger ecclesiastical sites were important consumer centres, such as Clonmacnoise in Ireland, whose faunal remains suggest it was a commercial hub like Viking Age Dublin (Sullivan *et al.* 2014, 177). Similarly on the Continent, some monasteries were on a par with trading settlements in terms of production (Henning 2009). Christian centres in Ireland were certainly important early adopters of mill technology and of fish trapping, but it is unclear whether the Church promoted economic developments or simply took part in changes taking place more generally (Davies and Flechner 2016). The abundant evidence for these innovations in Ireland compared to the more limited indications from Wales and Scotland led Davies to suggest that Ireland's economy was transformed more in the early medieval period than these other countries (Davies and Flechner 2016, 381–2, 384–5). However, in Pictland, apart from Portmahomack, few sites have been excavated on any scale, and we have few secular settlements of elite status or otherwise to compare to, but it is certainly the case that the monastic vallums at sites like Portmahomack and Kinneddar represent the largest enclosed settlements thus far identified in northern Pictland.

Overall, we can identify widespread evidence for the early Church in northern Pictland, though further field investigation of these sites will undoubtedly help clarify the timings and tempos surrounding the adoption of Christianity. Major ecclesiastical centres were certainly developing from the 7th and 8th centuries onwards, particularly in Easter Ross and Moray with smaller-scale Church establishments in Aberdeenshire. These Church establishments would have undoubtedly brought many changes to what may have largely been a pagan Pictland in the north in the 6th century. Early Christianity could be practised in the home or hall, but it also became an integral part of the wider public life, increasingly shaping social structure and secular politics. Indeed, it has been suggested that the Church may have played an important role in the consolidation of the kingdoms of Pictland and the rise to power of Fortriu (Carver 2016a, 107; Foster 2016, 151; J.E. Fraser 2009a, 259; Grigg 2015). However, Christianity offered competition for power as well as useful support: kings could benefit from the view that they were ordained by God, but this also could leave them requiring the support of ecclesiastics who were the earthly embodiment of Christianity. Moreover, the Church, especially in its monastic guise, had anti-war (see examples in Rekdal and Doherty 2016), anti-materialist and sometimes egalitarian streaks that did not always sit well with secular hierarchies and ideologies (Winterbottom 1978). The Church would have provided at times a competing rather than complementary power base for the kings of northern Pictland (cf. Higham 1993).

Assessing the impact of Christianity in northern Pictland also involves separating later history and mythology from the likely early medieval reality. On the textual side, increased critical study has enabled us to evaluate the evidence more effectively. This has often meant that old certainties about the origins and development of the Church, such as the missionary activities of Columba and Ninian, have been called into question, and gradually a new, more complex picture is tentatively emerging of the northern Pictish Church, with multiple saints, some Pictish, some Gaelic, others universal, coming to be venerated, and the existence of bishops, with Rosemarkie as one important centre. Pioneering studies of later patterns in the evidence relating to saints' dedications (e.g. Clancy 2008), place-names (Taylor with Márkus 2012), and landholdings and units such as davochs and parishes (Ross 2015) are gradually allowing scholars to differentiate between later medieval innovation and continuity from the earlier period. Nonetheless, how exactly the Church related to secular society, and whether it transformed it socially and economically or encouraged the creation of more centralised kingship are just some of the major research questions that will repay further investigation.

CHAPTER NINE

Coda

In this volume, Nick Evans has sketched out a historical narrative that we can use to help illuminate the Pictish period and the role of the regions of northern Pictland. It is worth briefly outlining the bones of that narrative once more. The first references to the Picts were by classical authors in the late 3rd century AD, and the Roman period was characterised by some political consolidation, with *Picti* perhaps best interpreted as a new collective term for the generally larger polities that had superseded smaller population groups referenced in earlier Roman sources. The 7th century seems to have been another key period of transition with the emergence of the overkingship of Fortriu. On his death in 692, Bridei son of Beli, the victor at Nechtanesmere in 685, was called rex Fortrenn, 'king of Fortriu' (AU [693].1), and the pre-eminence of Fortriu is reflected in the reign-lengths for the sons of Cruithne in the Pictish king-lists (Chapter 2; Evans 2011, 46–51). The 8th century was also a period of expansion and consolidation with King Onuist son of Uurguist (732–61), although viewed by some external commentators as a tyrant (Colgrave and Mynors 1969, 577), establishing a line of succession that became focused on an increasingly smaller dynasty. By the 9th century power in Pictland may have begun to shift southwards with the main royal centres recorded in the south around the Tay. By the end of the 10th century all reference to Picts and Pictish identity had ceased with the Gaelic kingdom of Alba in ascendancy, controlling an area from Fife to east of the Spey. The area of Moray is first mentioned in the 10th century and may have been, along with Ross, a term that replaced Fortriu in our sources. The kingdom of Alba attempted to be overlords of Moray, but control over the region to the west of the Spey was sporadic.

What light can the new archaeological data from northern Pictland shed on our limited historical sources? Increasingly, the archaeological evidence would certainly support major changes in late Roman society that coincide with the first references to a Pictish identity. The settlement evidence from 1st-millennium AD eastern and northern Scotland shows significant change around the 3rd century AD for example. Hunter (2007, 42–4) has linked these changes to political fragmentation rather than consolidation, but a different view might be gleaned from the evidence when we recognise that the Picts were able to coordinate on a large scale, conspiring with other major non-Roman groups in the 'Barbarian conspiracy' of 367, when they joined the *Scotti*, Franks and Saxons to wreak havoc on the Roman Empire. The fact that the Pictish symbol system may also originate in the same period (Chapter 7), would also suggest a degree of complexity and shared practices across a widespread area that became the core of the Pictish kingdoms when our historical sources become richer in the 7th century. The evidence from sites such as the promontory fort of Dunnicaer also suggests that the important re-emergence of fortified centres, a phenomenon rare in the Roman Iron Age, also began to take shape in the late Roman period. Promontory forts such as Dunnicaer are obvious sites through which changing power structures could be manifested, and in terms of political geography, sites where the connectivity possible through maritime networks could be harnessed, for these were ideal locations from where raids on the Roman Empire (and on other native groups) could be launched. The importance of the Roman period is also evident in the material culture record with late Roman objects being the model for certain early medieval artefact types, particularly in relation to elite symbols of power (Chapter 6). The Roman Empire and the use of Latin on public monuments may have also been the inspiration for the Pictish symbol tradition. Hence, while Roman military occupation of north-east Scotland was limited, the Roman presence clearly had long-term impacts on society well beyond the limits of the frontier.

Turning towards the second half of the 1st millennium AD, what we see at key sites such as Rhynie in north-east Scotland is an archaeological signature that suggests that a rich ideological language of rulership was being consolidated at major power centres. The archaeological discoveries at Rhynie have perhaps been particularly surprising because the extent to which the Picts were tied into wider international trade networks and trends was uncertain given the relative dearth of contextualised archaeological sites and sequences. The emerging evidence from Rhynie suggests that precocious power centres of a larger scale than Dunnicaer were rising to prominence in the immediate post-Roman period. The evidence from Rhynie shows that at least some of these had connections that ultimately extended to the eastern Mediterranean and western Continental Europe, via links that perhaps extended down both coasts of Britain. Our knowledge of the political geography of the Picts is so hazy that it is difficult to pin down which territory Rhynie may have been part of; it might be that it was the centre for a much smaller territory than what came to define Pictland in the later 1st millennium AD, but equally it may have been a key node of power for a relatively large polity. Here the growing archaeological record has much to contribute to refining our understanding of the nature and extent of polities in the immediate post-Roman period. What seems to mark Rhynie out from earlier fortified complexes is the explicit language of power and sacrality that is expressed in the monumental architecture of the site. As Evans-Pritchard (1966, 210) pointed out over 50 years ago, 'Kingship everywhere and at all times has been to some degree a sacred office.' Thus, while the overkingship of Pictland is not recorded in the historical sources till the 7th century, we can see at sites like Rhynie how the language and ideology of extensive rulership may have emerged earlier.

By the late 6th and into the 7th centuries we have more regular references to Pictish rulers, and the overkingship of Fortriu is documented by the late 7th century. Indeed, if Adomnán's portrayal of Bridei son of Mailcon's court was based on a 6th-century reality, we can see how northern Pictish kings had carved out extensive territories at a relatively early date. The presence of a *sub-regulus* from Orkney in Bridei's retinue as recorded by Adomnán implies that Pictish kings situated in the north had begun to dominate the islands and firths of eastern and northern Scotland. One obvious correlate of more developed maritime networks may be the construction and use of coastal sites. While Dunnicaer was abandoned by the early 5th century at the latest, recent work at Burghead suggests that larger promontory forts may have been in use by the 6th century. It may have been at a site like Burghead, with its extensive bay to the west of the fort, perfect for landing boats, that the 6th-century Bridei maintained dominance over the Orkneys. It may also have been sites such as Burghead from which the 7th-century king, Bridei, set out on his raid to decimate the Orkneys, a reference that implies that the maritime networks of power that may have been a key element of Pictish political success were being renewed or consolidated in the period in which the overkingship of Fortriu is first documented. The 7th century also saw the establishment of major early Christian centres in northern Pictland with important establishments at Portmahomack, Rosemarkie and Kinneddar found within the likely boundaries of Fortriu. An alignment with the Church might have helped cement the ideological position of increasingly powerful northern Pictish rulers, but through time the Church would have also been a competing power source.

Looking at the later 1st millennium AD, the growth in number of radiocarbon dates and the better chronologies beginning to be established will increasingly allow us to compare the historical record to the major trends in the archaeological record. The emerging pattern for the enclosed sites (Chapter 3) is for the more developed hill- and promontory forts to be a feature in particular of the 7th century, though more work needs to be done to confirm this (Noble *et al.* 2013, 1143). Sites like the stack site at Dunnottar and the 'nucleated' hillfort of Dundurn are first mentioned in the 7th century (Alcock *et al.* 1989, 192; Alcock and Alcock 1992, 267), though whether this is due to the scarcity of earlier sources and a limited excavation record is a moot point (Chapter 2). Nonetheless, the dating evidence that we do have suggests that the 7th century was a key phase for the development of these more complex fortified sites, and it may be that the more elaborate defences of these were a direct materialisation of the increasing client base of more powerful Pictish kings, with the hierarchical organisation of sites such as Burghead and Dundurn setting in stone a developed form of social stratification that was consolidated at this time. The presence of a probable chapel at Burghead also implies that Pictish rulers actively embraced the Christian faith as part of the trappings of kingship by the 7th or 8th century at the latest.

In terms of the end of Pictland, our historical sources again provide the outlines of a basic narrative. From the end of the 8th century onwards, Pictish kings also ruled Dál Riata, but seemingly paradoxically, by the end of the 10th century Gaelic identity, language and culture were in the ascendancy, with the elite tracing their origins back to Dál Riata and ultimately Ireland. Identified royal sites in the 9th century are only found in southern Pictland, and Pictish terminology ceased to be used for contemporary society in the first half of the 10th century. Clearly big changes were afoot, and in terms of identifying the catalysts of change the Scandinavian presence has to be seen as one major driver (Chapter 2). It is perhaps in the Viking presence and impact that we should seek the origins of the changes documented in 9th- and 10th-century eastern and northern Scotland. Scandinavian groups gained supremacy in former Pictish-dominated areas such as Caithness and the Northern and Western Isles, and gained ascendancy more widely across the western seaboard, a takeover which must have had huge repercussions for the Pictish kingdom as a whole, provoking social and political transformation, which combined with ongoing Gaelicisation to create the later kingdom of Alba. The historical sources reveal major Viking raids on Pictish territory in the late 1st millennium AD that must have caused a considerable drain on resources and huge stress on the Pictish overkings' ability to rule.

In terms of the archaeology, our evidence is scant at present (see also Carver 2008). Many of the sites outlined in this volume, such as Dunnicaer and Rhynie, ended well before the latter part of the 1st millennium AD. Recent work at Burghead and Kinneddar is beginning to reveal sequences that extend to the end of the millennium, but as the work is ongoing, only limited reflection can be brought to bear on the subject. The sequence at Portmahomack suggests that major changes occurred at some ecclesiastical settlements in the Viking Age with a vibrant centre of production and worship having much more modest archaeological signature from the 9th century onwards (Carver et al. 2016, 283). New excavations at Burghead suggest that this major secular centre of the northern Picts may have been destroyed in the 10th century. Dramatic events, such as the Viking raids that appear to have brought an end to the monastic phase at Portmahomack and perhaps ended the use of Burghead as a seat of rulership, may have led to the power shifts that characterised late Pictish kingship and the emergence of Alba. Once again with more intensive programmes of investigation, it is the archaeological evidence that can perhaps begin to occupy a more central role in a major long-standing debate concerning the demise of Pictland and the emergence of the kingdom of Alba.

Overall, what this volume represents most clearly is a renewed interest in an area of Pictland that had seen limited historical focus and archaeological investigation until recently. In terms of the archaeological record, few projects had specifically targeted the Pictish period as opposed to finding early medieval remains as part of investigation of multiperiod sites (e.g. Greig 1970, 1971, 1972; Small and Cottam 1972). Indeed, the possibility of a focused project on a part of Pictland has long been difficult due to the difficulties of identifying sites of this period, but through a better understanding of fort typology and a focus on the archaeological setting of symbol stones and early Christian cross-slabs we have ways to identify sites that will repay archaeological investigation. Undoubtedly Martin Carver's project at Portmahomack marked an important watershed in the scale and ambition of investigation at a Pictish site in northern Scotland, but the resources expended on the project were amply rewarded by the results (Carver 2016a; Carver *et al.* 2016). Having surveys such as the 2007 RCAHMS volume *In the Shadow of Bennachie* has also been crucial in establishing a baseline for analysis and a typology of settlement forms to work with. The success of these previous projects made the case for a project such as the University of Aberdeen Northern Picts project realisable.

This volume represents the first attempt to consolidate the historical and archaeological evidence for the Pictish areas of Fortriu and Ce of northern Pictland, but undoubtedly this volume is simply the start rather than end point for new perspectives on northern Pictland. The Northern Picts project and its sister project, the Leverhulme-funded Comparative Kingship project, also based at Aberdeen, are both ongoing, and undoubtedly some of the results presented here are perhaps already out of date. While that could be seen negatively, the pace of new findings is a testament to how vibrant this area of research has become.

In conclusion, we can point to many important new developments that can be capitalised on through new research and continuing reviews of the evidence. Alex Woolf's ground-breaking article on Fortriu was published just over ten years ago and the Northern Picts project began just over five years ago. It is remarkable how much our knowledge of northern Pictland has advanced in that period. Our historical understanding of the political organisation and development of the Pictish kingdoms has been questioned through renewed historical scholarship, but undoubtedly that work has also reinvigorated debate and will set the foundations for research on Pictland in the short to medium term. In terms of archaeology, we have gone from a demonstrable lack of identified and dated Pictish sites in northern Pictland to one of the best dated sequences from early medieval Scotland with a whole body of new and well-researched sites that will enrich our narratives of this period for years to come. I write this conclusion having just returned from the first season of large-scale investigation of Burghead by the University of Aberdeen. Our recent work has shown that, despite 19th-century destruction of a substantial part of the fort, much remains to be discovered. This includes an incredibly well-preserved timber-laced rampart of the fort and internal buildings that have preserved floor layers, hearths and structural detail of the type rarely preserved on Pictish sites in mainland Scotland. The ongoing work at Burghead will undoubtedly reveal in greater detail than ever before the nature of settlement at a major fort of northern Pictland. Overall, it is a very exciting time to be an archaeologist working with a diverse range of colleagues on Pictland, and we all look forward to the new results that future investigations will bring, helping to answer the big questions which still remain about the Picts and their kings in the north.

Gordon Noble
October 2018

Sites to visit

A list of sites to visit from Aberdeenshire to Easter Ross is highlighted below. Each site has its national monument site number listed followed by an OS map grid reference. More information on each site can be obtained by searching using the site number on the National Monuments Record Service online database, Canmore: https://canmore.org.uk/

Aberdeenshire

NJ81NE 8, Sheet 38, NJ 8752 1541
Dyce, St Fergus. There are a number of Pictish symbol stones and carved crosses from Dyce that indicate that this was an important site in the early medieval period and the focus of an early church. The stones include one stone with symbols only: a 'Pictish beast' and double-disc and Z-rod. Another has an elaborate interlaced cross with a crescent and V-rod and triple-disc on the left and a double-disc and Z-rod and 'mirror-case' on the right. There is also an ogham inscription on the side of this stone. The other stones consist of simple cross-inscribed stones. The stones are within a recess in the ruined chapel.

NJ72SE 23, Sheet 38, NJ 75992 22403
Brandsbutt, Inverurie. Now in the middle of a housing estate in Inverurie, this stone was broken up for a field-dyke in the 19th century. It has a crescent and V-rod, a serpent and Z-rod and an ogham inscription on the front. The stone may have been associated with, and reused from, a Late Neolithic/Bronze Age stone circle that stood nearby.

NO88SE 11, Sheet 45, NO 88128 83842
Dunnottar Castle. Technically there is nothing Pictish to see here, but

this spectacular medieval castle at Dunnottar stands on a site recorded as being under siege in the 7th century AD. In the next bay to the north stands the much degraded promontory upon which stood Dunnicaer, a fort of the 3rd–4th centuries AD where five Pictish stones were uncovered in the 19th century.

NJ72SE 11, Sheet 38, NJ 78043 20611
Inverurie kirkyard. Four symbol stones are displayed near the motte in Inverurie kirkyard. All but one is damaged, a charismatic horse carved on a small standing stone. The other three have the more abstract symbols including double-discs and a crescent and V-rod, although a serpent does make an appearance on the larger stone of the three.

NJ71NE 33, Sheet 38, NJ 7930 1628
Kintore churchyard. A single symbol stone displaying a salmon and triple-disc on one face and 'Pictish beast' and crescent and V-rod on the other. The stone stands just inside the church gate.

NO49NW 14, Sheet 37, NO 44000 99787
Loch Kinord. By Loch Kinord, a fine stone cross-slab carved with interlaced designs of probable 9th-century date. The stone overlooks the loch, which has two crannogs that have phases dated to the late 1st millennium AD.

NJ72SW 1, Sheet 38, NJ 70378 24714
Maiden Stone. To the west of Chapel of Garioch in the shadow of Bennachie is perhaps Aberdeenshire's most impressive Pictish stone. The tall pink granite slab has an elaborate but faded ring-headed cross with a human figure and two fish-monsters above on one face and a series of figures and symbols on the reverse. These include the mirror and comb on the bottom, a 'Pictish beast', a notched rectangle and Z-rod and a group of centaurs and other four-legged beasts. The stone stands in the shadow of the Pictish fort, the Mither Tap, Bennachie.

NJ40NW 2, Sheet 37, NJ 43668 06839
Migvie kirkyard. In the burial ground stands a stone with an elaborately carved interlaced cross. The cross frames four additional images, one in each quadrant defined by the cross. These are a horseman, a pair of shears, a double-disc and Z-rod, and a horseshoe. On

the reverse side there is another horseman. A smaller cross-incised stone is now built into the walls of the church.

NJ71NW 12, Sheet 38, NJ 703 151
Monymusk. Now in the church at Monymusk, but said to originally come from a field by the Don. A granite pillar with cross, triple-disc and curious 'stepped rectangle'.

NJ33NW 12, Sheet 28, NJ 3237 3928
Mortlach. Two symbol stones survive at Mortlach. One stands in the lower graveyard extension below the church and is carved with a cross, a pair of fish-monsters and a four-legged creature on one side and an eagle, snake, bull's head, mounted horseman and hunting dog on the other. The second stone is built into the vestibule of the church and is carved with a 'Pictish beast' and a curvilinear symbol.

NJ63SW 3, Sheet 37, NJ 60994 30259
Picardy Stone. Just over a mile to the north-west of Insch stands the Picardy Stone, an imposing pillar of whinstone with prominent veins of quartz. On one face there is a mirror, snake and Z-rod and a double-disc and Z-rod. Fine views of Dunnideer hillfort can be obtained from here.

NJ42NE 35 and NJ42NE 42, Sheet 37, NJ 49749 26345, NJ 4992 2649
Rhynie, the 'Craw Stane' and churchyard. The 'Craw Stane' is a block of grey granite that sits on top of a prominent rise just to the west of the churchyard at Rhynie. A salmon and 'Pictish beast' are carved on one side. Further stones can be found in a shelter built near the churchyard on the outskirts of the village down by the Water of Bogie. These are part of a group of eight stones known from Rhynie, which include the fearsome axe-wielding 'Rhynie Man', who now stands in the foyer of Woodhill House in Aberdeen. Recent excavations at Rhynie in association with the Craw Stane have shown that the symbol stones here stood in association with a high-status settlement and cemetery dating to the 4th to 6th centuries AD.

NO39NE 2, Sheet 37, NO 39050 97548
Tullich, St Nathalan's Kirk. A Pictish symbol stone and cross-incised slabs can be found in the churchyard of St Nathalan's. These relate to an important early church site here in the early medieval period.

Moray

NH95NE 3, Sheet 27, NH 98425 57665
Brodie, 'Rodney's Stone'. By driveway at entrance to Brodie Castle. This symbol stone was originally found during excavations of the foundations for Dyke Church in 1781. It bears on one face an elaborately carved interlaced cross and on the back two fish-monsters, a 'Pictish beast' and a double-disc and Z-rod. On the sides and back are the longest ogham inscription in Pictland, which includes the name EDDARRNONN. The inscription may be a dedication.

NJ16NW 1, Sheet 28, NJ 1090 6914
Burghead. At Burghead lie the remains of a very substantial promontory fort. The complex defences included a triple rampart cutting the promontory from the headland and an upper and lower enclosure within. Excavations and radiocarbon dating suggest the fort was in use from the 6th to the 10th century AD. Six carved stones of bulls survive from a much larger group found in the 19th century. Additional sculpture found near the churchyard and around, including fragments of a cross-slab and shrine, indicate an important Christian establishment here in the later 1st millennium AD. Within the fort lies an impressive rock-cut well. Some of the stones can be seen in the visitor centre at the end of the promontory.

NJ46NE 8, Sheet 28, NJ 4885 6877
Portknockie, Green Castle. Just to the north of the village a low bank cuts off a small area of headland, about 70m × 15m. Excavation has shown the site was occupied in the Pictish period from the 7th to the 9th centuries AD and was defended by an elaborate timber-laced rampart that enclosed a number of timber buildings within.

NJ17SE 1, Sheet 28, NJ 1750 7072
Covesea, Sculptor's Cave. Carved into the rock of this cave are a number of Pictish symbols. These include a fish, a crescent and V-rod, stars and a keyhole-shaped carving. The symbols are found near the mouths of the two entrance passages seemingly marking the transition between outside and in. Within the cave a substantial number of human bones have been found, including remains indicative of decapitation. Late Bronze Age metalwork and Roman coins and

jewellery have also been found. **Take great care accessing the site as the cave is cut off at high tide.**

NJ26SW 2, Sheet 28, NJ 2219 6305
Elgin Cathedral. Originally found near St Giles' Kirk in Elgin, but now within the grounds of Elgin Cathedral. This is an elaborately carved cross-slab decorated on one face with the cross, the four evangelists and a serpent. On the other side there is a hunting scene with figures on horseback and a crescent and V-rod, double-disc and Z-rod and at the top the hands of a fragmentary human figure, the upper portion of which has been broken off.

NJ13NE 7, Sheet 28, NJ 1828 3767
Inveravon churchyard. On the south wall of the church, there are four stones carved with symbols. The most impressive stone has an eagle, mirror or 'mirror-case' and a mirror and comb carved on one side.

NJ26NW 3, Sheet 28, NJ 223 696
Kinneddar stones (now in Elgin Museum). A very impressive collection of Pictish symbol stones, cross-slabs and other decorated stones. These were originally found at Kinneddar, a site of the bishopric in Moray. The stones suggest an important early Christian centre here with royal patronage.

NJ05NW 1, Sheet 27, NJ 04655 59533
Sueno's Stone. A remarkable example of early medieval carving dating to the late 1st millennium AD. Sueno's Stone is around 6m high, carved from sandstone and displays a great battle scene on one side and an enormous ring-headed cross on the other. On the front is an elaborately carved interlaced ring-headed cross with a group of figures below. The back is divided into four panels with almost 100 individual figures depicted. The top panel includes figures on horseback, while the panel below includes figures with swords and spears engaged in battle, piles of human heads and decapitated bodies. The panel below includes a canopy or bridge, beneath which are several decapitated bodies, while the final panel shows further human figures. Various interpretations have been proposed for the battle scene represented on the stone. The interpretations have revolved around three main ideas: a battle between the Picts and the Scots; Viking conflict

with the kings of Pictland/Alba; or a more specific battle in AD 967 at Forres when Dub son of Máel Choluim, king of Alba, was killed and his body hidden under a bridge at nearby Kinloss.

Inverness-shire/Easter Ross

NH64NW 6, Sheet 26, NH 6400 4527
Craig Phadrig. An impressive fort overlooking Inverness. Originally built in the Iron Age, the site was reoccupied in the Pictish period. Excavations in 1971 uncovered fragments of moulds and imported pottery dating to the 7th century AD. The site is one of the likely candidates for being the fort of King Bridei which Columba visited in the late 6th century.

NH78NW 2, Sheet 21, NH 7082 8507
Edderton. An impressively tall standing stone stands at Edderton. The stone may have originally been erected in the Bronze Age, but it bears on one face a 'salmon' and 'double-disc and Z-rod' symbols. The stone was recorded in the 18th century as standing on a circular mound of earth, which has now largely disappeared.

NH64SE 25, Sheet 26, NH 6567 4134
Knocknagael. An impressive boar and a 'mirror-case' symbol are carved on this huge slab of slate, which formerly stood in a field on the farm of Knocknagael to the south of Inverness till the 1990s. The stone now stands in the foyer of the Highland Council Headquarters, Glenurquhart Road, Inverness.

NH87SW 1, Sheet 21, NH 8049 7170
Nigg. One of a series of elaborately decorated cross-slabs from the Tarbat peninsula. The Nigg cross-slab is located in the present-day church. It displays on one side an impressively carved cross with representations of St Paul and St Anthony above the cross. On the back are scenes from the story of David and a series of Pictish symbols.

NH87SE 4, Sheet 21, NH 8555 7471
Shandwick cross-slab. The impressive monument at Shandwick stands in a glass box overlooking a beautiful sandy bay. The front has

a cross decorated with carved spiral bosses and on the back is an elaborate hunt scene with incredible panels of spirals, interlace and key-pattern.

Museums

Elgin (Sheet 28). Elgin Museum, Elgin town centre, is Scotland's oldest independent museum. It holds an impressive collection of Pictish sculpture including bulls from Burghead and a collection of sculpture from Kinneddar. It also has a small display on Covesea Cave.

Groam House (Sheet 27). Groam House Museum is located in the centre of the lovely village of Rosemarkie, on the Black Isle, north of Inverness. It holds extensive collections of Pictish sculpture including a magnificent cross-slab that was found in the floor of the old parish church.

Inverness Museum and Art Gallery (Sheet 26). The museum in Inverness has a number of Pictish stones on display including a beautiful slab carved with a wolf from Ardross and a bull from Kingsmills.

Tarbat Discovery Centre, Portmahomack (Sheet 21). A wonderful museum located in the former church of St Colman's, Portmahomack, which displays material found during University of York excavations. The excavations from 1996 to 2007 uncovered the remains of a major monastery of the Picts on land immediately to the south of the church. The displays include artefacts from the dig, information on the Picts and an impressive collection of early medieval sculpture. St Colman's gallery holds temporary exhibitions including displays from the Northern Picts project.

Learning resources

Teachers! Find out more. The Forestry Commission Scotland has produced a wonderful learning resource for the Picts. The resource contains excellent material to inspire young audiences:

https://scotland.forestry.gov.uk/managing/work-on-scotlands-national -forest-estate/conservation/archaeology/learning/the-picts

References

Primary sources

Anderson, A.O. (trans.) 1922 *Early Sources of Scottish History*, 2 vols (Edinburgh: Oliver and Boyd).

Anderson, M.O. (ed.) 2011 *Kings and Kingship in Early Scotland* (Edinburgh: John Donald).

Cary, E. (ed.) 1927 *Dio's Roman History*, vol. IX (London: Heinemann).

Colgrave, B. and Mynors, R.A.B. (eds and trans.) 1969 *Bede's Ecclesiastical History of the English People* (Oxford: The Clarendon Press).

Dobbs, M.E. (ed. and trans.) 1923 'The history of the descendants of Ir', *Zeitschrift für celtische Philologie* 14 (1923), pp. 44–144.

Hood, A.B.E. (ed. and trans.) 1978 *St. Patrick: His Writings and Muirchu's Life* (London and Chichester: Phillimore).

Ireland, S. (trans.) 1986 *Roman Britain: A Sourcebook* (London: Routledge).

Mac Airt, S. and Mac Niocaill, G. (eds and trans.) 1983 *The Annals of Ulster (To A.D. 1131) Part I Text and Translation* (Dublin: Dublin Institute for Advanced Studies).

Nixon, C.E.V. and Rodgers, B.S. (trans.) 1994 *In Praise of Later Roman Emperors: The Panegyrici Latini* (Oxford: University of California Press).

Rolfe, J.C. (ed.) 1972 *Ammianus Marcellinus*, vol. III (London: Heinemann).

Sharpe, R. (trans.) 1995 *Adomnán of Iona: Life of St Columba* (Harmondsworth: Penguin Books).

Stokes, W. (ed. and trans.) 1905 *Félire Óengusso Céli Dé. The Martyrology of Oengus the Culdee* (London: Henry Bradshaw Society; reprinted 1984, Dublin: Dublin Institute for Advanced Studies).

Webb, J.F. (trans) 2004 'Life of Wilfrid', in Webb. J.F. and Farmer, D.H. (eds), *The Age of Bede*, revised edition (London: Penguin), pp. 105–84.

Winterbottom, M. (ed. and trans.) 1978 *Gildas: On the Ruin of Britain and other Writings* (London and Chichester: Phillimore).

Secondary sources

Ahlqvist, A. 1982 *The Early Irish Linguist: An Edition of the Canonical Part of the Auraicept na nÉces* (Helsinki: Societas Scientiarum Fennica).

Alcock, L. 1972 *'By South Cadbury is that Camelot . . .': The Excavation of Cadbury Castle 1966–70* (London: Thames and Hudson).

Alcock, L. 1981 'Early Historic fortifications in Scotland', in G. Guilbert (ed.), *Hillfort Studies: Essays for A.H.A. Hogg* (Leicester: Leicester University Press), pp. 150–80.

Alcock, L. 1988 'The activities of potentates in Celtic Britain, AD 500–800: a positivist approach', in S.T. Driscoll and M.R. Nieke (eds), *Power and Politics in Early Medieval Britain and Ireland* (Edinburgh: Edinburgh University Press), pp. 22–46.

Alcock, L. 1996 'Ur-symbols in the pictograph-system of the Picts', *Pictish Arts Society Journal* 9, pp. 2–5.

Alcock, L. 2003 *Kings and Warriors, Craftsmen and Priests in Northern Britain AD 550–850* (Edinburgh: Society of Antiquaries of Scotland).

Alcock, L. and Alcock, E.A. 1990 'Reconnaissance excavations on Early Historic fortifications other royal sites Scotland, 1974–84: excavations at Alt Clut, Clyde Rock, Strathclyde, 1974–75', *Proceedings of the Society of Antiquaries of Scotland* 120, pp. 95–149.

Alcock, L. and Alcock, E.A. 1992 'Reconnaissance excavations on Early Historic fortifications and other royal sites in Scotland, 1974–84; 5: A, Excavations and other fieldwork at Forteviot, Perthshire, 1981; B, Excavations at Urquhart Castle, Inverness-shire, 1983; C, Excavations at Dunnottar, Kincardineshire, 1984', *Proceedings of the Society of Antiquaries of Scotland* 122, pp. 215–287.

Alcock, L., Alcock, E.A. and Driscoll, S.T. 1989 'Reconnaissance excavations on Early Historic fortifications and other royal sites in Scotland, 1974–84; 3: Excavations at Dundurn, Strathearn, Perthshire, 1976–77', *Proceedings of the Society of Antiquaries of Scotland* 119, pp. 189–226.

Aldhouse-Green, M. 2004 *An Archaeology of Images: Iconology and cosmology in Iron Age and Roman Europe* (London: Routledge).

Alexander, D. 2000 'Dell Farm, Whitebridge, Highland (Boleskine and Abertarff parish), barrow', *Discovery and Excavation in Scotland* 1, p. 49.

Alexander, D. 2005 'Redcastle, Lunan Bay, Angus: the excavation of an Iron Age timber lined souterrain and a Pictish barrow cemetery', *Proceedings of the Society of Antiquaries of Scotland* 135, pp. 41–118.

Allen, J.R. and Anderson, J. 1903, reprinted 1993. *The Early Christian Monuments of Scotland*, vols. 1 and 2 (Balgavies: The Pinkfoot Press).

Andrén, A., Jennbert, K. and Raudvere, C. 2006 'Old Norse religion: some problems and prospects', in A. Andrén, K. Jennbert and C. Raudvere (eds) *Old Norse Religion in Long-Term Perspectives: Origins, Changes and Interactions* (Lund: Nordic Academic Press), pp. 11–16.

Armit, I. and Ginn, V. 2007 'Beyond the grave: human remains from domestic contexts in Atlantic Scotland', *Proceedings of the Prehistoric Society* 73, pp. 115–36.

Armit, I., Schulting, R., Knüsel, C.J. and Shepherd, I.A.G. 2011 'Death, decapitation and display? The Bronze Age and Iron Age human remains from the Sculptor's Cave, Covesea, north-east Scotland', *Proceedings of the Prehistoric Society* 77, pp. 251–78.

Atkinson, D. 2006 *Mither Tap Fort, Bennachie, Aberdeenshire: Results of an Archaeological Watching Brief*, Unpublished Data Structure Report (Edinburgh: Headland Archaeology).

Atkinson, D. 2007 'Mither Tap, Bennachie, Aberdeenshire (Oyne parish), watching brief, radiocarbon dating' *Discovery and Excavation in Scotland* 8, p. 28.

Baines, J. 1995 'Communication and display: the integration of early Egyptian art and writing', *Antiquity* 63, pp. 471–82.

Barnes, M. P. 2012 *Runes: A Handbook* (Woodbridge: Boydell Press).

Barrett, J.C. 1988 'The living, the dead, and the ancestors: Neolithic and early Bronze Age mortuary practices', in J.C. Barrett and I. Kinnes (eds), *The Archaeology of Context in the Neolithic and Early Bronze Age: Recent Trends* (Sheffield: Sheffield University Department of Archaeology and Prehistory), pp. 30–41.

Barrett, J.C. 1994 *Fragments from Antiquity: An Archaeology of Social Life in Britain, 2900–1200 BC* (Oxford: Blackwell).

Bassett, S. 1989 'In search of the origins of the Anglo-Saxon kingdoms', in S. Bassett (ed.), *The Origins of Anglo-Saxon Kingdoms* (London and New York: Leicester University Press), pp. 3–27.

Bell, C. 1992 *Ritual Theory, Ritual Practice* (Oxford: Oxford University Press).

Bhreathnach, E. 2014 *Ireland in the Medieval World, AD 400–1000: Landscape, Kinship and Religion* (Dublin: Four Courts Press).

Bigelow, G. F. 1984 'Two kerbed cairns from Sandwick, Unst, Shetland', in Friell and Watson 1984, pp. 115–29.

Blackwell, A. 2012 'Individuals', in Clarke *et al.* 2012, pp. 3–68.

Blackwell, A. and Goldberg, M. in press 'Widening the context of the Norrie's Law hoard', in A. Blackwell (ed.) *Scotland in Early Medieval Europe* (Edinburgh: Society of Antiquaries of Scotland).

Blackwell, A., Goldberg, M. and Hunter, F. 2017 *Scotland's Early Silver* (Edinburgh: National Museums Scotland).

Blair, J. 1995 'Anglo-Saxon shrines and their prototypes', *Anglo-Saxon Studies in Archaeology and History* 38, pp. 1–28.

Bland, R., Moorhead, S. and Walton, P. 2013 'Finds of late Roman silver coins from Britain: the contribution of the Portable Antiquities Scheme', in Hunter and Painter 2013, pp. 117–66.

Bourke, C. 1983 'The hand-bells of the early Scottish church', *Proceedings of the Society of Antiquaries of Scotland* 113, pp. 464–68.

Bradley, J. 2011 'An early medieval crannog at Moynagh Lough, Co. Meath', in C. Corlett and M. Potterton (eds), *Settlement in Early Medieval Ireland in the Light of Recent Archaeological Excavations*, Research Papers in Irish Archaeology 3 (Dublin: Wordwell), pp. 11–34.

Bradley, R. 1987 'Time regained: the creation of continuity', *Journal of the British Archaeological Association* 140, pp. 1–17.

Bradley, R. 2000 *The Good Stones: A New Investigation of the Clava Cairns* (Edinburgh: Society of Antiquaries of Scotland).

Bradley, R. 2007 *The Prehistory of Britain and Ireland* (Cambridge: Cambridge University Press).

Brennan, N. and Hamerow, H. 2015 'An Anglo-Saxon great hall complex at Sutton Courtenay/Drayton, Oxfordshire: a royal centre of early Wessex?', *The Archaeological Journal* 172, pp. 325–50.

Bronk Ramsey, C. 1995 'Radiocarbon calibration and analysis of stratigraphy: the OxCal program', *Radiocarbon* 37, pp. 425–30.

Bronk Ramsey, C. 1998 'Probability and dating', *Radiocarbon* 40:1, pp. 461–74.

Bronk Ramsey, C. 2001 'Development of the radiocarbon calibration program', *Radiocarbon* 43, pp. 355–63.

Bronk Ramsey, C. 2009 'Bayesian analysis of radiocarbon dates', *Radiocarbon* 51:1, pp. 337–60.

Brookes, S. and Reynolds, A. 2011 'The origins of political order and the Anglo-Saxon state', *Archaeology International* 13/14, pp. 84–93.

Broun, D. 1998 'Pictish kings 761–839: integration with Dál Riata or separate development?', in S.M. Foster (ed.), *The St Andrews Sarcophagus and its International Connections* (Dublin: Four Courts Press), pp. 71–83.

Broun, D. 2007 *Scottish Independence and the Idea of Britain from the Picts to Alexander III* (Edinburgh: Edinburgh University Press).

Broun, D. 2008 'The property records in the Book of Deer as a source for early Scottish society', in Forsyth 2008a, pp. 313–60.

Brundle, A., Home Lorimer, D. and Ritchie, A. 2003 'Buckquoy revisited', in Downes and Ritchie 2003, pp. 95–104.

Buck, C.E., Cavanagh, W.G., and Litton, C. D. 1996 *Bayesian Approach to Interpreting Archaeological Data* (Chichester: John Wiley & Sons, Ltd).

Byrne, F.J. 1973 *Irish Kings and High-Kings* (London: B.T. Batsford).

Cameron, K. 1995 'Kinneddar archaeological field evaluation, Lossiemouth, Moray District', unpublished report: CFA Archaeology Data Structure Report No. 243.

Campbell, E. 1996 'Trade in the Dark Age West: a peripheral activity?', in B. Crawford (ed.), *Scotland in Dark Age Britain* (St Andrews: Scottish Cultural Press), pp. 79–91.

Campbell, E. 2001 'Were the Scots Irish?', *Antiquity* 75, pp. 285–92.

Campbell, E. 2007 *Continental and Mediterranean Imports to Atlantic Britain and Ireland, AD 400–800* (York: Council for British Archaeology Research Report 157).

Campbell, E. and Maldonado, A. forthcoming 'The Pictish cemetery and other features', in E. Campbell and S.T. Driscoll (eds), *Royal Forteviot: Forteviot in the 1st and 2nd Millennia*, Council for British Archaeology Research Report.

Carver, M. 1999 *Surviving in Symbols: A Visit to the Pictish Nation* (Edinburgh: Birlinn).

Carver, M. 2002 'Reflections on the meaning of Anglo-Saxon barrows', in Lucy and Reynolds 2002, pp. 132–43.

Carver, M. 2005 *Sutton Hoo: A Seventh-Century Princely Burial Ground and its Context* (London: British Museum Press).

Carver, M. 2008 *Post-Pictish Problems: The Moray Firthlands in the 9th–11th Centuries* (Rosemarkie: Groam House).

Carver, M. 2011 'Lost, found, repossessed or argued away – the case of the Picts', *Antiquity* 85, pp. 1479–83.

Carver, M. 2016a *Portmahomack: Monastery of the Picts*, 2nd edition (Edinburgh: Edinburgh University Press).

Carver, M. 2016b. 'Ideological Transitions in Pictland', in Flechner and Ní Mhaonaigh 2016a, pp. 305–20.

Carver, M., Barrett, J., Downes, J. and Hooper, J. 2012, 'Pictish byre houses at Pitcarmick and their landscape: Investigations 1993–5', *Proceedings of the Society of Antiquaries of Scotland* 142, pp. 145–200.

Carver, M., Garner-Lahire, J. and Spall, C. 2016 *Portmahomack on Tarbat Ness: Changing Ideologies in North-East Scotland, Sixth to Sixteenth Century AD* (Edinburgh: Society of Antiquaries of Scotland).

Charles-Edwards, T.M. 1993 *Early Irish and Welsh Kinship* (Oxford: Clarendon Press).

Charles-Edwards, T.M. 2000 *Early Christian Ireland* (Cambridge: Cambridge University Press).

Charles-Edwards, T.M. 2008 'Picts and Scots. A review of Alex Woolf, *From Pictland to Alba 789–1070*', *The Innes Review* 59, pp. 168–88.

Charles-Edwards, T.M. 2013 *Wales and the Britons, 350–1064* (Oxford: Oxford University Press).

Cherry, J.F. 1978 'Generalisation and the archaeology of the state', in D. Green, C. Haselgrove and M. Spriggs (eds), *Social Organisation and Settlement* (Oxford: British Archaeological Reports International Series 47), pp. 411–37.

Clancy, T.O. 2008 'Deer and the early church in North-Eastern Scotland', in Forsyth 2008a, 363–97.

Clancy, T.O. 2010 'Atholl, Banff, Earn and Elgin: "New Irelands" in the east revisited', in W. McLeod, A. Burnyeat, D.U. Stiùbhart, T. Clancy and R. Ó Maolalaigh (eds), *Bile ós Chrannaibh: A Festschrift for William Gillies* (Ceann Drochaid: Clann Tuirc), pp. 79–102.

Clarke, D.V. 2007 'Reading the multiple lives of Pictish symbol stones', *Medieval Archaeology* 51, pp. 19–39.

Clarke, D.V. 2012 'Communities', in Clarke *et al.* 2012, pp. 69–140.

Clarke, D.V. and Heald, A. 2008 'A new date for "Pictish" symbols', *Medieval Archaeology* 52:1, pp. 291–310.

Clarke, D.V., Blackwell, A. and Goldberg, M. 2012 *Early Medieval Scotland: Individuals, Communities and Ideas* (Edinburgh: National Museum of Scotland).

Close-Brooks, J. 1980 'Excavations in the Dairy Park, Dunrobin,

Sutherland, 1977', *Proceedings of the Society of Antiquaries of Scotland* 110, pp. 328–45.

Close-Brooks, J. 1986 'Excavations at Clatchard Craig, Fife', *Proceedings of the Society of Antiquaries of Scotland* 116, pp. 117–184.

Collins, R. 2013 'Soldiers to warriors: renegotiating the Roman frontier in the fifth century', in Hunter and Painter 2013, pp. 29–44.

Cook, M.J. 2003 'Grantown Road, Forres (Forres parish)', *Discovery and Excavation in Scotland* 4, p. 96.

Cook, M.J. 2010 'New light on oblong forts: excavations at Dunnideer, Aberdeenshire', *Proceedings of the Society of Antiquaries of Scotland* 140, pp. 79–91.

Cook, M.J. 2011a 'Maiden Castle, Insch, Aberdeenshire: choice and architecture in Pictland', *Tayside and Fife Archaeological Journal* 17, pp. 25–35.

Cook, M.J. 2011b 'New evidence for the activities of Pictish potentates in Aberdeenshire: the hillforts of Strathdon', *Proceedings of the Society of Antiquaries of Scotland* 141, pp. 207–31.

Cook, M.J. and Dunbar, L. 2008 *Rituals, Roundhouses and Romans: Excavations at Kintore, Aberdeenshire, 2000–2006* (Edinburgh: Scottish Trust for Archaeological Research).

Cramond, W. 1887 'The stone circles at Ley: excursion to Deskford', *Transactions of the Banffshire Field Club* 1887, pp. 92–93.

Crawford, B.E. 2011 'F.T. Wainwright and *The Problem of the Picts*', in Driscoll *et al.* 2011, pp. 3–14.

Crawford, B.E. and Taylor, S. 2003 'The Southern Frontier of Norse Settlement in North Scotland', *Northern Scotland* 23, pp. 1–76.

Curle, A.O. 1923 *The Treasure at Traprain* (Glasgow: Maclehose, Jackson & Co).

Cusack, C. M. 1999 *The Rise of Christianity in Northern Europe, 300–1000* (London: Cassell).

Davies, W. and Flechner, R. 2016 'Conversion to Christianity and economic change: consequence or coincidence?', in Flechner and Ní Mhaonaigh 2016a, pp. 377–96.

Diack, F.C. 1944 *The Inscriptions of Pictland* (Aberdeen: Spalding Club).

Dickinson, T.M. 2011 'Overview: Mortuary ritual', in Hamerow *et al.* 2011, pp. 221–37.

Dickinson, T.M. and Griffiths, D. (eds) 1999 *The Making of Kingdoms*, Anglo-Saxon Studies in Archaeology and History 10 (Oxford: Oxford University Press).

Dobat, A.S. 2006 'The king and his cult: the axe-hammer from Sutton Hoo and its implications for the concept of sacral leadership in early medieval Europe', *Antiquity* 80, pp. 880–93.

Dobbs, M.E. 1949 'Cé: the Pictish name of a district in eastern Scotland', *Scottish Gaelic Studies* 6, pp. 137–38.

Doherty, C. 1985 'The monastic towns in early medieval Ireland', in P. Ní Chatháin and M. Richter (eds), *Ireland and Europe: The Early Church* (Stuttgart: Klett-Cotta), pp. 89–101.

Downes, J. and Ritchie, A. (eds) 2003 *Sea Change: Orkney and Northern Europe in the Later Iron Age AD 300–800* (Balgavies: Pinkfoot Press).

Dransart, P. 2001 'Two shrine fragments from Kineddar, Moray', in M. Redknap, N. Edwards, S. Youngs, A. Lane and J. Knight (eds) *Pattern and Purpose in Insular Art* (Oxford: Oxbow Books), pp. 233–40.

Dransart, P. 2016 'Bishop's palaces in the medieval dioceses of Aberdeen and Moray', in J. Geddes (ed.), *Medieval Art, Architecture and Archaeology in the Dioceses of Aberdeen and Moray*, British Archaeological Association Conference Transactions 40 (Abingdon: Routledge), pp. 58–81.

Driscoll, S.T. 1988 'Power and authority in Early Historic Scotland: Pictish symbol stones and other documents', in J. Gledhill, B. Bender and M. Larsen (eds) *State and Society: The Emergence and Development of Social Hierarchy and Political Centralization* (London: Taylor & Francis), pp. 215–36.

Driscoll, S.T. 1998a 'Picts and prehistory: cultural resource management in early medieval Scotland', *World Archaeology* 30:1, pp. 142–58.

Driscoll, S.T. 1998b 'Political discourse and the growth of Christian ceremonialism in Pictland, the place of the St Andrews Sarcophagus', in S.M. Foster (ed.) *St Andrews Sarcophagus: A Pictish Masterpiece and its International Connections* (Dublin: Four Courts Press), pp. 168–78.

Driscoll, S.T. 2011 'Pictish archaeology: persistent problems and structural solutions', in Driscoll *et al.* 2011, pp. 245–80.

Driscoll, S.T., Hall, M. and Geddes, J. (eds) 2011 *Pictish Progress. New Studies on Northern Britain in the Early Middle Ages*, The Northern World 50 (Leiden: Brill).

Dumville, D.N. 1996 'Britain and Ireland in *Táin Bó Fráich*', *Études Celtiques* 32, pp. 175–87.

Dumville, D.N. with Abrams, L., Charles-Edwards, T.M., Corrêa, A., Dark, K.R., Maund, K.L. and Orchard, A.P.McD. 1993 *Saint Patrick. A.D. 493–1993* (Woodbridge: Boydell).

Dunbar, L. 2012 'Greshop Farm cropmark (Site 13), Forres (River Findhorn and Pilmuir) FAS, topsoil strip, evaluation and excavation: data structure report', unpublished report, AOC Archaeology.

Dunbar, L. and Maldonado, A. 2012 'A long cist cemetery near Auchterforfar Farm, Forfar, Angus: Christian or pre-Christian?', *Tayside and Fife Archaeological Journal* 18, pp. 63–80.

Dyhrfjeld-Johnsen, M. 2013 'Danish Hacksilver hoards: a status report', in Hunter and Painter 2013, pp. 321–38.

Earl of Southesk 1893 *Origins of Pictish Symbolism with Notes on the Sun Boar and a New Reading of the Newton Inscriptions* (Edinburgh: David Douglas).

Edwards, K.J. and Ralston, I.B.M. 1978 'New dating and environmental evidence from Burghead Fort, Moray', *Proceedings of the Society of Antiquaries of Scotland* 109, pp. 202–10.

Edwards, N. (ed.) 2009 *The Archaeology of the Early Medieval Celtic Churches*, Society for Medieval Archaeology Monograph 29 (Leeds: Maney).

Elliott, T.G. 1983 *Ammianus Marcellinus and Fourth Century History* (Toronto: Samuel Stevens).

Enright, M.J. 1982 'The Sutton Hoo whetstone sceptre: a study in iconography and cultural milieu', *Anglo-Saxon England* 11, pp. 119–34.

Etchingham, C. 1999 *Church Organisation in Ireland A.D. 650 to 1000* (Maynooth: Laigin Publications).

Evans, N. 2008 'Royal succession and kingship among the Picts', *The Innes Review* 59:1, pp. 1–48.

Evans, N. 2011 'Ideology, literacy, and matriliny: approaches to medieval texts on the Pictish past', in Driscoll *et al.* 2011, pp. 45–65.

Evans, N. 2013 'Circin and Mag Gerginn: Pictish territories in Irish and Scottish sources', *Cambrian Medieval Celtic Studies* 66, pp. 1–36.

Evans, N. 2014 *A Historical Introduction to the Northern Picts* (Aberdeen: Tarbat Discovery Centre/University of Aberdeen).

Evans-Pritchard, E.E. 1966 'The divine kingship of the Shilluck of the Nilotic Sudan' (Frazer Lecture 1948), in E.E. Evans-Pritchard, *Social Anthropology and Other Essays*. (New York: Faber and Faber).

Feachem, R.W. 1955 'Fortifications', in Wainwright 1955a, pp. 66–86.

Findell, M. 2014 *Runes* (London: British Museum).

Fitzpatrick, A. 2007 'Druids: towards an archaeology', in C. Gosden, H. Hamerow, P. de Jersey and G. Lock (eds) *Communities and Connections: Essays in Honour of Barry Cunliffe* (Oxford: Oxford University Press) pp. 287–315.

Fitzpatrick, E. 2004 *Royal Inauguration in Gaelic Ireland c. 1100–1600: A Cultural Landscape Study* (Woodbridge: Boydell).

Flechner, R. and Ní Mhaonaigh, M. (eds) 2016a *The Introduction of Christianity into the Early Medieval Insular World. Converting the Isles*, vol. 1 (Turnhout: Brepols).

Forsyth, K. 1997a *Language in Pictland: The Case Against 'non-Indo-European Pictish'* (Utrecht: Nodus).

Forsyth, K. 1997b 'Some thoughts on Pictish symbols as a formal writing system', in D. Henry (ed.) *The Worm, the Germ and the Thorn* (Balgavies: The Pinkfoot Press), pp. 85–98.

Forsyth, K. 1998 'Literacy in Pictland', in H. Pryce (ed.) *Literacy in Celtic Societies* (Cambridge: Cambridge University Press), pp. 39–61.

Forsyth, K., 2000, with an appendix by J.T. Koch, 'Evidence of a lost Pictish source in the *Historia Regum Anglorum* of Symeon of Durham', in Taylor 2000, pp. 19–34.

Forsyth, K. (ed.) 2008a *Studies on the Book of Deer* (Dublin: Four Courts Press).

Forsyth, K. 2008b 'The Stones of Deer', in Forsyth 2008a, pp. 313–60.

Forsyth, K., Brown, D. and Clancy, T. 2008 'The property records: text and translation', in Forsyth 2008a, pp. 131–44.

Foster, S.M. 1996. *Picts, Gaels and Scots* (London: Batsford).

Foster, S.M. 2014, *Picts, Gaels and Scots*, revised edition (Edinburgh: Birlinn).

Foster, S.M. 2015 'Physical evidence for the early church in Scotland', in P. S. Barnwell (ed.) *Places of Worship in Britain and Ireland, 300–950* (Donnington: Paul Watkins Publishing), pp. 68–91.

Fraser, I.A. 1995 'Norse settlement on the north-west seaboard', in B.E. Crawford (ed.) *Scandinavian Settlement in Northern Britain* (London: Leicester University Press), pp. 92–107.

Fraser, I.A. and Halliday, S. 2011 'The early medieval landscape of Donside, Aberdeenshire', in Driscoll *et al.* 2011, pp. 307–34.

Fraser, J.E. 2009a *From Caledonia to Pictland: Scotland to 795* (Edinburgh: Edinburgh University Press).

Fraser, J.E. 2009b 'Rochester, Hexham and Cennrígmonaid: the movements of St Andrew in Britain, 604–747', in S. Boardman, J.R. Davies and E. Williamson (eds) *Saints' Cults in the Celtic World* (Woodbridge: Boydell), pp. 1–17.

Fraser, J.E. 2011 'From ancient Scythia to *The Problem of the Picts*: thoughts on the quest for Pictish origins', in Driscoll *et al.* 2011, pp. 15–43.

Friell, J.G.P. and Watson, W.G. (eds) 1984 *Pictish Studies: Settlement, Burial and Art in Dark Age Northern Britain* (Oxford: British Archaeological Reports British Series 125).

Fulford, M., Handley, M. and Clarke, A. 2000 'An early date for Ogam: the Silchester Ogam stone rehabilitated' *Medieval Archaeology* 44:1, pp. 1–23.

Gammeltoft, P. 2001 *The Place-Name Element* bólstaðr *in the North Atlantic Area* (Copenhagen: C. A. Reitzel).

Gavin, F. 2013 'Insular military-style silver pins in late Iron Age Ireland', in Hunter and Painter 2013, pp. 427–41.

Geake, H. 1992 'Burial practice in seventh- and eighth-century England', in M. Carver (ed.) *The Age of Sutton Hoo: The Seventh Century in North-Western England* (Suffolk: Boydell), pp. 83–94.

Geddes, J., Murray, H.K. and Murray, J.C. 2015 'Tullich, Aberdeenshire: a reappraisal of an early ecclesiastical site and its carved stones in the light of recent excavations', *Proceedings of the Society of Antiquaries of Scotland* 145, pp. 229–81.

Gibson, C. and Stevens, C. 2007 'Iron Age and Pictish activity at Wemyss Caves, Fife', *Tayside and Fife Archaeological Journal* 13: 91–9.

Gleeson, P. 2012 'Constructing kingship in early medieval Ireland: power, place and ideology', *Medieval Archaeology* 56, pp. 1–33.

Gleeson, P. 2014 'Landscapes of Kingship in Early Medieval Ireland, AD 400–1100', unpublished PhD thesis, University College Cork.

Gleeson, P. 2015 'Kingdoms, communities, and Óenaig: Irish assembly practices in their north-west European context', *Journal of the North Atlantic* 8, pp. 33–51.

Gleeson P. and Carty N. 2013 'Kingship, violence and Loch Dá Gabhor: royal landscapes and the production of authority in early medieval Brega', *Ríocht na Midhe* 24, pp. 29–72.

Goldberg, M. 2012 'Ideas and ideology', in Clarke *et al.* 2012, pp. 141–204.

Goldberg, M. 2015 'At the western edge of the Christian world, c. AD600–90', in J. Farley and F. Hunter (eds) *Celts: Art and Identity* (London: British Museum/National Museums Scotland), pp. 172–205.

Goldberg, M. forthcoming 'Conventions and carving: a relative chronology for the Pictish symbol system', *Medieval Archaeology*.

Goldberg, M. and Blackwell, A. 2013 'The different histories of the Norrie's Law hoard', in J. Hawkes (ed.) *Making Histories: Proceedings of the Sixth International Insular Arts Conference, York 2011* (Donington: Shaun Tyas), pp. 326–38.

Gondek, M. 2006 'Investing in sculpture: power in Early Historic Scotland', *Medieval Archaeology* 50, pp. 105–42.

Gondek, M. 2010 'Constructing sacred space – soil, stone, water and symbols: early medieval carved stone monuments from Tillytarmont, Aberdeenshire', in A. George *et al.* (eds), *Early Medieval Enquiries* (Bristol: Clifton Antiquarian Club), pp. 318–33.

Gondek, M. 2015 'Building blocks: structural contexts and carved stones', in H. Williams, J. Kirton and M. Gondek (eds) *Early Medieval Stone Monuments: Materiality, Biography, Landscape* (Woodbridge: Boydell and Brewer), pp. 87–112.

Goody, J. 1968 'Introduction', in J. Goody (ed.) *Literacy in Traditional Societies* (Cambridge: Cambridge University Press), pp. 1–26.

Graham, B.J. 1987 'Urban genesis in early medieval Ireland', *Journal of Historical Geography* 13 (1), pp. 3–16.

Graham-Campbell, J. 1991 'Norrie's Law, Fife: on the nature and dating of the silver hoard', *Proceedings of the Society of Antiquaries of Scotland* 121, pp. 241–59.

Grant, A. 1993. 'Thanes and thanages, from the eleventh to fourteenth centuries', in A. Grant and K. Stringer (eds) *Medieval Scotland: Crown, Lordship and Community: Essays Presented to G.W.S. Barrow* (Edinburgh: Edinburgh University Press), pp. 39–81.

Grant, A. 2000 'The construction of the early Scottish state', in J.R. Maddicott and D.M. Palliser (eds) *The Medieval State: Essays Presented to James Campbell* (London and Rio Grande: Hambledon Press), pp. 47–71.

Grant, A. 2005 'The province of Ross and the kingdom of Alba', in E.J. Cowan and R.A. McDonald (eds) *Alba: Celtic Scotland in the Middle Ages* (Edinburgh: John Donald), pp. 88–126.

Gregory, R.A. and Jones, G.D.B. 2001 'Survey and excavation at Tarradale, Highland', *Proceedings of the Society of Antiquaries of Scotland* 131, pp. 241–66.

Greig, J.C. 1970 'Excavations at Castle Point, Troup, Banffshire', *Aberdeen University Review* 43, pp. 274–83.

Greig, J.C. 1971 'Excavations at Cullykhan, Castle Point, Troup, Banffshire', *Scottish Archaeological Forum* 3, pp. 15–21.

Greig, J.C. 1972 'Cullykhan', *Current Archaeology* 3:8, pp. 227–31.

Greig, J.C., Greig, M. and Ashmore, P. 2000 'Excavation of a cairn cemetery at Lundin Links, Fife in 1965–6', *Proceedings of the Society of Antiquaries of Scotland* 130, pp. 586–636.

Greig, M. 1994 'Sites identified while checking aerial photographs and maps held by GRC, or as the result of an aerial reconnaissance programme', *Discovery and Excavation in Scotland* 1994, p. 26.

Grigg, J. 2015 *The Philosopher King and the Pictish Nation* (Dublin: Four Courts Press).

Guest, P. 2013 'Siliquae from the Traprain Law treasure: silver and society in later fourth- and fifth-century Britain', in Hunter and Painter 2013, pp. 93–106.

Guggisberg, M. 2013 'Silver and donatives: non-coin exchange within and outside the Roman empire', in Hunter and Painter 2013, pp. 193–212.

Gwilt, A. and Haselgrove C. (eds) 1997 *Reconstructing Iron Age Societies: New Approaches to the British Iron Age* (Oxford: Oxbow).

Hamerow, H. 2012, *Rural Settlements and Society in Anglo-Saxon England* (Oxford: Oxford University Press).

Hamerow, H., Hinton, D.A. and Crawford, S. (eds) 2011 *The Oxford Handbook of Anglo-Saxon Archaeology* (Oxford: Oxford University Press).

Hamilton, D. and Kenney, J. 2015 'Multiple Bayesian modelling approaches to a suite of radiocarbon dates from ovens excavated at Ysgol yr Hendre, Caernarfon, North Wales', *Quaternary Geochronology* 25, pp. 72–82.

Hamilton, J.R.C. 1968 *Excavations at Clickhimin, Shetland* (Edinburgh: Her Majesty's Stationery Office).

Harding, D. 2004 *The Iron Age in Northern Britain: Celts and Romans, Natives and Invaders* (London: Routledge).

Harvey, A. 1987 'Early literacy in Ireland: the evidence from Ogam', *Cambridge Medieval Celtic Studies* 14, pp. 1–15.

Heather, P. 2009 *Empires and Barbarians: Migration, Development and the Birth of Empire* (London: Macmillan).

Hedeager, L. 2011 *Iron Age Myth and Materiality: An Archaeology of Scandinavia AD 400–1000* (London: Routledge).

Hencken, H.O'N. 1950 'Lagore Crannog: an Irish royal residence of the seventh to tenth centuries AD', *Proceedings of the Royal Irish Academy* 53, pp. 1–248.

Henderson, G. and Henderson, I. 2004 *The Art of the Picts: Sculpture and Metalwork in Early Medieval Scotland* (London: Thames and Hudson).

Henderson, I. 1958 'The origin centre of the Pictish symbol stones', *Proceedings of the Society of Antiquaries of Scotland* 91, pp. 44–60.

Henderson, I. 1967 *The Picts* (London: Thames and Hudson).

Henderson, I. 1971 'North Pictland', in Inverness Field Club, *The Dark Ages in the Highland: Ancient Peoples, Local History, Archaeology* (Inverness: Inverness Field Club), pp. 37–52.

Henderson, I. 1972 'The Picts of Aberdeenshire and their monuments', *The Archaeological Journal* 129, pp. 166–74.

Henderson, I. 1989 'The arts of late Celtic Britain (AD 600–900)', in B.

Ford (ed.) *The Cambridge Guide to the Arts in Britain*, vol.1: *Prehistoric, Roman and Early Medieval* (Cambridge: Cambridge University Press), pp. 207–19.

Henderson, I. 1998 '*Primus inter pares*: the St Andrews Sarcophagus and Pictish sculpture', in S.M. Foster (ed.) *The St Andrews Sarcophagus: A Pictish Masterpiece and Its International Connection*s (Dublin: Four Courts Press), pp. 97–168.

Henderson, J.A. 1907 *Aberdeenshire Epitaphs and Inscriptions: With Historical, Biographical, Genealogical, and Antiquarian Notes* (Aberdeen: Aberdeen Daily Journal Press).

Henning, J. 2009 'Revolution of relapse? Technology, agriculture and early medieval archaeology in Germanic central Europe', in G. Ausenda, P. Delogu and C. Wickham (eds), *The Lombards Before the Frankish Conquest: An Ethnographic Perspective* (Woodbridge: Boydell Press), pp. 149–73.

Henry, D. (ed.) 1997 *The Worm, the Germ and the Thorn: Pictish and Related Studies Presented to Isabel Henderson* (Balneaves: Pinkfoot Press).

Henshall, A.S. 1956 'A long cist cemetery at Parkburn sand pit, Lasswade, Midlothian', *Proceedings of the Society of Antiquaries of Scotland* 89, pp. 252–83.

Higham, N. 1993 *The Kingdom of Northumbria: A.D. 350–1100* (Dover, NH: A. Sutton).

Hingley, R. 1996 'Ancestors and identity in the later prehistory of Atlantic Scotland: the reuse and reinvention of Neolithic monuments and material culture', *World Archaeology* 28, pp. 231–43.

Hingley, R., Moore, H., Triscott, J. and Wilson, G. 1997 'The excavation of two later Iron Age homesteads at Aldclune, Blair Atholl, Perth and Kinross', *Proceedings of the Society of Antiquaries of Scotland* 127, pp. 407–66.

Hope-Taylor, B. 1977 *Yeavering: An Anglo-British-British Centre of Early Northumbria* (London: Her Majesty's Stationery Office).

Hughes, K. 1970, *Early Christianity in Pictland*, Jarrow Lecture 1970 (Jarrow: St Paul's Church). Reprinted in Hughes 1980, pp. 1–21.

Hughes, K. 1980 *Celtic Britain in the Early Middle Ages: Studies in Scottish and Welsh Sources*, Studies in Celtic History II, ed. D. Dumville (Woodbridge: Boydell).

Hunter, F. 2001 'The carnyx in Iron Age Europe', *Antiquaries Journal* 81, pp. 77–108.

Hunter, F. 2007a *Beyond the Edge of the Empire: Caledonians, Picts and Romans* (Rosemarkie: Groam House Museum).

Hunter, F. 2007b 'Silver for the barbarians: interpreting denarii hoards in north Britain and beyond', in R. Hingley and S. Wills (eds) *Roman Finds: Context and Theory* (Oxford: Oxbow), pp. 214–24.

Hunter, F. 2009 'Digging Birnie, 1998–2009: the story (so far) of an Iron Age power centre', in J. Trythall and B. Dalgarno (eds) *Beakers, Bones and Birnie* (Elgin: Elgin Museum), pp. 69–80.

Hunter, F. and Painter, K. (eds) 2013 *Late Roman Silver: The Traprain Treasure in Context* (Edinburgh: Society of Antiquaries of Scotland).

Hunter, F. and Ralston, I.B.M. (eds) 2015 *Scotland in Later Prehistoric Europe* (Edinburgh: Society of Antiquaries of Scotland).

Hunter, J., Bond, J.M. and Smith, A.N. 2007. *Investigations in Sanday, Orkney: Excavations at Pool, Sanday* (Kirkwall: Orcadian).

Innes, C. (ed.) 1837 *Registrum episcopatus Moraviensis* (Edinburgh: Bannatyne Club).

Innes, M. 1998 *Memory, Orality and Literacy in an Early Medieval Society* (Oxford: Oxford University Press).

Isaac, G.R. 2005 'Scotland', in J. de Hoz, E.R. Luján and P. Sims-Williams (eds) *New Approaches to Celtic Place-Names in Ptolemy's Geography* (Madrid: Ediciones Clásicas), pp. 189–214.

Jackson, A. 1984 *The Symbol Stones of Scotland: A Social Anthropological Resolution of the Problem of the Picts* (Stromness: The Orkney Press).

Jackson, K.H. 1950 'Notes on the Ogam inscriptions of southern Britain', in C. Fox and B. Dickins (eds) *The Early Cultures of Northwest Europe* (Cambridge: H.N. Chadwick Memorial Studies), pp. 197–213.

Jackson, K.H. 1953 *Language and History in Early Britain: A Chronological Survey of the Brittonic Languages 1st to 12th century AD* (Edinburgh: Edinburgh University Press).

Jackson, K.H. 1955 'The Pictish language', in Wainwright 1955a, pp. 129–60, 161–6, 173–6.

Johnston, G. 1999 'Cunningsburgh: Pictish power centre?', *New Shetlander* 208, pp. 15–20.

Kelly, F. 1988 *A Guide to Early Irish Law* (Dublin: Dublin Institute for Advanced Studies).

Keynes, S. 2001 'Mercia and Wessex in the ninth century', in M.P. Brown and C.A. Farr (eds) *Mercia* (Leicester: Continuum), pp. 310–28.

Laing, L. 1990 'The beginnings of "Dark Age" Celtic art', in A. Bammesberger and A. Wollman (eds) *Britain 400–600: Language and History* (Heidelberg: C. Winter), pp. 37–50.

Laing, L. and Laing, J. 1984 'The date and origin of the Pictish symbols', *Proceedings of the Society of Antiquaries of Scotland* 114, pp. 261–76.

Laing, L. and Laing, J. 1993 *The Picts and the Scots* (Stroud: Alan Sutton).

Lane, A. and Campbell, E. 2000 *Dunadd: An Early Dalriadic Capital* (Oxford: Oxbow).

Lane, P. 2001 'The archaeology of Christianity in global perspective', in T. Insoll (ed.) *Archaeology and World Religion* (London: Routledge), pp. 148–81.

Lee, R. 2010 'The use of information theory to determine the language character type of Pictish symbols', *Scottish Archaeological Journal* 32:2, pp. 137–76.

Lee, R., Jonathan, P. and Ziman, P. 2010 'Pictish symbols revealed as a written language through application of Shannon entropy', *Proceedings of the Royal Society* 10, pp. 1–16.

Logan, J. 1829, 'Observations on several monumental stones in the north of Scotland', *Archaeologia* 22, pp. 55–58.

Longley, D. 2009 'Early medieval burial in Wales', in Edwards 2009, pp. 105–34.

Lucy, S. and Reynolds, A. (eds) 2002 *Burial in Early Medieval England and Wales*, Society for Medieval Archaeology Monograph 17 (Leeds: Maney).

Mac Cana, P. 1980 *The Learned Tales of Medieval Ireland* (Dublin: Dublin Institute for Advanced Studies).

MacDonald, A. 1994 *Curadán, Boniface and the Early Church of Rosemarkie*, Groam House Lecture (Rosemarkie: Groam House Museum).

MacDonald, J. 1862 'Historical notes of the "Broch" or Burghead, in Moray, with an account of its antiquities', *Proceedings of the Society of Antiquaries of Scotland* 4, pp. 321–69.

Mack, A. 2007 *Symbols and Pictures: The Pictish Legacy in Stone* (Brechin: The Pinkfoot Press).

Macquarrie, A. (ed.) 2012 *Legends of the Scottish Saints: Readings, Hymns and Prayers for the Commemorations of Scottish Saints in the Aberdeen Breviary* with R. Butter and contributions by S. Taylor and G. Márkus (Dublin: Four Courts Press).

Maldonado, A. 2011 'What does early Christianity look like? Mortuary archaeology and conversion in Late Iron Age Scotland', *Scottish Archaeological Journal* 33, pp. 39–54.

Maldonado, A. 2013, 'Burial in early medieval Scotland: new questions', *Medieval Archaeology* 57, pp. 1–34.

Marzinzik, S. 2013 'The Coleraine treasure from Northern Ireland: a consideration of the fittings', in Hunter and Painter 2013, pp. 175–92.

Maxwell, G.S. 1978 'Air photography and the work of the Royal Commission for the Ancient and Historical Monuments of Scotland', *Aerial Archaeology* 2, pp. 37–45.

McGill, C. 2001 'Pottery', in Gregory and Jones 2001, pp. 255–58.

Miller, M. 1982 '"Matriliny by treaty": the Pictish foundation-legend', in D. Whitelock, R. McKitterick and D. Dumville (eds) *Ireland in Early Mediaeval Europe: Studies in Memory of Kathleen Hughes* (Cambridge: Cambridge University Press), pp. 133–61.

Mitchell, J. and Noble, G. 2017 'The monumental cemeteries of northern Pictland', *Medieval Archaeology* 61, pp. 1–40.

Mizoguchi, K. 1993 'Time in the reproduction of mortuary practices', *World Archaeology* 25, pp. 223–35.

Murray, D. and Ralston, I.B.M. 1997 'The excavation of a square-ditched barrow and other cropmarks at Boysack Mills, Inverkeilor, Angus', *Proceedings of the Society of Antiquaries of Scotland* 127, pp. 359–86.

Nash-Williams, V.E. 1950 *The Early Christian Monuments of Wales* (Cardiff: University of Wales).

Needham, S.T. 2001 'When expediency broaches ritual intention: the flow of metal between systemic and buried domains', *The Journal of the Royal Anthropological Institute* 7:2, pp. 275–98.

Neighbour, T., Knott, C., Bruce, M.F. and Kerr, N.W. 2000 'Excavation of two burials at Galson, Isle of Lewis, 1993 and 1996', *Proceedings of the Society of Antiquaries of Scotland* 130, pp. 559–84.

Newman, C. 2007, 'Procession and symbolism at Tara: analysis of Tech Midchuarta (the Banqueting Hall) in the context of the sacral campus', *Oxford Journal of Archaeology* 26:4, pp. 415–38.

Nicolaisen, W.F.H. 1993 'Names in the landscape of the Moray Firth', in W.D.H. Sellar (ed.) *Moray: Province and People* (Edinburgh: Scottish Society for Northern Studies), pp. 253–62.

Nicolaisen, W.F.H. 2001 *Scottish Place-Names*, revised edition (Edinburgh: John Donald).

Noble, G. and Gondek, M. 2011 'Symbol stones in context: excavations at Rhynie, an undocumented Pictish power centre of the 6th–7th centuries AD?', *Medieval Archaeology* 55, pp. 317–21.

Noble, G., Gondek, M., Campbell, E. and Cook, M. 2013 'Between prehistory and history: the archaeological detection of social change among the Picts', *Antiquity* 87, pp. 1136–50.

Noble, G., Goldberg, M., McPherson, A. and Sveinbjarnarson, O. 2016 '(Re)discovering the Gaulcross hoard', *Antiquity* 90, pp. 726–41.

Noble, G., Goldberg, M., and Hamilton, D. 2018 'The development of the Pictish symbol system: inscribing identity beyond the edges of empire', *Antiquity* 92, pp. 1329–48.

Noble, G., Gondek, M., Campbell, E., Evans, N., Hamilton, D., Ross, A., and Taylor, S. forthcoming 'A powerful place of Pictland: interdisciplinary perspectives on a post-Roman power centre', submitted to *Medieval Archaeology*.

O'Brien, E. 2009 'Pagan or Christian? Burial in Ireland during the 5th to 8th centuries AD', in Edwards 2009, pp. 135–54.

O'Brien, E. and Bhreathnach, E. 2011 'Irish boundary *ferta*, their physical manifestation and historical context', in F. Edmonds and P. Russell (eds) *Tome: Studies in Medieval Celtic History and Law in Honour of Thomas Charles-Edwards*, Studies in Celtic History 31 (Woodbridge: Boydell), pp. 53–64.

Ó Carragáin, T. 2010 *Churches in Early Medieval Ireland: Architecture, Ritual and Memory* (New Haven, CT: Yale University Press).

Ó Corráin, D. 1998 'Creating the past: the early Irish genealogical tradition', *Peritia* 12, pp. 177–208.

Odenstedt, B. 1990 *On the Origin and Early History of the Runic Script: Typology and Graphic Variation in the Older Futhark* (Stockholm: Almqvist and Wiksell).

O'Grady, O.J.T. 2014 'Judicial assembly sites in Scotland: archaeological and place-name evidence of the Scottish court hill', *Medieval Archaeology* 58, pp. 104–35.

Oram, R. 2007 'Capital tales or Burghead bull?', in S. Arbuthnot and K. Hollo (eds) *Fil súil ngais: A Grey Eye Looks Back: A Festschrift in Honour of Colm Ó Baoill* (Ceann Drochaid: Clann Tuirc), pp. 241–62.

Ó Riain, P. 2009 'The Metz Version of *Lebor Gabála Érenn*', in J. Carey (ed.) *Lebor Gabála Érenn: Textual History and Pseudohistory*, Subsidiary Series 20 (Dublin: Irish Texts Society), pp. 33–47.

Ó Riain, P. 2011 *A Dictionary of Irish Saints* (Dublin: Four Courts Press).

O'Sullivan, A., McCormick, F., Kerr, T.R. and Harney, L. 2014, *Early Medieval Ireland AD 400–1100: The Evidence from Archaeological Excavation* (Dublin: Royal Irish Academy Monograph).

Painter, K. 2013 'Hacksilver: a means of exchange', in Hunter and Painter 2013, pp. 215–42.

Papdopoulos, J.K. 2016 'The early history of the Greek alphabet: new evidence from Eretria and Methone', *Antiquity* 90, pp. 1238–1254.

Peteranna, M. and Birch, S. forthcoming. 'Storm Damage at Craig Phadrig Hillfort, Inverness: Results of the Emergency Archaeological Evaluation'.

Postgate, N., Wang, T. and Wilkinson, T. 1995 'The evidence for early writing: utilitarian or ceremonial?', *Antiquity* 69, pp. 459–80.

Rae, A. and Rae, V. 1953 'A bowl barrow at Pityoulish, in Strathspey', *Proceedings of the Society of Antiquaries of Scotland* 87, pp. 153–60.

Ralston, I.B.M. 1980, 'The Green Castle and the promontory forts of north-east Scotland' *Scottish Archaeological Forum* 10, pp. 27–40.

Ralston, I.B.M. 1987 'Portknockie: promontory forts and Pictish settlement in the North-East', in A. Small (ed.) *The Picts: A New Look at Old Problems* (Dundee: University of Dundee), pp. 15–26.

Ralston I.B.M. 2004 *The Hill-forts of Pictland since the Problem of the Picts* (Rosemarkie: Groam House Museum).

Ralston, I.B.M. and Inglis, J. 1984 *Foul Hordes: the Picts in the North-East and their background* (Anthropological Museum: University of Aberdeen).

Rau, A. 2013 'Where did the late empire end? Hacksilber and coins in continental and northern Barbaricum, *c* AD 340–500', in Hunter and Painter 2013, pp. 339–58.

RCAHMS 1978 *The Archaeological Sites and Monuments of the Lunan Valey, Montrose Basin, Angus District, Tayside Region* (Edinburgh: RCAHMS).

RCAHMS 1984 *The Archaeological Sites and Monuments of North Kincardine, Kincardine and Deeside District, Grampian Region* (Edinburgh: RCAHMS).

RCAHMS 2007 *In the Shadow of Bennachie: A Field Archaeology of Donside, Aberdeenshire* (Edinburgh: Society of Antiquaries of Scotland/ RCAHMS).

RCAHMS 2008 *The Pictish Symbol Stones of Scotland* (Edinburgh: RCAHMS).

Reimer, P.J., Bard, E., Bayliss, A., Beck, J.W., Blackwell, P.G., Bronk Ramsey, C., Buck, C.E., Cheng, H., Edwards, R.L., Friedrich, M., Grootes, P.M., Guilderson, T.P., Haflidason, H., Hajdas, I., Hatté, C., Heaton, T.J., Hoffmann, D.L., Hogg, A.G., Hughen, K.A., Kaiser, K.F., Kromer, B., Manning, S.W., Niu, M., Reimer, R.W., Richards, D.A., Scott, E.M., Southon, J.R., Staff, R.A., Turney, C.S.M. and van der Plicht, J. 2013

'IntCal13 and Marine13 radiocarbon age calibration curves 0–50,000 years cal BP', *Radiocarbon* 55, pp. 1869–87.

Rekdal, J.E. and Doherty, C. (eds) 2016 *Kings and Warriors in Early North-West Europe* (Dublin: Four Courts Press).

Reynolds, A. 2002 'Burials, boundaries and charters in Anglo-Saxon England: a reassessment', in Lucy and Reynolds 2002, pp. 171–94.

Ringtved, J. 1999 'The geography of power: south Scandinavia before the Danish kingdom', in Dickinson and Griffiths 1999, pp. 49–64.

Ritchie, A. 1989 *Picts* (Edinburgh: HMSO).

Ritchie, A. 1994 *Perceptions of the Picts: from Eumenius to John Buchan* (Rosemarkie: Groam House Museum).

Ritchie, A. 2003 'Paganism among the Picts and the conversion of Orkney', in Downes and Ritchie 2003, pp. 3–10.

Ritchie, A. 2011 'Cemeteries of platform cairns and long cists around Sinclair's Bay, Caithness', *Proceedings of the Society of Antiquaries of Scotland* 141, pp. 125–43.

Ritchie, J.N.G. 1976 'The Stones of Stenness, Orkney', *Proceedings of the Society of Antiquaries of Scotland* 107, pp. 1–60.

Rivet, A.L.F. and Smith, C. 1979, *The Place-Names of Roman Britain* (London: Batsford).

Ross, A. 1999 'Pictish matriliny?', *Northern Studies* 34, pp. 11–22.

Ross, A. 2006 'The Dabhach in Moray: a new look at an old tub', in A. Woolf (ed.) *Landscape and Environment in Dark Age Scotland* (St Andrews: St John's House Papers No 11), pp. 57–74.

Ross, A. 2011 *The Kings of Alba* c. *1000–*c. *1130* (Edinburgh: John Donald).

Ross, A. 2015 *Land Assessment and Lordship in Medieval Northern Scotland* (Turnhout: Brepols).

Samson, R. 1992 'The reinterpretation of the Pictish symbols', *Journal of the British Archaeological Association* 145, pp. 29–65.

Scott, I.A.G. 2005 'The bulls of Burghead and Allen's technique of illustration', in S. Foster and M. Cross (eds) *Able Minds and Practised Hands: Scotland's Early Medieval Sculpture in the 21st Century*, Society for Medieval Archaeology Monograph 23 (Leeds: Maney), pp. 215–20.

Scull, C. 2009 *Early Medieval (Late 5th – Early 8th Centuries AD) Cemeteries at Boss Hall and Buttermarket, Ipswich, Suffolk*, Society for Medieval Archaeology Monograph 27 (London: Society for Medieval Archaeology).

Sellar, W.D.H. 1985 'Warlords, holy men and matrilineal succession' (review article), *The Innes Review* 36, pp. 29–43.

Schot, R., Newman, C. and Bhreathnach, E. 2011 *Landscapes of Cult and Kingship* (Dublin: Four Courts Press).

Shepherd, I.A.G. 1986 *Grampian: Exploring Scotland's Heritage* (Edinburgh: HMSO).

Shepherd, I.A.G. 1993 'The Picts in Moray', in W.D.H. Sellar (ed.) *Moray: Province and People* (Edinburgh: Scottish Society for Northern Studies), pp. 75–90.

Shepherd, I.A.G. and Shepherd, A.N. 1978, 'An incised Pictish figure and a new symbol stone from Barflat, Rhynie, Gordon District', *Proceedings of the Society of Antiquaries of Scotland* 109, pp. 211–22.

Simpson, W.D. 1930 'Craig Castle and the Kirk of Auchindoir', *Proceedings of the Society of Antiquaries of Scotland* 64, pp. 48–96.

Small, A. 1969 'Burghead', *Scottish Archaeological Forum* 1, pp. 61–9.

Small, A. 1974 'Cairn o' Mount: a Pictish routeway', *The Deeside Field* 3:1, pp. 8–11.

Small, A. and Cottam, M.B. 1972 'Craig Phadrig', Department of Geography Occasional Paper 1 (Dundee: University of Dundee).

Smith, B. 2016 'Did the broch of Mousa have a roof? – and why not!', *The New Shetlander* 276, pp. 4–17.

Smyth, A.P. 1984 *Warlords and Holy Men: Scotland AD 80–1000* (Edinburgh: Edinburgh University Press).

Sproat, R. 2010 'Ancient symbols, computational linguistics, and the reviewing practices of the general science journals', *Computational Linguistics* 36(3), pp. 585–94.

Stevenson, J.B. 1984 'Garbeg and Whitebridge: two square-barrow cemeteries in Inverness-shire', in Friell and Watson 1984, pp. 145–50.

Stevenson, R.B.K. 1949 'The nuclear fort at Dalmahoy, Midlothian, and other Dark Age capitals', *Proceedings of the Society of Antiquaries of Scotland* 83, pp. 186–98.

Stevenson, R.B.K. 1955 'Pictish art', in Wainwright 1955a, pp. 97–128.

Stevenson, R. and Emery, J. 1964 'The Gaulcross hoard of Pictish silver', *Proceedings of the Society of Antiquaries of Scotland* 97, pp. 206–11.

Stewart, J. 1987 *Shetland Place-Names* (Lerwick: Shetland Library and Museum).

Stout, M. 1997 *The Irish Ringfort* (Dublin: Four Courts Press).

Strathern, M. 1988 *The Gender of the Gift: Problems with Women and Problems with Society in Melanesia* (Berkeley: University of California Press).

Stratigos, M. and Noble, G. 2014 'Crannogs, castles and lordly residences: new research and dating of crannogs in northeast Scotland', *Proceedings of the Society of Antiquaries of Scotland* 144, pp. 205–22.

Stuart, J. 1867 *Sculptured Stones of Scotland*, vol. 2 (Aberdeen: Spalding Club).

Stuiver, M. and Reimer, P.J. 1993 'Extended ^{14}C data base and revised CALIB 3.0 ^{14}C calibration program', *Radiocarbon* 35:1, pp. 215–30.

Sundqvist, O. 2002 *Freyr's Offspring: Rulers and Religion in Ancient Svea Society* (Uppsala: Acta Universitatis Upsaliensis).

Swift, C. 1997 *Ogam Stones and the Earliest Irish Christians* (Maynooth: Maynooth Monograph Series Minor 2).

Swift, C. 1998 'Forts and fields: a study of "monastic towns" in seventh and eighth century Ireland', *Journal of Irish Archaeology* 9, pp. 105–25.

Taylor, D.B. 1990 *Circular Homesteads in North-west Perthshire* (Dundee: Abertay Historical Society publication no. 29).

Taylor, S. 1996 'Place-names and the early Church in eastern Scotland', in
    B.E. Crawford (ed.) *Scotland in Dark Age Britain*, St John's House
    Papers No. 6 (St Andrews: Scottish Cultural Press), pp. 93–110.

Taylor, S. (ed.) 2000 *Kings, Clerics and Chronicles in Scotland, 500–1297:
    Essays in Honour of Marjorie Ogilvie Anderson on the Occasion of her
    Ninetieth Birthday* (Dublin: Four Courts Press).

Taylor, S. 2008 'The toponymic landscape of the Gaelic notes in the Book
    of Deer', in Forsyth 2008a, pp. 275–308.

Taylor, S. 2011 'Pictish place-names revisited', in Driscoll *et al.* 2011, pp.
    67–120.

Taylor, S. forthcoming *Fortrose, Fortriu and the place-names of northern
    Pictland* (Rosemarkie, Groam House lecture publications).

Taylor, S. with Márkus, G. 2012 *The Place-Names of Fife*, vol. 5
    (Donnington: Shaun Tyas).

Thomas, A. 1858 'Notice of sculptured stones found at "Dinnacair", a rock
    in the sea, near Stonehaven', *Proceedings of the Society of Antiquaries
    of Scotland* 3, pp. 69–75.

Thomas, C. 1961 'The animal art of the Scottish Iron Age and its origins',
    The Archaeological Journal 117, pp. 14–64.

Thomas, C. 1963 'The interpretation of the Pictish symbols', *The
    Archaeological Journal* 120, pp. 31–64.

Thomas, G. 2013 'Life before the minster: the social dynamics of monastic
    foundation at Anglo-Saxon Lyminge, Kent', *Antiquaries Journal* 93, pp.
    109–45.

Toolis, R. and Bowles, C. 2016 *The Lost Dark Age Kingdom of Rheged:
    The Discovery of a Royal Stronghold at Trusty's Hill, Galloway*
    (Oxford: Oxbow Books).

Turner, V. 1994 'The Mail stone: an incised Pictish figure from Mail,
    Cunningsburgh, Shetland', *Proceedings of the Society of Antiquaries of
    Scotland* 124, pp. 315–25.

Valante, M. 1998 'Reassessing the Irish monastic town', *Irish Historical
    Studies* 31, pp. 1–18.

Veitch, K. 1997 'The Columban Church in northern Britain, 664–717: a
    reassessment', *Proceedings of the Society of Antiquaries of Scotland* 17,
    pp. 627–47.

Wainwright, F.T. (ed.) 1955a *The Problem of the Picts* (Edinburgh: Nelson;
    reprinted 1980, Perth: The Melven Press).

Wainwright, F.T. 1955b 'Houses and graves', in Wainwright 1955a, pp.
    87–96.

Wainwright. F.T. 1955c 'The Picts and the problem', in Wainwright 1955a,
    pp. 1–53.

Walker, D.W. and Woodworth, M. 2015 *The Buildings of Scotland.
    Aberdeenshire: North and Moray* (London: Yale University Press).

Warner, R. 1988 'The archaeology of Early Historic kingship', in S. Driscoll
    and M. Nieke (eds) *Power and Politics in Early Medieval Britain and
    Ireland* (Edinburgh: Edinburgh University Press), pp. 47–68.

Warner, R. 2000 'Clogher: an archaeological window on early medieval

Tyrone and mid-Ulster', in C. Dillon and H. Jefferies (eds) *Tyrone: History and Society* (Dublin: Geography Publications), pp. 39–54.

Watkins, T. 1981 'Excavation of an Iron Age open settlement at Dalladies, Kincardineshire', *Proceedings of the Society of Antiquaries of Scotland* 110, pp. 122–64.

Watson, W.J. 1926 [2011] *The Celtic Place-names of Scotland* (Edinburgh: Birlinn).

Watt, M. 1999 'Kings or gods? Iconographic evidence for Scandinavian gold foil figures', in Dickinson and Griffiths 1999, pp. 173–83.

Wedderburn, L.M. and Grime, D. 1984 'The cairn cemetery at Garbeg, Drumnadrochit', in Friell and Watson 1984, pp. 151–68.

Welch, M. 2011 'The mid Saxon "Final Phase"', in Hamerow *et al.* 2011, pp. 266–87.

Whittle, A. 1997 *Sacred Mound Holy Rings: Silbury Hill and the West Kennet Palisade Enclosures: a Later Neolithic Complex in North Wiltshire* (Oxford: Oxbow Monograph 74).

Wickham, C. 2005 *Framing the Early Middle Ages: Europe and the Mediterranean, 400–800* (Oxford: Oxford University Press).

Wickham, C. 2016 'The comparative method and early medieval religious conversion', in Flechner and Ní Mhaonaigh 2016a, pp. 13–37.

Williams, H. 2007 'Depicting the dead: commemoration through cists, cairns and symbols in early medieval Britain', *Cambridge Archaeological Journal* 17:2, pp. 145–64.

Winlow, S. 2011 'A review of Pictish burial practices in Tayside and Fife', in Driscoll *et al.* 2011, pp. 335–50.

Woodham, A.A. 1975 'Tillytarmont cairn', *Discovery and Excavation in Scotland* 6.

Woolf, A. 1998 'Pictish matriliny reconsidered', *The Innes Review* 49, pp. 147–67.

Woolf, A. 2006 'Dún Nechtain, Fortriu and the geography of the Picts', *Scottish Historical Review* 85, pp. 182–201.

Woolf, A. 2007a 'The cult of Moluag, the See of Mortlach and Church organisation in northern Scotland in the eleventh and twelfth centuries', in S. Arbuthnot and K. Hollo (eds) *Fil súil ngais: A Grey Eye Looks Back: A Festschrift in Honour of Colm Ó Baoill* (Ceann Drochaid: Clann Tuirc), pp. 311–22.

Woolf, A. 2007b *From Pictland to Alba, 789–1070*, New Edinburgh History of Scotland 2 (Edinburgh: Edinburgh University Press).

Woolf, A. 2013, *The Churches of Pictavia*, Kathleen Hughes Memorial Lecture 11 (Cambridge: Department of Anglo-Saxon, Norse and Celtic).

Woolf, A. 2017 'On the Nature of the Picts', *Scottish Historical Review* 96:2, pp. 214–17.

Wormald, P. 1996 'The emergence of the *Regnum Scottorum*: a Carolingian hegemony?', in B.E. Crawford (ed.) *Scotland in Dark Age Britain*, St John's House Papers No. 6 (St Andrews: Scottish Cultural Press), pp. 131–60.

Yeoman, P.A. 1988 'Mottes in Northeast Scotland', *Scottish Archaeological Review* 5, pp. 125–33.

Young, H.W. 1890 'The ancient bath at Burghead, with remarks on its
    origin, as shown by existing baths of the same shape and design',
    Proceedings of the Society of Antiquaries of Scotland 24, pp. 147–56.
Young, H.W. 1891 'Notes on the ramparts of Burghead, as revealed by
    recent excavations', *Proceedings of the Society of Antiquaries of
    Scotland* 25,
    pp. 435–47.
Young, H.W. 1893 'Notes on further excavations at Burghead', *Proceedings
    of the Society of Antiquaries of Scotland* 27, pp. 86–91.
Youngs, S. (ed.) 1989 *The Work of Angels: Masterpieces of Celtic
    Metalwork, 6th–9th Centuries AD* (London: British Museum Press).
Youngs, S. 2013 'From chains to brooches: the uses and hoarding of silver
    in north Britain in the Early Historic period', in Hunter and Painter
    2013,
    pp. 403–26.

Index

Note: Page numbers in *italics* refer to illustrations